The Firm Building Series

# How to Capture and Keep Clients

## Marketing Strategies for Lawyers

jennifer j. rose, editor

AMERICAN BAR ASSOCIATION
Defending Liberty
Pursuing Justice

GP | Solo

ABA General Practice, Solo & Small Firm Section

Cover design by ABA Publishing.

"Sometimes Bigger Is Better" by Eileen M. Letts, "How to Manage the Rising Waters in a Small Town" William G. Schwab, "The Fine Art of Turning Clients Away" by Lonny H. Dolin, "A Blueprint for Marketing with Staff" by Robert A. Kraft, "How to 'Partner' with Other Lawyers" by Joseph A. DeWoskin, "The Virtual Law Firm" by Patrick W. Begos, "Can the Rainmaker and the IRS Be Business Partners?" by Dennis Jacknewitz and Patrick E. Stark, "Isn't It Time to Get a Web Page?" by Keith B. McLennan, "Do You Still Need to Join Kiwanis?" by Lynne J. Stadjuhar, and "Rainmaking Tips from Solosez" by Carolyn J. Stevens originally appeared in *GPSolo* magazine, Volume 20, Number 5 (July/August 2003).

Printed in the United States of America
09 08 07 06 05  5 4 3 2 1

### Library of Congress Cataloging-in-Publication Data

Rose, Jennifer (Jennifer J.)
    How to capture and keep clients : marketing strategies for lawyers / by Jennifer Rose.
      p.   cm.
    Includes bibliographical references and index.
    ISBN 1-59031-526-X
    1. Legal services—United States—Marketing. 2. Lawyers—United States—Marketing. 3. Practice of law—United States. I. American Bar Association. General Practice, Solo and Small Firm Section. II. Title.

KF316.5.R67  2005
340'.068'8—dc22

                                                    2005017031

# Contents

# About the Editor

JENNIFER J. ROSE was a solo practitioner practicing family law in Shenandoah, Iowa, for 20 years before moving to Morelia, Michoacán, Mexico, eight years ago. In that life, she was listed in *Best Lawyers in America,* rated AV by Martindale-Hubbell, and served a term as chair of the Iowa State Bar Association Family and Juvenile Law Section.

She has been editor-in-chief of *GPSolo,* the flagship magazine of the American Bar Association General Practice, Solo and Small Firm Section, for a decade; has served on the Section's Council; and has served on too many committees and boards to enumerate. She is list manager of the Section-sponsored listserve Solosez. She has been a contributing editor to *Matrimonial Strategist* and *Internet Law Researcher* and regularly serves as a judge of *Law Office Computing*'s annual law firm Web site competition.

# About the Contributors

DAVID J. ABESHOUSE is the principal of the Law Offices of David J. Abeshouse (http://www.lawyers.com/abeshouselaw), located in Uniondale, Long Island, New York, with a practice concentrating on business litigation and alternative dispute resolution, including business arbitration and mediation. He also is a professional neutral, serving as an arbitrator on the commercial arbitration panels of two national ADR forums. His e-mail address is davidlaw@optonline.net.

JEFFREY ALLEN is sole practitioner in the firm of Graves & Allen in Oakland, California, with a practice emphasis in real estate, bankruptcy, and litigation. He is editor-in-chief and columnist of the *Technology Practice Guide* issues of the magazine *GPSolo*, published by the American Bar Association General Practice, Solo and Small Firm Section. His e-mail address is jallenlaw@aol.com.

PATRICK W. BEGOS is a partner in Begos & Horgan, LLP, and practices commercial litigation in Connecticut and New York. He is a founding member of RiverSide West and can be reached at begos@attglobal.net.

STEVEN R. BOUTWELL is director of client services at Kean, Miller, Hawthorne, D'Armond, McCowan & Jarman (http://www.keanmiller.com) in Baton Rouge, Louisiana.

MELANIE D. BRAGG is a former briefing attorney and adjunct professor, and was the first woman president of the Houston Young Lawyers Association. She has served as a director in the ABA Young Lawyers Division and as editor of *Fellows Fodder*, and on the General Practice, Solo and Small Firm Section Publications Board. Bragg is a mediator/arbitrator and, as President of Legal Insight, Inc., she has authored and performed 14 medical/legal programs, the four most recent of which are currently distributed worldwide. Her e-mail address is mdbragg@earthlink.net.

MARK A. CHINN, a principal in Chinn & Associates, PLLC, (http://www.chinnandassociates.com) in Jackson, Mississippi, has been chair of the Mississippi Bar Association Family Law Section twice and is a member of the governing council of the American Bar Association Family Law Section. He lectures at the Ole Miss Law School and has been an adjunct professor at Mississippi College School of Law.

CORINNE COOPER is the principal of Professional Presence® (http://www.professionalpresence.com), a communication consulting firm that specializes in professional communication consulting for legal organizations. She was on the faculty of University of Missouri–Kansas City School of Law for almost two decades, teaching contracts and commercial law. She has written two books about the use of graphics to teach law: *Getting Graphic* and *Getting Graphic2*. A member of the *ABA Journal* Board of Editors, Cooper has also served as Editor of *Business Law Today*. Professor Cooper is a member of the American Law Institute.

JOSEPH A. DEWOSKIN, licensed in Missouri and Kansas, practices law in Kansas City, Missouri. He is programs group coordinator for the ABA General Practice, Solo and Small Firm Section. He can be reached at j.dewoskin@cwbbh.com.

LONNY H. DOLIN practices employment law in the firm of Dolin, Thomas & Sullivan (http://www.dts-esq.com) in Rochester, New York.

CAROLYN ELEFANT is principal attorney in the Law Offices of Carolyn Elefant, an energy regulatory and litigation practice in Washington, D.C., and the creator of MyShingle.com, a Web log for solo and small firm lawyers and those who yearn to hang their own shingle. Her e-mail address is loce@his.com.

BARBARA GLESNER FINES has been on the faculty of University of Missouri–Kansas City School of Law for almost 20 years, teaching professional responsibility, civil procedure, remedies, and family law. Her research interests focus on professional responsibility issues and aspects of legal education. She serves as president of the Center for Computer-Assisted Legal Education (CALI) and is the immediate past chair of the AALS Section on Academic Support. Her e-mail address is glesnerb@umkc.edu.

ANDREA GOLDMAN practices in the two-person firm of Gately & Goldman (http://www.gately-goldman.com) in Newton, Massachusetts, focusing on business, employment, construction, and consumer law. She is also general counsel to Dango Designs, Inc., a software consulting company. Goldman has been a mediator since 1996, and she is certified as an arbitrator for the National Association of Securities Dealers, Inc., and the American Arbitration Association.

MATTHEW W. HOMANN is an attorney and mediator practicing in a two-person firm in Highland, Illinois. Homann shares hundreds of inventive and original ways to bring meaningful and satisfying change to the practice of law in his blog "the [non]billable hour" (http://www.nonbillablehour.com), where he demonstrates how innovative billing strategies, creative marketing techniques, cutting-edge ideas from other industries and professions, and proven customer service principles can combine to revolutionize the ways lawyers serve their clients—and enjoy their lives. His e-mail address is Matt@SilverLakeLaw.com.

DENNIS JACKNEWITZ, who formerly worked with the Internal Revenue Service and is a member of the ABA General Practice, Solo and Small Firm Section, practices law in Belleville, Illinois. He can be reached at djjesqslu@aol.com.

RONALD A. JONES has a solo practice in Summerfield, Florida, concentrating on estate planning, probate, and real estate. His e-mail address is rajones@iag.net.

FRANK J. KAUTZ II is a sole practitioner in the Kautz Law Office (http://www.kautzlaw.com) in Woburn, Massachusetts. He serves on the Technology Board of the ABA General Practice, Solo and Small Firm Section.

ROBERT A. KRAFT is a principal in Kraft & Associates (http://www.kraftlaw.com) a Dallas personal injury firm. He is currently a director emeritus of the Dallas Trial Lawyers Association and is president of the North Dallas Bar Association. Kraft is a fellow of the College of the State Bar of Texas and a sustaining member of the National Organization of Social Security Claimants Representatives and the Texas Trial Lawyers Association.

DAVID LEFFLER is a member of the New York City law firm Leffler Marcus & McCaffrey LLC, where he represents technology clients, women-owned businesses, and other entrepreneurial and growing companies. Leffler has been engaged in a wide variety of transactions and matters in the areas of corporate, business, real estate, employment, Internet/new media, and intellectual property law. He writes the *Being Solo* column and serves on the editorial board of *GPSolo* magazine, published by the ABA General Practice, Solo and Small Firm Section. His e-mail address is lefflermailbox@aol.com

EILEEN M. LETTS is a founding partner of Greene and Letts (http://www.greeneandletts.com), an African-American owned Chicago firm that specializes in litigation, discrimination, and employment law defense. She has served as president of the Chicago Bar Foundation.

JEAN MANEKE, of The Maneke Law Group, L.C., (http://firms
.findlaw.com/jmaneke) Kansas City, Missouri, practices primarily
in the areas of media, entertainment, and probate law, serving
for nearly 15 years as counsel to the Missouri Press Association.
She represents authors, publishers, film producers, photographers,
musicians, and others in creative arts fields. She sits on the board
of the Missouri Broadcasters Association and on the Missouri
Press-Bar Commission, and is chair of the Missouri Bar Media
Law Committee.

KEITH B. MCLENNAN is a partner with the law firm of Miller,
Turetsky, Rule & McLennan, P.C. (http://www.millerturetsky.com),
with an office in Collegeville, Montgomery County, Pennsylvania.
His practice is concentrated in business law, estate planning and
administration, commercial litigation, contracts, copyrights, trademarks, and elder law. He has served as president of the Montgomery Bar Association, as past chair of the Pennsylvania Bar
Association Solo and Small Firm Practice Section, and is vice-
chair of the ABA General Practice, Solo and Small Firm Section.

ALAN O. OLSON is a sole practitioner in Des Moines, Iowa, concentrating in personal injury. He was chair of the ABA Young
Lawyers Division in 2002–03 and serves on the ABA Standing
Committee on Membership and in the House of Delegates. His
e-mail address is AOO@Olson-law.net.

NERINO J. PETRO JR. is a practicing attorney in Loves Park,
Illinois, concentrating in real estate and small business law.

He is also CEO and senior legal technologist for CenCom, a division of Centro, Inc., providing professional and legal technology services to businesses, lawyers, and their staff throughout the country. He serves on the ABA General Practice, Solo and Small Firm Section Legal Technology Committee and the ABA TechShow Advisory Board. He is an authorized independent consultant for TimeMatters and Billing Matters software. He can be reached at njpetro@lawofficetech.com.

WILLIAM G. SCHWAB maintains a four-attorney general practice in Lehighton, Pennsylvania, where he also wears hats as a bankruptcy trustee, assistant public defender, and school solicitor. He can be reached at schwab@uslawcenter.com.

LISA SOLOMON was one of the first attorneys to recognize and take advantage of the technological advances that make outsourcing legal research and writing services practical and profitable for law firms of all sizes. Since 1996, Solomon has limited her practice, in Ardsley, New York, to assisting attorneys with all of their legal research and writing needs, including preparing and arguing appeals and drafting substantive motions and trial memoranda. She has worked in almost every area of law, and has developed particular expertise in insurance coverage, employment, negligence, and contract matters. Her Web site is http://www.questionoflaw.net/.

VICTORIA TRAN SOOD is a Vietnamese attorney in San Jose, California. She practices probate and trust dispute, probate, estate planning, and international tax. She thanks all the attorneys who shared their experience and ideas on marketing to the Vietnamese community in the San Jose area. Her e-mail address is vtranlaw @hotmail.com.

LYNNE J. STADJUHAR currently practices with a small firm, McConaughy & Sarkissian, P.C., in Englewood, Colorado, focusing upon insurance defense, insurance coverage litigation, and general corporation representation. Her e-mail address is lstadjuhar @mslawpc.com

PATRICK E. STARK is a certified public accountant with Grace Advisors, Inc., in St. Louis, Missouri; he can be reached at pes@graceadvisors.com.

CAROLYN J. STEVENS is a solo family law practitioner in Lolo, Montana, and can be reached at cjstevens@abanet.org.

NATALIE R. THORNWELL is the director of the State Bar of Georgia's Law Practice Management Program. She is also an adjunct professor at John Marshall Law School in Atlanta, teaching law office management. Thornwell is a certified consultant for Timeslips, Amicus Attorney, ABACUS Law, TimeMatters, TABS III, Practice Master, and PC Law legal software. She is active in the ABA Law Practice Management and General Practice, Solo and Small Firm sections. She is a member of the Practice Management Advisors Committee; was a member of the 2002 Publishing Board and 2003 and 2004 Techshow Boards of the Law Practice Management Section; and serves on the Technology Practice Guide

editorial board of *GPSolo* magazine. Her e-mail address is
natalie@gabar.org

TED A. WAGGONER practices in a small firm, Peterson & Waggoner, LLP (http://www.peterson-waggoner.com/), in Rochester, Indiana. Practicing general law with an emphasis on real estate, estate planning, and business issues, Ted has focused on business planning concerns for a variety of clients and is a civil mediator. He is active with the Indiana State Bar Association and the Indiana Bar Foundation, where he serves as chair of the Fellows. Ted is a Fellow of the American Bar Foundation.

ROBIN PAGE WEST practices with the small firm Cohan & West (http://www.cohanwest.com) in Baltimore, Maryland, where she specializes in qui tam and whistleblower litigation, negligence, and products liability. She has been editor-in-chief of the ABA General Practice, Solo and Small Firm Section newsletter *SOLO* since its inception, and she is the author of *Advising the Qui Tam Whistleblower.*

WILLIAM H. WILHOIT runs a small firm (http://www.wilhoitlaw .com) in his hometown of Grayson, Kentucky, focusing on personal injury litigation representing both plaintiffs and defendants. He formally chaired the Kentucky Young Lawyers Section and was active in the American Bar Associations Young Lawyers Division serving as the Meetings Coordinator and National Conferences Chair. He is now active in the ABA General Practice, Solo and Small Firm Section, serving on the Corporate Sponsorship

Committee and as the Litigation Group Coordinator. He currently is a representative in the Kentucky House of Delegates and has been elected to the Kentucky Bar Associations Board of Governors.

YOLANDA WILLIAMS-FAVORS is a sole practitioner (http://www .yolandafavors.com) in Stone Mountain, Georgia, specializing in commercial and residential real estate and bankruptcy law. Her clientele has consisted of buyers, sellers, builders, developers, mortgage brokers, and lenders in the real estate department, and debtors and creditors in the bankruptcy department. She also represents the Fulton County's Office of Economic Development, closing all loans for its Business Improvement Loan and Revolving Loan Programs.

ROBERT ZUPKUS is a principal in the Denver firm of Zupkus & Angell (http://www.zalaw.com). He has extensive experience in insurance coverage and bad faith, employment, and commercial litigation matters and specializes in providing general corporate legal counsel geared toward high-tech industries, particularly telecommunications. He is secretary of the American Bar Association General Practice, Solo and Small Firm Section.

# Instructions for Using This Book

## *How to Read This Book*

If you're like most lawyers, you'll probably read this page last, or at least after you've broken the rules by reading a few chapters first. If you're reading this page before proceeding to the rest of the book, you're probably the kind of reader who also reads the copyright notice before anything else.

Do not read this book at one sitting. You will not gain full benefit from this book if you do. This book is not intended to be read all at once and thereafter placed on the bookshelf for others to admire.

Don't even read the chapters in consecutive order. The table of contents is intended for consultation after you read this book. Read the chapters in this book more than once and over a respectable interval of time. What strikes you as not-so-important today may have greater meaning two months from now. Your practice changes over time, and so too must your need to bring in clients.

If you want to know about the lawyers who contributed to this book, read "About the Contributors" first. In fact, I strongly suggest that you do, because the folks who wrote this book are real, in-the-trenches lawyers who practice in a variety of styles across America, from the 14th floor of a tall building in New York City to very small towns in Indiana and Kentucky. The contributors aren't the fancy-pants kind of lawyers who dole out unproven advice; each of them has put the lessons offered to use in real-life practices. Feel free to contact any of the contributors with questions or comments. Some of them may even respond.

Chapter 5, How to Build a Law Firm Brand, is practically a novella.

## Putting the Lessons into Use

Under no circumstances should you attempt to put into use all of the lessons contained in this book at one time. Doing so will leave you no time to practice law. Take no more than three ideas and implement those approaches over a six-month period. Find out what works for you, and adapt the authors' techniques.

## How to Use this Book

This book is not printed on sacred paper. Feel free to mark it up, highlighting important passages, dog-earing favorite chapters, and even tearing out entire pages. You have my permission to bend, spindle, and mutilate it, even to break its spine. You paid good money to buy this book, and it's yours to use. In five years, I do not expect to find this book reposing in pristine condition in your office library. By then, it should resemble a well-used *Joy of Cooking,* replete with the smudges of dirty fingerprints.

## Where to Store This Book

After removing this book from the plain brown wrapper in which it was delivered to you, place it in a conspicuous place to ensure further consumption and enjoyment. Suggested places to store this book include

- The upper right-hand corner of your desk, available for reading while you're on hold, downloading a long file, or waiting for a client.
- Inside your briefcase for reading on the train or while you're waiting in court.
- In your car.
- On your bedroom nightstand.
- Among the reading material contained in the smallest, most frequently used room of your house.

Placement of this book on the bookshelf is absolutely prohibited.

## Don't Be Selfish!

When you have gained complete benefit from this book and can no longer accept one more client, do not keep this book to yourself. Permit your office mates and staff, spouse, significant other, and adult children to read this book. Give it to another lawyer who's looking for clients.

Are you looking for the perfect gift? Buy extra copies of this book for new lawyers, lawyers transitioning to private practice, lawyers who've sent clients your direction, struggling lawyers, and even your friends and relatives. If you buy enough copies of this book, the ABA may even give you a quantity discount.

# 1

# The Hardest Part: Asking for Business

*Lawyers are trained to practice law,
and most just hope it walks in the door.*

# §1.1 Marketing Is Not a Dirty Word

### Mark A. Chinn

Many lawyers view marketing as either an unpleasant or an unprofessional task. However, if viewed from the proper perspective, marketing is neither. In fact, marketing can be rewarding and enhance professionalism. Other lawyers say they don't have to market because they already have more work than they can do. These lawyers are missing opportunity for their practices and their lives.

Marketing can be fun. In its most basic format, it is nothing more than developing trusting referral relationships: friends. Now, unless you have an objection to creating positive, trusting relationships with as many people as possible, you can see that an effective marketing program will add to your personal life.

In my view, the greatest threat to professionalism is a lawyer who is not making it financially. Lawyers who are struggling financially may cut corners, provide inadequate representation, and "borrow" client funds. Therefore, it is critical to professionalism that lawyers have thriving businesses.

Finally, those lawyers who say they don't have to market are missing the opportunity to improve their business. Effective marketing for the established lawyer can lead to higher hourly rates, more challenging or sophisticated clientele and business, and less labor for more dollars. Moreover, marketing for the established lawyer can insure against downward cycles, which happen in all businesses.

No one can afford not to market. It is ironic, is it not, that the most established and profitable of all businesses market the most! Businesses like Coca-Cola, McDonald's, and Anheuser-Busch, which are clearly number one in their markets by large margins, zealously protect their market share with aggressive marketing.

In short, you can choose the style of your marketing, but you cannot choose whether or not to market.

## Marketing Must Become a Way of Life

Perhaps the most powerful point of this book—after developing missions and goals—is the need to develop a marketing mentality. Marketing must become a part of your mentality and your daily life; it cannot be a one-shot thing. For example, I have worked out at the gym for many years. Every year around New Year's, the gym is full of people who are fulfilling New Year's resolutions to get in shape. The regulars in the gym like to bet on how long the "New Year's Eve-ers" will stay, whether it will be four or five weeks. As it turns out, most are gone by February. These "New Year's Eve-ers" fail to realize that getting in shape is not a project; it is a way of life.

To effectively market, you must—like the person who leads a healthy lifestyle—develop the mentality that marketing is a way of life. For example, you cannot simply have an office party, send some letters, run an ad in the paper, and think this campaign will propel your practice to success. The office parties must be regular and identifiable, the letters must flow out of your office without interruption for your entire career, and the newspaper exposure must be relatively frequent. If you intend to use television, for example, you cannot decide to invest in television advertising for six months and expect that to be enough. You must commit to long term, unending advertising, or else all of the investment will be wasted. Just as fitness is a lifelong commitment, so must marketing be a lifelong commitment.

## Determining Your Target Audience

The most critical step in marketing is determining whom you want to attract as referral sources and customers. This can be done only after creating personal and firm mission statements. The personal mission statement tells you what kind of life you want to have. The firm mission statement must be structured

**Short List of Marketing Tips**

1. Make marketing a way of life.
2. Look people in the eye and greet them in a friendly way.
3. Carry your business card at all times and present it whenever possible.
4. Speak.
5. Write.
6. Participate in state, local, and ABA bar work.
7. Participate in community groups.
8. Join national specialty associations.
9. Keep track of referrals and contact them regularly.
10. Stay in touch with former clients.
11. Develop a good Web site.

to deliver to you the kind of life you want. Marketing must be designed to bring the firm the business it is designed to have.

Years ago, I contemplated using large Yellow Pages advertising. A client of mine sold the advertising and worked hard to sell me on the benefits of it. She was able to quote statistics on the large number of calls that such an ad would generate for me. She showed me impressive full-page ads to consider. The thought of receiving hundreds of calls for new business was quite alluring. But I thought I should investigate this change in my marketing direction very carefully. I decided to ask the opinions of people who sent me business and of the clients I most wanted to have. The key discussion took place with a local doctor, the type of client I wanted to continue to attract. He said, "I don't think you should do it. I don't want a lawyer who advertises [in the Yellow Pages]." That was all I needed to hear.

Let's be clear on what I am saying here. I am not saying a lawyer should not have a large, attractive Yellow Pages ad. As a matter of fact, such ads are wonderful for obtaining lots of a certain kind of business. The question is, "Will the ad (or any other marketing activity) yield the business you want?" And a caveat to mass advertising such as the Yellow Pages is this: Be prepared with enough staff and phone lines to handle the calls, and be prepared to lose profitable billable hours screening the calls for paying business.

## Profiling and Targeting Your Clients

To assist you in targeting your business, it is helpful to profile your prospective clients. What will they look like? The more detailed the description, the better focus for your marketing efforts. Focus is necessary to prevent waste of effort and money. For example in the early years of my practice, I sought to profile my most preferred client. As it turned out at that stage in my career as a matrimonial lawyer, the clients that I enjoyed the most and had the most success with were doctors' wives between the ages of 35 and 50. These were the most profitable type of case I was able to get at the time, and the most rewarding. Later in the development of my business, I changed my focus to the client with at least a million dollars involved in the estate and a professional occupation or successful small business. In short, I wanted to target millionaires.

Once you have described your ideal prospective clients, you must learn everything you can about them. For example, since I was targeting millionaires, I needed to research where they were, who they were, what they enjoyed doing, what their hobbies were, and what type of medium or referral source they might use to find a lawyer. I read books, specifically *How to Meet Millionaires* and *The Millionaire Next Door.* Interesting things turned up. I learned that many millionaires like to go have coffee in the mornings and talk. So I changed my daily routine from getting to work at eight in the morning to going to the local bakeries and coffeehouses at eight in the morning. To my shock and amazement, all the people that I thought were at work like me all those years were drinking coffee! In *The Millionaire Next Door,* I learned that most millionaires do not look like I thought they did. They were electricians or plumbers, or construction business owners, or restaurateurs. They didn't hang out at the richest shops. As a matter of fact, they might wear less expensive clothes and drive a used car. Once again, this helped me focus my marketing efforts.

A useful metaphor for understanding market targeting is fishing. You can have the best fishing boat on the ocean and the most sophisticated rods and reels and lures and a great coastal fishing guide, but you won't catch a single thing in a Mississippi lake where the bring will leap to a cricket at the end of a bobber and a cane pole. The point is, you must know your fish, their environment, and their desires. You don't see fine wines advertised on stock cars.

You have to know what fish you are trying to catch so you can fish in the right lake with the right lures. You can have the fanciest boat and gear on the gulf, but it won't help you a bit in catching a catfish in a pond. Profile your desired clients. Know who they are, who their friends are, where they go.

## *Profiling and Targeting Your Referral Sources*

Most law business for most of us comes from referrals. This means that lawyers should not only market to potential clients, they must target and market referral sources. You should profile your referral sources. One way to do that is to examine the most profitable and rewarding cases you have already received. Where did those cases come from? Who sent them to you? Are there any consistencies there? When I did this many years ago, I found the number one source of referrals to me was lawyers about my age in the big firms in town, firms that did not do divorce cases. I knew then that I should focus my efforts on those lawyers. Where do you find such lawyers? In bar associations. So I dedicated myself to serving the bar as much as I could. This service allowed me to give back to the public and helped me build relationships and name recognition with literally hundreds of lawyers who are potential referral sources.

## *Marketing 101*

### The Color of Their Eyes

Marketing is about building trusting relationships with people. The grassroots of marketing for the lawyer lies in every single personal contact. Whenever you are seen or interact with others, impressions are being created. First impressions are critical. In most interpersonal contact, the most critical element is eye contact. It is my opinion that 99 percent of people never learn the wonderful art of total and concentrated eye contact with the people they meet. In seminars, I will ask the audience to turn and face another audience member and say "hello." Then, I ask them to cover their eyes and see if they can remember the color of the eyes of the person they have just met. Most often, they cannot. The reason: They have not truly focused on the individual in front of them, but only on the ceremony of the greeting. I promise you will enjoy enhanced relationships with all you meet or see, if you will pause and study their eyes long enough to learn the color. The old saying that the eyes are the window to the soul is true. One caveat: Do not hold the gaze into the eyes too long, as it could be unnerving to some.

### The Use of the Business Card

The business card can be an extremely effective marketing tool. It can also be meaningless. It all depends on how you use it.

**CARRY CARDS AT ALL TIMES.** Never, never, never be without your business cards. Failure to have a card with you sends the signal that you do not take your profession seriously. Men should carry their cards in their shirt pocket. This allows for a "quick draw" of the card, signaling that your business is first on your mind. Women who don't wear shirts with pockets might keep a striking carrying case in their purse. In either case, the card should be easy to access. Fumbling or searching for the card destroys the momentum of the marketing moment.

**PRESENTING THE CARD.** Jay Foonberg teaches that the manner of presentation of the card is critical. He teaches that you should hold your card in both hands and present it as though it is a treasured gift. This communicates that your profession and your business is something valuable. Something that is treasured is well taken care of, and that is what people who might send you business want to know.

Foonberg also teaches that you should receive a card from someone in just the same manner as you present your own, that is with two hands, as though it is a treasured gift. This makes the presenter remember you fondly as someone who respected him or her. And when you get the card, comment on some favorable characteristic of the card. If the card features gold scales of justice, you might say, "What a wonderful gold scales of justice on your card!" Again, this makes the other person feel good, and feel good about you.

Give people three cards instead of one. I learned this technique from a very successful personal injury lawyer in Alabama.

Carry business cards in your front pocket and give three to every person you see.

The Alabama lawyer never used newspaper or television advertising, but he was covered up in good business. His technique is to give three business cards to every single person he meets. Even when he is in an elevator with people he doesn't know, he gives them all three cards. Now, what, you ask, is the reason for three cards? Well, I think there are several reasons. First, if someone has three cards, they will still have a card if they lose one, or two. Second, the giving of three cards is special. No one else does it. It's distinctive. And third, the receiver is less likely to throw away three cards, because it just seems too wasteful. So they are more likely to keep at least one.

**STYLE**. Give thought to the style of your card. The style should convey the type of message you want to send. It should speak to the people you want reach. And it should be consistent with your stationery and all of your other marketing efforts.

When I first started my practice, I wanted to be perceived as a bold, aggressive, but distinguished litigator. I did not want to appear flashy. I wanted to appear solid and established, even though I wasn't. So I took care to design a card

(and stationery) that was bold. I carefully chose a typeface that was classic—a little bit of style, but no flash. The card was white and the print was a rich, embossed black. It was no-nonsense. I wanted to be taken seriously.

There are many distinctive things you can do with cards. You can put your picture on them. You can add a dash of color. You can add a word, mark, or symbol. You can add the scales of justice. Take the time to carefully consider how your card should look, as it is a basic marketing symbol.

## Stationery

The use of stationery has changed dramatically in the last 20 years. We used to spend a lot of time deciding about the texture and color of paper and whether or not to emboss the stationery. However, the ability to print your own stationery changed all of that. Of course, fine, embossed stationery is nice, but I rarely see it anymore. It seems completely acceptable now to use the computer to generate your own letterhead. The use of faxes and e-mails is also significantly affecting stationery.

Of course, it is important to take time and care in designing your stationery.

## The Next Level—Speaking and Writing

Speaking and writing are magnificent tools for developing lawyer referrals and elevating professional standing. When you agree to speak for a continuing education program, many marketing forces go to work for you. The first thing that happens is that you are listed on a program as a speaker. This creates the impression of expertise and excellence. Second, program brochures are mailed to every member of the bar to which the program is targeted, placing your name and purported expertise in front of literally thousands of your peers. Even if they are not interested in the seminar, they will likely open the brochure out of curiosity to see who is speaking. And, finally, if you speak well, you will be remembered by your audience not only as a competent and perhaps expert lawyer, but also as someone who took the time to help them become better. Many times in jurisdictions in which I am not familiar, I have had lawyers come up to me and say, "You don't know me, but I heard you speak."

WRITING. Writing, like speaking, reaches your audience and conveys an impression of expertise. There are many, many places you can write. For starters, your local or state bar section may have a periodical or newsletter. They may have a recent case discussion that you could author. State bars and continuing legal education providers such as private companies and universities are always looking for authors. Call them and ask if they need an author.

Write an opinion or advice column in a local newspaper. You can call the editors and ask if they need articles, or you could write an article and send it to them. There are some small or local newspapers that will accept just about any article, as long as you write it for them.

## Bar Work

Your fellow members of the bar are responsible in large part for your professional reputation and standing and for sending you business. You should take every opportunity to associate, socialize, and work with them. There is no better inroad into connections with members of the bar than bar work.

Many lawyer-ranking services base their rankings on the opinions of your fellow lawyers. Martindale-Hubbell provides one of the most prestigious ranking services. They rank lawyers in terms of ability and integrity. The highest rating is "AV." The "A" stands for the highest ability ranking and the "V" stands for the highest integrity ranking. This coveted ranking can be obtained only from fellow lawyers. Obviously, professional standing enhances business.

Lawyers are a leading source of referrals. Most lawyers do not advertise, so the public usually asks for referrals from trusted sources. People routinely ask their lawyer friends what lawyer would be good for a certain type of case. Moreover, most large firms do not do family law, so when a family law question comes up, they usually refer it to a family law specialist. That would be you—that is, if they are familiar with you.

## Local and State Bars

There are many different levels of bar work: local bars, young lawyers associations, and state bars. You are better off the more bars you serve in. The more bars you become involved in, the more lawyers you reach. Most bars are starving for volunteers and would welcome your request to become involved.

There are many ways to serve the bar. The basic options are committee work, section membership and work, and elective office. It is easy to join a committee. Call the bar, ask for a list of committees, and join the ones that interest you. I have found that committee projects—although important—often become less important than the relationships forged with other lawyers while working on the projects. A good example of this is my long tenure as chairman of the Hinds County Bar Golf Committee. Our objective was to run a golf tournament once a year for the bar. When we started, the tournament was for recreation and fellowship. But when I finished my five years as chair of the committee, we had turned the tournament into a moneymaking spectacle that was revered by the entire bar. Tens of thousands of dollars were raised for the Mississippi Bar Volunteer Lawyers Project and other charities. Today, the charity dollars are even higher. Despite the great achievements of the committee, the greatest reward was the development of life-long relationships with members of the committee. Those friendships have also led to enhanced professional standing and business referrals.

All state bars, most young lawyer associations, and many local bars have sections. If you practice family law, you should join the family law section of every bar you can. How could you consider yourself an expert in a field if you are not a member of every available grouping of experts in your field? In my opinion, you cannot.

Section membership involves a wide range of activity, depending on the section. I would suppose that most sections are relatively inactive, with perhaps one meeting or CLE a year. Some, of course, are more active. But make it a point to be involved as much as you can. Other members of the bar will be aware of your involvement. If they know you are at the heart of activity for your trade, they will regard you as an expert worthy of referral. Moreover, you will learn about your trade in your area. You will learn what the other lawyers and judges are thinking and doing. You will develop relationships with them that may enhance your dealings with them or give you enhanced credibility in counties where you are not familiar. I can go just about anywhere in Mississippi and the judges and lawyers have heard of me from my bar work. This makes me more comfortable when I go into counties or courts where I have never been before or do not go very often.

Taking office with the bar is an excellent way to advance your reputation. There are many, many offices to run for. They range from local bar directors to state bar representatives and local and state bar officer ships. Usually, these positions are selected by nominating committees and later submitted for vote. The best way to obtain these positions is to find out when the nomination process takes place and who serves on the nominating committee, and then solicit a nomination from the committee members (check your bar regulations on this before you do it, though). If you are not nominated but still desire the position, you can probably obtain candidacy through a petition process. I never sought nomination to any office, but the nominations came anyway because I worked very hard in each organization of which I have been a member. If you work hard and are diligent and productive, the leaders of the organization will usually lift you up.

## American Bar Association

Membership in an ABA Section and participation in its meetings and seminars produces many benefits. First, your membership in the ABA establishes you as a lawyer who is interested in learning and adhering to a national standard of professional development. Lawyers in your community and state will appreciate this and be more willing to make referrals to you. I get many referrals each year from lawyers in my state where interstate issues are involved because they know I am involved in the ABA and have national contacts (there are usually only 200 lawyers from across the country who attend the ABA meetings, so it should be relatively easy for you to establish yourself in your community as having these contacts). Second, you will make contacts with lawyers from around the country. Believe it or not, this can lead to referrals of business. One of the best examples of this is a referral from a good friend of mine in Cleveland of a pro basketball player for the Los Angeles Lakers who had a paternity problem in Mississippi. Another benefit is the CLE and publications of the ABA.

## Other Legal Organizations

There are many organizations related to your area of practice that you can join or seek induction into. Joining these state, national, or local groups of lawyers has many benefits. First, it serves as notice to the world that you are doing everything you can to enhance your professional skills by giving time and effort and money to meet with fellow lawyers to exchange information and ideas on improving your practice. Second, it creates professional contacts for potential referral. Finally, you will learn from the other members of the organization.

**AWARDS AND HONORS.** You will probably have the opportunity to apply for membership in "Who's Who" type societies. The true benefits of this is unproven, but I have applied for and been accepted for many of these honors. The reason is that it provides one more link, one more source for someone to see or get my name, one more source of professional accreditation. There is usually an expense to these "honors," and you will just have to determine which ones, if any, you will chose to pay for.

**CERTIFICATES.** There are societies that test and certify lawyers for competence. One such society that I obtained certification from was the National Board of Trial Advocacy. Many years ago, when my solo practice was just beginning to grow, I tested for and received certification as a civil trial expert. It gave me confidence that I had been certified by a national organization as having special skills. The value of these certifications cannot be quantified, but wouldn't you agree that you should seek every possible advantage to enhance your professional standing?

## Community Organizations

Community work is a necessary ingredient to becoming what I call "a pillar in your community." It is my opinion that lawyers should be pillars in their community. First, service to the community is the right thing to do. But from a practice-management standpoint, it is an important thing to do. Lawyers are advocates for people. This means that when a lawyer speaks for someone, he or she must be believed. People want to hire someone who will have credibility. They also want to hire someone who has good judgment. If people know that you are serving the community in a constructive way, they are more likely to perceive you as having good judgment. Finally, community service gets your name out in the public, which enhances your "top of mind awareness" for referrals. For example, for many years, I was involved with a festival in Jackson, Mississippi, called Jubilee Jam. City residents love this event and flock to it every year to listen to music of all kinds and party in the streets of downtown Jackson. My involvement with the Jam got me on TV many, many times. Reporters always covered the event and would interview the volunteers who were organizing the event. I was also at the festival each year in my volunteer uniform, so my friends and acquaintances could see I was working for the community. And, of course, the countless hours of organizational work with literally thousands of volunteers, city officials, local businesspeople, and the media enhanced my name recognition and reputation in the community. Finally, it was fun!

It is my opinion that the community work I have done has never directly led to quality referrals. This may prove different for you. But there is no mistaking that the community work has helped me take my place as a pillar in the community, which has enhanced my professional standing.

*One caveat:* Never do community or church work just because you are trying to get business. I believe people will see through that and it will not be productive.

## Rotary, Chamber of Commerce, and Their Ilk

Join community groups that have businesspeople as their members. Join as many as you can. Some examples are Rotary, the Chamber of Commerce, Optimist Club, and Junior League. Many of these business groups meet at lunch or breakfast. This means you can invest in marketing without taking time away from your business or your home life. Most of these organizations are designed to create networking opportunities for their members. For example, our local Chamber of Commerce has a breakfast meeting designed solely for networking. Groups of eight meet at a table to describe their businesses and pass out cards.

After a few minutes, a bell is rung and the composition of the tables changes, so new people can be met.

## Religious Affiliation

An essential part of being a pillar of your community is joining the organization of your faith. If you have faith, you ought to be participating. Such participation leads to business. Your congregation is nothing more than a microcosm of your community, and there will be many problems among your members that need your expertise. Moreover, I believe people will trust you more if they see you exercising your faith. They will be more likely to see you as someone who is stable and trustworthy.

## *Brochures*

Brochures can be an important part of the total marketing package. A brochure should be carefully designed to give the prospective customer or referral source just the right amount of information in a fairly short amount of time and space. I recommend that a brochure be a single, folded sheet of paper. I also recommend you use a fairly stiff, glossy paper. The brochure does not have to be in color, but it should probably have a good picture of you. The brochure should describe your firm mission, contain biographical information, and describe the service you provide. A brochure should not be long or detailed, as it is my experience that people do not want to read a lot of material.

If you have employees, I recommend that you do not picture or mention any staff. The reason: They will leave the week after you pay for the brochures, and your brochure will be outdated immediately.

You may be able to generate your brochure with desktop publishing. Just make sure the quality is good, as you want to make a good impression.

Brochures can be distributed in many ways. You should pass brochures out to every member of any audience you speak to. You should carry brochures to bar or business meetings and hand them to people you meet. You can send brochures to prospective referral sources such as counselors, accountants, and other lawyers.

Brochures are a nice marketing touch. However, if funds are limited, this should be one of the last pieces of your marketing package.

## *Advanced Marketing: Media Matters*

### People in the News

There is a great, hidden source of free mass marketing. Usually called something like "People in the News," it's the section in almost every newspaper that prints announcements such as hiring and promotions. Banks and insurance companies seem to have discovered this wonderful source of free publicity, but lawyers seem to be oblivious to it. Our firm uses People in the News as much as possible. We use it to announce new hires, promotions, and awards or honors. We simply write a sentence or two and send it to the paper(s) with a digital photo. I always include a photo because I firmly believe that many people read only the announcements accompanied by a photo. I know I do. Our firm keeps on file the names and addresses of the People in the News editors at nearly every newspaper in the state. We also keep a healthy supply of photos to send. You should use a picture whenever possible—not just in People in the News, but in all media.

### Local Publications

There are many publications that are designed to reach people in places such as malls, bars, coffeehouses, and other retail establishments. These publications are usually free to the public. Some develop almost cult-like followings. You should check out these publications in your area. Ask them the demographics of their readership. Make sure their demographics fit with your target audience. Check the fees.

Last year I started a mediation business called "Divorce in a Day." It is designed to bring mediation services in divorce directly to the public. I advertised this new service in a local publication, *Coffee News*. *Coffee News* is one sheet of paper printed on both sides. Each page is rimmed with two-by-two-inch ads. Only one ad for each kind of business is permitted. The middle of *Coffee News* contains short stories and news items suitable for reading while one drinks a cup of coffee before work. Hey, don't knock this type of advertising. According to *The Millionaire Next Door*, millionaires like to go to coffeehouses. The cost for a month of ads was in the neighborhood of $250.

Years ago, I was speaking to the Gulf Coast Bar Association in Gulfport, Mississippi, about marketing. A very attractive young woman came up to me after the speech and told me she was starting her own practice. I said, "The first thing you should do is take out a yellow page ad with a *big* picture of you." I signalled the picture size with my hands. "You will be covered up in business." I forgot about my contact and then several years later I ran into a young woman at a bar meeting. She said, "Do you remember me?" I said, "Of course I do, but I am sorry I cannot remember your name." She said, "I am Kathleen Smiley. I came up to you after you spoke to our bar in Gulfport several years ago. Do you remember what you said to me?" I said, "No." She repeated what I had said and mimicked my hand motion when I described the *big* picture of her. She said, "Well, I didn't get a Yellow Pages ad, but I put a *big* picture of me"—she mimicked me again—"in the local shopping mall paper, and it worked!" She continued, "I got so much business, I couldn't begin to do the work. Thank you," she said, "for inspiring me to take those steps, because they made my career." Today, Kathleen Smiley operates the largest female-owned firm on the Mississippi Gulf Coast.

So, if you want to advertise to jump-start a business or product, this type of advertising may be just what the doctor ordered.

## Yellow Pages

The Yellow Pages is a wonderful place for almost any business to advertise. I think it is essential for any business to have a listing in the Yellow Pages—that's where people who already know who you are will look for your phone number. Failing to be there could send the message of inattention to good business practices.

But the larger issues is how big and what kind of an ad you should have. To answer this question, you must first answer the threshold question of what kind of business you would like to have. If you wish to appeal to the masses, irrespective of income, the Yellow Pages are a good choice. Lawyers who use large Yellow Page ads tell me that the ads work so well, they have to add phone lines and staff just to answer the calls. The problem is that many of the calls do not translate into paying business, and it requires many staff hours to screen the calls. So if you wish to receive only calls from the type of person you want to represent, a huge Yellow Pages ad may be a disaster for you.

Our firm has always maintained a dignified, bold-print listing. The purpose of the bold print is to make it easier for people who are already looking for me to find my number.

## TV

I have not seen much television advertising for family law practices. Perhaps you have in your area. I don't see any reason why television cannot work for family law. Of course, this type of advertising is expensive. It can be expensive to create the ads and then expensive to run them.

The number one caveat for television advertising: Be prepared for a long-run commitment. I wouldn't even begin to embark on this type of advertising unless you are prepared to advertise for an entire year, regardless of the success. Short-term television advertising is like pouring money down a drain.

If you are thinking of television, talk carefully with the marketing representatives of each television station in your broadcast area. Carefully analyze the demographics of each show to see how they compare with your desired client types.

## Radio

I think radio may be the most overlooked form of advertising for lawyers. There are many ways to advertise on radio. The obvious way is to create an ad and pay to have it run on a show. Costs of production of a radio ad can be almost negligible. It can be as simple as you writing a script and visiting the station one day for a few minutes to record it.

Another way to advertise is to appear as a guest on an existing show. If you want to do this, you might call some of the local AM talk shows and ask them if they are interested in having you as a guest to discuss a topic of interest, such as "How to Tell If Your Spouse Is Having an Affair." They may invite you as a guest (after you already invited yourself). Or you may be able to purchase time as a "guest."

Another way to advertise on radio is to host your own show, perhaps a call-in show on the issues of family law. This will cost you a fee with the station. Again, call your local AM station and ask them how to do this.

If you want to jump-start your practice, or if you are just starting out, radio is an excellent medium for this.

## Internet

The Internet is a vast new frontier for advertising. The intricacies of this form of advertising could occupy a separate book. For the purposes of this book, we will discuss some basics.

First, every reputable firm and every firm seeking to establish itself should endeavor to have a state-of-the-art Web page. Marketing experts tell me that people are turning more and more to the Internet to find lawyers and that the demographics of the people using this resource are higher income. My prediction is that the average income of Internet users will decrease as computers spread though our society.

The key to successful Internet marketing is search engines. You must be connected with a search engine that will lead to people finding your page. I am affiliated with Martindale-Hubbell. People who access http://www.lawyers.com will find my page easily. To check out how available your page is to the public, conduct your own search.

### Internet Marketing Companies

You will receive contact from companies who want to serve as a purveyor of your firm or Web site on the Internet. These companies can lead to many referrals or none at all. You must carefully investigate any commitment to an Internet purveyor to avoid wasting your money.

## Contact Management Software

Periodic contact with people who might refer business to you increases the likelihood of referrals. If you are on the "top of the mind" of a referral source, you have a better chance of getting the referral. How many times have you run into a friend who sent a piece of business else-where, either because they forgot what you do or because they hadn't seen you in awhile? The best way to stay at the top of someone's mind is to make regular contact.

Contact management software makes periodic contact easy. This software can be used to automatically remind you to contact someone. You can program in birthdays, anniversaries, graduations, or regular periodic contact, such as every 90 days.

Many case management programs have this capacity built into the program. For example, our firm uses Amicus case management. All persons that our firm contacts, whether clients, lawyers, judges, referral sources, or court personnel, are entered into the system. The system allows us to categorize the people in the system. For example, a lawyer who refers business is reflected both as a lawyer and as a referral source. This allows you to sort.

Our firm asks every potential client who referred them to us. This name and contact information is placed in the system as a referral source. The Amicus software allows us to select how often we wish to contact the referral source. We usually select "every 90 days." Then, every 90 days, the computer reminds us to contact that person. We usually do that with a letter or e-mail. Sometimes we will follow up with a call or lunch invitation. If the firm has been featured in an article or received some distinction, we might send that to the referral sources. Often, I include a picture of my children at an event or vacation. This personalizes the message and makes the referral source aware of the family they are helping with the income generated from referrals.

Here's an example of the type of note we send to referral sources every 90 days or so.

"I was just up at the office this past weekend doing some thinking and planning for my divorce practice, and I thought of you and how much you helped me with referrals in the past. I just want you to know how much I appreciate you for helping me."

Here's another example:

"I just got back from the Bar convention where my family won the sand castle building contest. Enclosed is a picture of my daughters and me in front of our prize-winning castle. Thanks for everything you have done for me in the past."

I usually write one generic note that can be used for several weeks for many people. My office manager generates the e-mails or letters for me. When you mass-produce letters, however, you should take care to make sure you don't send the same letter twice. You should also make sure the letter is appropriate for each person. There is a good chance that the receiver will know that you are mass-producing contact letters, but, as long as you are careful with it, this does not seem to diminish accomplishing the goal, which is "top of mind awareness."

If you want to make your contacts more personal, you can, but it takes more time. Instead of mass-producing letters, block out an hour or so each week to make personal calls. Another way to personalize your contact is to take postcards with you on flights or long car rides (with someone else driving) and write out personal notes to persons on a list printed from the computer.

A friend of mine who is a specialist in business valuation, Jim Koerber of Hattiesburg, Mississippi, sends me cases, articles, or other material with his card stapled to it with a short personal note inscribed on the card, such as, "Mark, thought you would benefit from this article."

These short notes keep Jim at the top of my mind, and I usually benefit from the material he sends.

## Saying Thank You

I refer many cases to lawyers every year, and it just amazes me how few thank me. I would say that I get a thank-you letter for one out of every 30 referrals I make. I find that absolutely appalling. When you refer someone to a lawyer, it means many things. It means that you are putting your own reputation on the line. It means that you are publicizing your belief that the person whom you are referring is competent. It also means that you are sending the person income. How in the world can someone accept such riches without thanks? Since so few people say thank you, you will stand out when you do.

The first question you should ask every person who calls your firm—whether you take the business or not—is "Who referred you to us?" This valuable information should then be stored and used to keep regular contact with the referral source. The best way to do this is with contact management software, as discussed in the previous section.

The most memorable thank you is a gift. My friend Steve Riley, an estate-planning specialist in Tampa, Florida, takes a picture of his new clients, puts the picture on a plaque, and sends the plaque to the referral sources. He says some referral sources have a wall of plaques and actu-ally compete with other referral sources to see who has the most plaques. My friend Joel Kirsch-baum from Fort Lauderdale, Florida, sends me very fine Christmas gifts every year. I would send business to Joel whether he sent me a gift or not, but the gift certainly makes an impression and makes the relationship special (actually, I think Joel's wife Karin picks out the presents).

## Events

Events can be excellent marketing tools. Examples include holiday parties, golf tournaments, deep-sea fishing excursions, seminars, and cocktail parties. One key to a successful marketing event is to carefully select the event so that the people you want to influence will enjoy and remember it. Don't just select an event because you think it would be fun. A well run, fun event that does not influence people to send you business is not a successful marketing event.

On the other hand, the event that you select as being fun to potential referral sources must also be fun to you. The reason is that it is critical to success to make your personal life and business life compatible.

Another key element to marketing success with events is to plan on making the event an institution. In other words, try to plan the event so that it will take place every year at the same time. This allows people to enjoy the event and then enjoy looking forward to it again the next year. This creates top of mind awareness through anticipation. It also creates a bond between you and your referral sources.

Selecting something unique enhances marketing success of events. For example, if most lawyers in town are already having Christmas parties, it will be hard for you to distinguish your party and create top of mind awareness. The competition might also make it hard to draw a healthy crowd.

Marketing events for former divorce clients are difficult to plan, as most divorce clients desire privacy. This does not mean they cannot be invited to events. One event I had for former clients was a "divorce client seminar." I made lists of ten to twelve of my past clients with whom I had a good relationship and invited them to my office to meet and socialize with other past clients. I had two groups of women. They chose to meet over lunch. We discussed the divorce experience, what they learned, and how our firm could improve our service. Each of the women had been the victim of adultery by her spouse, and the discussions in the group were very therapeutic. Listening to the discussions taught me a

great deal about what it was like to go through divorce and be represented by me. I also had a group of men. They preferred to meet on Friday afternoon over some beer. Almost every one of them had committed adultery on their spouse. It was interesting to hear them discuss their regret. Of course, the beer flowed and the men had a good time.

## Sponsorships

Sponsoring events is a viable way to market. This method is very indirect, because it is rare that you will receive business directly from such an effort. However, sponsoring events is a vital part of the total package of top of mind awareness and credibility. Sponsorships can include golf hole sponsorships; charitable events for the Kidney Foundation, Cancer League, Junior League, 100 Black Men, and symphony and opera leagues; and Little League and YMCA teams. Our firm does all of these things.

I always sponsor my daughters' soccer and YMCA basketball teams. The sponsorship places the firm name on the jerseys for the team. This sends a strong message that we are giving back to the community. This creates credibility. What's more, I find that the kids wear the jerseys even when they are not playing and perhaps for years after the season is over. They become walking billboards.

Our firm buys as many sponsorships in local charitable events as we can afford. We usually spend just enough to get a couple of tickets and program listing. We charge this expense to advertising. Since we are interested in "high asset" divorce, we feel this money is well spent since successful people with lots of money usually attend charitable events. Also, contributions to local charities enhance the reputation of the firm as a credible, upright contributor to the welfare of the community as a whole.

## Consistency

Make sure that all of your marketing attempts have a consistent image. Consistency enhances the awareness of the public of your product. I have worked for years for local events where we have solicited businesses to sponsor the events. The more sophisticated of these business marketers zealously guard their brand and its presentation. They will not allow you, for example, to alter their trademark or name one bit. The design must be the same. The colors must be the same. You should be the same way with your marketing. For example, if you have a style or logo on your letterhead, make sure that same style of print or character is used on all items of marketing, from business cards, to large envelopes, to your e-mail signature, to the jerseys of sports teams you might sponsor.

Be consistent. Make sure all of the material that you generate has the same look and theme. Gary Player, the famous golfer, says his father told him to do that, so he developed the image of always wearing all black. This distinguished him from other golfers and helped him become known all over the world.

# §1.2 Attracting and Keeping Clients
## Alan O. Olson

The ability to generate legal work is the foundation of any successful law practice. Without clients, there is simply no business to conduct. Rainmaking is the art of generating business and is primarily a function of the lawyer's *known value* to those in need of legal services. Success depends upon two factors: (1) the lawyer's commitment to becoming valuable, and (2) the lawyer's willingness and ability to demonstrate value.

First and foremost, the lawyer must be valuable. How valuable a lawyer is depends upon the lawyer's competence, capability, responsiveness, reliability, and creativity. These traits make up the lawyer's reputation, and reputation is the backdrop against which all rainmaking occurs. Only after becoming valuable can the lawyer demonstrate value, and successful rainmaking requires both.

Demonstrating value is the art of exemplifying why potential clients should hire the lawyer and why referral sources should find the lawyer trustworthy. Some label this art "marketing." Regardless of its title, its success depends upon strategy and a comprehensive approach. The key is to recognize the need to "prime the pump" and to avoid wasted moves.

To make rain, the atmospheric conditions must be right in four coexisting climates: (1) attracting the client; (2) signing the client; (3) keeping the client; and (4) retaining the client after the representation concludes.

- The ability to generate legal work is the foundation of any successful law practice.

- "Rainmaking" is the art of generating business and is primarily a function of the lawyer's *known value* to those in need of legal services.

- Success depends upon two factors: (1) the lawyer's commitment to becoming valuable, and (2) the lawyer's willingness and ability to demonstrate value.

- How valuable a lawyer is depends upon the lawyer's competence, capability, responsiveness, reliability, and creativity.

- Demonstrating value is the art of exemplifying why potential clients should hire the lawyer and why referral sources should find the lawyer trustworthy.

### Climate for Rainmaking

To make rain, the atmospheric conditions must be right in four coexisting climates: (1) attracting the client, (2) signing the client, (3) keeping the client, and (4) retaining the client after the representation concludes.

#### Attracting the Client

The lawyer should determine the ideal type of client to be attracted.

Determining an ideal type depends upon the lawyer's area of legal expertise and the type of legal service the lawyer intends to provide.

- The lawyer must determine where the ideal type is most likely to look for a lawyer and upon what information that type is most likely to form an opinion.
- Networking is the process of people interacting, bonding, and, in the process, discovering each other's interests and strengths. Building meaningful relationships with a variety of people in a diverse array of settings will also build business.

Generating referrals from other lawyers generally involves being contacted by a person or entity in need of legal services that the referring lawyer has decided not to provide or with which the referring lawyer has a conflict of interest.

- Referrals are primarily generated by word of mouth based upon the performing lawyer's past achievement.
- Advertising is another method of demonstrating value and is most effective when the message to be communicated is narrowly crafted, recognizable, and repeated frequently. Advertising presents numerous options and most commonly appears on business cards, brochures, newsletters, telephone books, legal directories, publications, the Internet, a Web site, and even on television.
- Driving clients to your Web page is a key to success, along with the creative design genius, ease of use, and informative nature of the Web page itself.

#### Signing the Client: The Initial Interview

- In generating legal business, it is critical for the first impression be an honest reflection of the lawyer's value. The lawyer should strive to hold the initial interview in a physically impressive location that exudes the lawyer's past success to send the message that the lawyer is capable of handling the legal matter and is worthy of the potential client's trust.

The lawyer's challenge in the initial interview is to foster a relationship of trust and an environment of credibility.

Creating this environment begins with fundamental good manners and requires the lawyer to be sincerely empathetic to the potential client's plight.

- After gaining rapport, the lawyer should segue into educating the potential client that he or she would be well served to hire a lawyer who specializes in the area of law relevant to the problem at hand.

## Attracting the Client

The first step in producing rain is attracting clients. To maximize the likelihood of attracting clients, the lawyer should determine the ideal type of client to be attracted. Determining an ideal type depends upon the lawyer's area of legal expertise and the type of legal service the lawyer intends to provide. The lawyer should decide the type of legal work he or she is good at and determine what types of challenges inspire and satisfy the lawyer's need to help others.

- The lawyer should provide the client with an overview of the steps involved in pursuing his or her legal rights and should thoroughly explain, in clearly understandable terms, the cost of pursuing the legal rights.

### Keeping the Client

The lawyer should stress the office's commitment to personal service—and to the ultimate quality and success of the representation—by keeping the client informed and affording an opportunity for meaningful input.

Servicing clients starts with being accessible. When the client inquires, the lawyer must respond quickly, thoroughly, and accurately.

- Proactivity is the ounce of prevention that avoids the need for cure. The lawyer must strive be sensitive to the client's developing plight in order to anticipate potential questions, concerns, and needs.
- The lawyer should advise the client of all developments in the case in a timely fashion. Advising includes ensuring that the client thoroughly understands the options, the recommended plan of action, and the next step.
- A key to client satisfaction is the lawyer's ambition and efficiency.

### Retaining the Client

The reason the lawyer must work so hard to attract, to sign, and to keep the client satisfied is to achieve the ultimate goal of the legal representation: leaving the client ecstatic.

- Leaving the client ecstatic also facilitates staying in touch with the client on an ongoing basis. In turn, staying in touch promotes the opportunity for the lawyer and the client's relationship to continue to grow and, in doing so, also facilitates future referrals. Known value is the centrifugal force that churns new clients.

Once these decisions are made, the next step is to learn as much about the ideal type as possible in order to formulate a strategy of attracting that type of client. The lawyer must determine where the ideal type is most likely to look for a lawyer and upon what information that type is most likely to form an opinion.

Traditional marketing involves cultivation of clients through a combination of referral sources, networking, and advertising. Networking is simply the process of people interacting, bonding and, in the process, discovering each other's interests and strengths. It typically includes active involvement in one or more bar associations, continuing legal education presentations, committees, or community activities, organizations or boards. Potential referral sources ultimately include all of the lawyer's family, friends, and acquaintances—social, business, and professional. Past and present clients are a particularly important referral source. Depending upon the lawyer's practice area, court appointments may be available once the lawyer has been approved for assuming such responsibilities. Of course, the court itself is a potential referral source, and few things are as gratifying professionally as receiving a client referral from a respected judge.

Advertising is another method of demonstrating value and is most effective when the message to be communicated is narrowly crafted, recognizable, and repeated frequently. Ultimately, in addition to meeting interesting people, the purpose of networking and advertising is to increase the universe of situations likely to yield potential clients.

Generating referrals from other lawyers generally involves two scenarios. The first situation involves a lawyer who has been contacted by a person or entity in need of legal services that the referring lawyer has decided not to provide. Typically, this scenario presents when the necessary legal services are outside the scope of the referring lawyer's interest, availability, or expertise. Nonetheless, the referring lawyer may want to stay involved in the representation, while expecting the performing lawyer to take the lead in delivering the needed services. Here, it is important to openly discuss the referring lawyer's expectation in the relationship so he or she may agree upon a fee-split arrangement consistent with the distribution of responsibility and risk. Whether or not the referring lawyer wishes to remain involved in the case, the performing lawyer should be sure to thank the referring lawyer and to make a note of the referring lawyer's area of practice in order to reciprocate.

The second scenario involves the referring lawyer having a conflict of interest regarding a particular situation or need of an existing client. In this scenario, it is extremely important for the lawyer performing the legal services to satisfy the referring lawyer that the performing lawyer understands that he or she is being called upon to serve the client for the particular matter at hand only. Similarly, the performing lawyer should ensure the existing client understands this as well.

Referrals are primarily generated by word of mouth based upon the performing lawyer's past achievement. However, while most referrals are made based upon the performing lawyer's perceived value (based upon reputation), occasionally a referral is made because the referring lawyer expects something (other than a job well done for the client) in return from the performing lawyer. When the performing lawyer senses such a situation, the lawyer should consider the expected cost of accepting the referral before deciding to do so.

Advertising presents numerous options and most commonly appears on business cards, brochures, newsletters, telephone books, legal directories, publications, the Internet, a Web site, and even on television. Threshold determinations include budget and message platform. Before advertising in any form, however, the lawyer should carefully study all governing rules and ensure compliance. In print advertising, location, size, and color matter.

A rapidly growing trend in legal advertising is office Web sites. Driving clients to the Web page is the key to success, along with the creative design genius, ease of use, and informative nature of the Web page itself. Impressive Web pages include features such as lawyer, staff, and office photographs, articles about the lawyer's successes and achievements, professional publications authored by the lawyer, links to related sites on the information highway, and a commitment to keeping the page updated, novel, and informative.

## Signing the Client: The Initial Interview

Attracting the client is just the beginning. The second—and critical—step in producing rain is signing the client. All the resources expended in getting the client through the door are invested for one primary reason: the initial interview. Most new clients are understandably uneasy about the prospective of trusting a stranger with their confidential, highly sensitive, and extremely important personal and business affairs. The lawyer's challenge—in a relatively short period of time—is to foster a relationship of trust and an environment of credibility.

Creating this environment begins with fundamental good manners and requires the lawyer to be sincerely empathetic to the potential client's plight. It is critical for the lawyer to exude an attitude of being more interested in understanding and resolving the potential client's problem than in obtaining a signature on a lawyer fee agreement. While doing so, the lawyer must subtly demonstrate legal expertise while anticipating the potential client's questions and concerns. Achieving this atmosphere requires striking a healthy balance between speaking and listening.

In addition, the lawyer should stress the office's commitment to personal service and demonstrate an understanding of the importance to the client—and to the ultimate quality and success of the representation—of keeping the client informed and of affording him or her the opportunity for meaningful input. The client will be impressed to discover the lawyer recognizes the importance of a healthy partnership between the lawyer and the client. One sure way to alienate a potential client is to send the message that, if hired, the lawyer will expect the client to remain uninvolved unless called upon by the lawyer. Instead, the lawyer should illustrate a genuine commitment to active client involvement by stressing that the client will be copied on all correspondence or otherwise informed of each development. The lawyer should explain that the reason for this is twofold: (1) to ensure the client always knows what is happening in the case; and (2) to ensure, as the client sees what is happening in the case, that the client is given a timely opportunity to seek clarifications, to ask questions, and to offer input.

As well as demonstrating a commitment to keeping the potential client informed and to affording opportunities for meaningful, ongoing input, the lawyer should provide an overview of the steps involved in pursuing the client's legal rights. Discussion of the various stages of pursuing the claim should include a likely timeline and should expand on those stages that will have a tendency to unnerve the client, e.g., responding to discovery requests, being deposed, and participating in alternative dispute resolution.

After gaining rapport, the lawyer should segue into explaining that the potential client would be well served to hire a lawyer who specializes in the relevant area of law needed to successfully address the problem at hand. If a lawyer is merited—given the potential client's situation—the lawyer should be sure to inform the client that, indeed, the client has a good-faith basis to pursue a claim.

The lawyer should then go on to thoroughly explain, in clearly understandable terms, the cost of pursuing those legal rights. For example, in a plaintiff's personal injury case, the client should be advised there are two costs to pursuing a claim: the lawyer fee and the expenses. It is critical to establishing credibility and to gaining trust to address head-on the arrangement under which the lawyer is willing to represent the potential client. Doing so gives the potential client a fair opportunity—up front—to ask questions and to seek clarifications. The attorney-client relationship can thrive only after a mutual commitment to full disclosure concerning every aspect of the representation. When the attorney fee contract is presented for signature at the initial interview, the lawyer should read through the entire contract with the client, pausing where necessary to ensure a meeting of the minds.

Where possible, the lawyer should strive to hold the initial interview in a physically impressive location. Toward this end, at least one room in the lawyer's office should exude the lawyer's past success. Such an environment will go a long way to sending a message to the potential client that the lawyer is capable of handling the legal matter and is most worthy of the potential client's trust.

As with all relationships, the lawyer must be mindful that one never gets a second chance to make a first impression. And, in generating legal business, it is critical for the first impression be an honest reflection of the lawyer's value.

## Keeping the Client

By now, the central message is emerging: Generating business is about building meaningful relationships with a variety of people in a diverse array of settings. From these relationships come the opportunities to demonstrate value. Known value is the centrifugal force that churns new clients.

The best way for a lawyer to create known value is to service existing clients. Serving clients starts with being accessible. It has been said that

when momma is happy, everyone is happy. So it is with clients. Happy clients make for winning cases. Accordingly, the lawyer must strive to keep the client satisfied. Doing so requires the lawyer to be sensitive to the client's developing plight in order to anticipate potential questions, concerns, and needs—before they arise. And, when the client does inquire, the lawyer must respond quickly, thoroughly, and accurately.

Proactivity is the ounce of prevention that forestalls the need for a pound of cure. The lawyer should advise the client of all case developments in a timely fashion. Advising the client includes ensuring that the client thoroughly understands the developments, the options, a recommended plan of action, and the next step. This includes preparing the client to successfully handle each situation requiring the client's participation. Of course, such situations vary with the nature of the legal issues, but may include discovery review and response, the client's deposition, presenting and considering formal offers of settlement, medical examinations, mediation, arbitration, and trial.

Clients are especially impressed when, for seemingly no reason at all, the lawyer inquires how the client is doing and whether he or she needs anything. This inquiry may be in the form of a letter, a telephone call, an e-mail message, or even a quarterly Confidential Report of Client to Attorney for completion.

Another key to client satisfaction is the lawyer's ambition and efficiency. These traits will ensure that the legal matter is resolved as quickly as possible. Swift resolution, to the extent possible, is of great importance to the client. The sooner the case is resolved, the sooner clients can experience closure, thereby potentially reducing their stress and "freeing" them to move forward with their life.

## Retaining the Client after the Representation

The reason why the lawyer must work so hard to attract, to sign, and to keep the client satisfied is to achieve the ultimate goal of the legal representation: leaving the client ecstatic. Ecstatic clients are staunchly loyal and constitute the single most effective billboards imaginable. Their emotionally moving testimonials will naturally work themselves into conversational nooks and crannies in which the lawyer would otherwise never appear.

Leaving the client ecstatic also facilitates staying in touch with the client on an ongoing basis. In turn, staying in touch promotes the opportunity for the lawyer and the client to continue to grow and, in doing so, also facilitates future referrals. The bond that develops between lawyer and client over time is deep—and lasting! The terrain traversed together is titanic! But the journey cannot begin until the lawyer and the client intersect. And, for the lawyer, the only thing more rewarding than seeing a smile on the client's face is knowing who put it there and, eventually, what comes of it.

# §1.3 Is Time Spent Rainmaking Time Not Spent Making Money?
## *Frank J. Kautz II*

It was a pretty slow weekend on the ABA's Solosez listserve when John posted a question with the subject line "Is time spent rainmaking time not spent making money?" In the body of his message he complained: "I am a fairly new solo lawyer and I do not see how I can make any money at this business. I have had my door open for two years and only two people have walked inside of it. I started off with a bunch of clients that my old firm did not want, but now I have finished up most of their cases. While I love hanging around Solosez and chatting, I still need to eat. How do the rest of you manage to get clients?"

In typical Solosez fashion, John started receiving answers within hours. The folks that make up Solosez love to talk about law practice management. It is the one thing that almost everyone on Solosez does for himself or herself, and it always affects the bottom line. Also predictably, for every five people, there are seven opinions on how things should be done. Some people are contentious and some downright helpful.

Sue answered first: "Marketing is easy. All you need is a large family, a bunch of friends, and a lot of cards. My family hands my cards out to everyone and I am constantly getting business."

George chimed in next with, "What is your practice area? What works in one practice area might not in another. I wine and dine my corporate clients and make sure that they have a good time. But that would not work in other fields. Nobody could afford to take all their clients to dinner all the time."

Brian, an older lawyer who likes to remind people that he has been practicing for almost 40 years in the Midwest, wrote, "Do not advertise. That is the bane of the profession. I see all of those billboards asking 'Have you been injured?' and I just want to scream. Advertising is for plumbers, not lawyers. We are professionals and should not have to do stuff like that. Build yourself a good reputation and the clients will flock to your door."

Sarah noted, "Not everyone has a large family or a lot of friends, Sue. Some of us just have to do it ourselves. George, while rainmaking is somewhat different from practice area to practice area, some of the principles are the same.

Oh, Brian, some of us are right out of school in large urban areas. We have to advertise or we will not get a reputation. In areas like Boston, there are seven law schools turning out hundreds of lawyers a year. Some of us just cannot find jobs and end up on our own by default. We have little money, no experience, maybe one client, and a lot of time on our hands. Without advertising we will never get noticed.

"John, I really think that you should spend some time at your local bar association. Go there for their lunch programs. If your bar does not have lunch programs, ask to start some or start a lunch group in your area. The time you spend there will make you a lot of good contacts. Other lawyers will send you cases. Another thing to do is lecture in your practice area. If you handle landlord/tenant problems, see if your local library will host a discussion for you. You can discuss the problems that both landlords and tenants have. If you are an estate planner, talk to people about the necessity of wills and the usefulness of trusts. If you handle business clients, talk about how to run a small business. If you are a personal injury lawyer, tell people what to expect after an accident. The point is to just get out there and let people know you are around."

Sarah was not the only one to add some good advice. Jane, an older and wiser member of the collective, had this to say: "Rainmaking is important. Time spent doing it is definitely neither wasted nor lost money. If you do not go out and spend some time rainmaking, you will not have any clients. Rainmaking can take many forms. You can spend time visiting bar association functions, you can join a club that interests you, you can set up functions to speak at, or you can spend your time on listserves. What you need to do is spend some of your time every week doing some sort of rainmaking, no matter what your practice area is.

"If your practice is one that lends itself well to referrals from other lawyers, then by all means, spend a lot of time at the bar association or on listserves. If, on the other hand, your practice does not involve referrals from other lawyers, then you would be wiser to spend your time with nonlawyers. Join a social group that focuses on something in which you are interested. Do not come out and immediately announce that you are a lawyer; let it come out as part of normal conversation. Be helpful without crossing the line into legal advice. Be generous with your time. If your practice lends itself well to giving a small discount to the people that you meet through the organization, by all means, give them a small discount.

"Brian," Sarah added, "there are many forms of advertising. Not all of it is bad. Those of us who have been around a while forget that it is a different world. If the younger lawyers do not advertise, they will never have the chance to really succeed. We grew up in a very different world from the one that they did. Besides, we did advertise. Our advertising was not the same as what lawyers do today, but never forget that it was there."

In the end, all of the replies from Solosez aside, time spent rainmaking *is* time spent making money. We all need clients. They are the lifeblood of whatever type of practice you have. Whether you are an associate, a partner, or a solo, you need clients if you want to improve your lot in life. Associates who want to move up the ladder need clients. Without clients, your chances of being considered for a partnership are slim. It is your ability to attract and keep clients that will affect your ability to make money for the partnership. If you cannot make money for the partnership, then you will not be offered a chance join the partnership. Partners need to keep their current clients and continue to get more for many of the same reason that associates need clients.

Those of us in solo practices are even more in need of clients. A solo who does not have clients will be out of business and money very quickly. That time that you spend rainmaking *is* time spent making money. A solo who does not do rain dances regularly will quickly find himself or herself in serious trouble. Now, this does not mean that a solo has to do a rain dance daily (although this certainly helps), but solos do have to do them regularly. Far more regularly than other lawyers, because we do not have anyone helping us in our rain dances.

For those who have never heard of Solosez (http://www.solosez.net), I will point out that the names used here are fictional and only vaguely resemble real people. Once described as "the water cooler of the '90s," Solosez (pronounced "so-low-says") is an electronic mail discussion list that has matured into a worldwide community of more than 1,100 solo and small firm practitioners. Solosez is an online resource for lawyers to share information on a wide range of personal and professional subjects: legal questions, client referrals, topical issues, practice technology problems and solutions, travel information, jokes, or just to gloat about a court victory or vent about a local judge. Hosted by the ABA General Practice, Solo and Small Firm Section, this Internet tool has changed the way many solos practice law.

The knowledge and resources of the Solosez community are amazing. There are lawyers from almost every U.S. jurisdiction, Canada, Great Britain—even American lawyers practicing in Mexico, Korea, Germany, Israel, and Japan. Lawyers with experience in virtually every practice niche known to mankind! Techie lawyers, big-city lawyers, country lawyers, new lawyers, senior lawyers, fat lawyers, skinny lawyers, even lawyers who climb on rocks. But most important: This online community has solo and small firm lawyers who are willing to generously share their thoughts and expertise with their colleagues. And sometimes without anyone asking!

Come, join us on Solosez. It is a lot of e-mail, but more than worth the time it takes.

So, what little things can you do to make rain that do not take a lot of time? Change how your secretary answers the phone. You have a name; make sure that people remember it. Your name is one of your biggest rainmaking assets; do not waste it. If you are a solo, make sure that your office staff uses your name when answering the phone. If you are in a larger firm, make sure that your personal secretary uses your name when answering your office phone. If you answer the phone, make sure that you use your own name and do not just say "hi."

If you bring a client into your firm who is already represented by another lawyer, make sure you check up with that other lawyer. Let the client know that you care about them even if you are not handling the case. A five-minute call wherein you know what is going on in their case could well be the difference between you keeping the client or the other lawyer keeping the client.

What do you do when you finish a case? Well, you should always include a business card in your closing letter. A short letter thanking the client for the business and stating what else your firm does is another good way to make some rain. How many times do you think that a client who is looking to have a will drawn does not think of his or her personal injury lawyer? Or clients who are preparing their estate look for another lawyer to handle incorporating their small business? If a client does not know what type of work you can handle, they will not necessarily think of you when it comes to other legal problems. Even if you do not handle a particular type of work, let your clients know that you know other lawyers who can handle it.

> Time spent rainmaking is time spent making money. We all need clients. They are the lifeblood of whatever type of practice you have.

> If you bring a client into your firm and another lawyer is actually handling the case, make sure you check up with the other lawyer. Let the client know that you care even if you are not handling the case.

There are also more time-consuming ways of making it rain in your firm. Joining a club that contains mostly nonlawyers is a very good way of going about this. Just make sure it is an organization in whose cause you really believe or an activity that you enjoy. If you do not agree with the aims of the organization or you do not find pleasure in the activity, the other members will know. This will reduce your chance of getting clients immensely. People like dealing with lawyers who care about the things that they care about. If they think you are just there fishing for clients, they will be more likely to take their business elsewhere.

Another way of attracting clients is to get your name in the newspaper and on television and the radio. Let reporters know that you will answer legal questions in your area of expertise. Just remember, if they call, you must answer or call them back quickly. Reporters are on a deadline and if you do not return their calls, they will go with someone else. And do not ignore the legal-specific publications in your city, state, or practice area. Contribute to the "fluff" pieces as well as to the substantive pieces in such publications. You want your name noticed in any positive way. While potential clients may not see these publications, other lawyers do and often think that the other lawyers in these publications, regardless of whether or not they are in the substantive articles, are important individuals in the field. Being thought of as important generates business.

Advertising is another method of rainmaking. Now, many in our profession hear "advertising" and immediately think of mediocre television ads or lurid billboards asking "Are you injured?" That is not all there is to advertising, though. Advertising can be tasteful and simple. It can be holiday and birthday cards, small reminders that you care about the client and the client's family. Advertising can also be more complex and still remain tasteful. The focus should remain on the lawyer's name or firm name. Name recognition is extremely important and is the key to rainmaking. If no one knows your name or that of your firm, how will you ever make it rain?

One thing to remember is that rainmaking involves not just marketing and advertising but also some personal charm. While many in our profession have the charm, few put it together with the marketing and advertising to make it really pay off. Sure, it costs money and time to make rain, but without spending both the money and the time, you are not likely to keep your practice moving in the right direction.

What are you waiting for? Get out there and make some rain!

# §1.4 Sometimes Bigger Is Better

## *Eileen M. Letts*

When should a small firm turn away preferred business out of concern that the workload will be too great and the quality of representation (along with the firm's reputation) may suffer? The answer is simple—never.

New clients are the lifeblood for a firm looking to expand. When a law practice generates excessive rain, it should never run for shelter, but must fashion itself an umbrella: Change the firm, expand the firm, or partner the firm with another outfit, but don't turn away clients, as they may never come calling again. Whenever a firm accepts additional work, however, it must take care to best serve these new clients.

In devising a strategy to upgrade a firm's functional capacity, the first priority is to conduct an honest self-assessment to determine the office's current capabilities and needs. An internal evaluation will often reveal that existing resources are not being used as efficiently as possible, and that a firm can readily handle supplemental challenges while retaining its current size. Examine the billable hours of lawyers and the workload allocation among support staff to identify where additional productivity may be wrung from existing assets. With better delegation and increased team effort, small firms may discover that simply utilizing untapped potential will allow the management of added challenges without the need to expand.

Where it is determined that the requirements of a new client will outstrip the current capabilities of a practice, a firm must choose whether to increase its size or to partner with another firm on the project. Partnering may seem the easier and economically safer option, but it carries certain pitfalls: alienation of the client who didn't hire the third-party firm; loss of quality control; and the potential for theft of an account. If at all possible, keeping files in-house is recommended over outside partnering.

When designing an expansion plan, further appraisal should be performed to determine whether the firm will require additional lawyers, paralegals, office staff, information technology, or a combination thereof. Often these needs will depend upon the nature of the work at hand.

In class action suits that focus more on document organization than courtroom time, support staff may be the primary need; where procedural complexities will demand extensive research, paralegals may be called for; with intricate fact patterns entailing extensive depositions and investigation, the enlistment of additional lawyers may be required.

Other factors to consider with new hires are whether they will be needed on a permanent basis, and whether the demands of the representation will require lawyers with specialized skills, practice areas, or experience.

Finally, during expansion a small firm must conscientiously balance the need for additional resources with an eye toward cost-effectiveness and profitability. With new clients, critical attention must be paid to superior representation and relationship management, as smaller test assignments may lead to more lucrative associations. With this in mind, expenses should not be spared—but they should be controlled.

Investing in your practice and enlarging the payroll entail an element of risk and can be daunting, but ultimately this is the only way to develop beyond small firm status. When my partner and I set up our own practice, we had only our own talents and an office administrator. Twelve years and several expansions later, Greene and Letts comprises two dozen employees and is still growing to handle our swelling client list. Timidity or self-doubt was never in our business plan.

Common sense, pride, and legal ethics all compel a law firm to provide optimal representation. Solid business practices dictate that a firm never turn away opportunity. An ambitious practice should earn a reputation neither for taking work that it cannot handle nor for being unwilling to accept assignments. Always acquire the client, and always ensure that the work will be managed professionally (even if it means altering your firm accordingly).

"Be careful what you wish for; you might just get it" is a cynical adage to which success-minded individuals should pay no heed. Strive for the business that you wish for, obtain it, and then make whatever changes are necessary to accommodate the work. By gradually enhancing your "umbrella," your small firm will eventually find itself able to handle any rain that comes its way—and it may no longer be considered "small" by potential clients.

# §1.5 How to Manage the Rising Waters in a Small Town
## *William G. Schwab*

I practice in small-town America—not the type of place one normally assumes a lawyer would have too much work, but unfortunately that is what I face each day of my practice. I chose to practice in a small county where I knew personally all the lawyers in the bar. What I didn't count on was that after 25 years, only six of the original 14 lawyers and firms in my town would remain to serve the community's needs—and two of the surviving lawyers are now in their 80s. I also benefited from unplanned marketing as my three children became unintentional recruiters for Dad's practice whenever I met other parents at scouts, 4-H, soccer, Little League, midget basketball— you get the point. The law in the meantime has become more and more involved, and people are resorting much more to litigation to solve their problems.

When I first began generating too much business in the 1980s, I attempted unsuccessfully to recruit associates to join me in the practice. Few law school graduates saw opportunities in a small town that didn't even have a movie theater or a McDonald's. The basic necessities of life seemed missing to them.

At that point I chose not to turn away clients or limit my practice. Instead I initially turned to technology. I invested heavily in networked word processors with big, eight-inch disks. Suddenly I was the "quick" lawyer who put out good work promptly. Paralegals were unheard of at that time in my town, so I recruited heavily of the best of the local high school's secretarial students and trained them to function as paralegals. At one time I had eight support staff working directly for me. New work and clients continued to overwhelm me, and for a while I used a national research service to provide support, but that still was not a solution, since I couldn't control the turnaround time.

Finally, after the sixth year without a vacation, I recruited an associate to join me. My associate liked family law and developed a niche in that area. Pretty soon "my help" needed help. Eventually I lost my associate, who wanted to practice in his nearby hometown. I panicked.

How could I cover the settlements and all the court appearances by myself? In many ways this was a blessing in disguise, as I gave my associate more than 75 family law files to help him with his new practice. I immediately decided not to take any family law cases. I reviewed my accounts receivable and found that criminal defense work was not all that profitable, so that went, too. I started to refer both to my former associate.

Not only had I limited my practice, I also increased my hourly fees at the same time to discourage new business. Funny, but that decision had the opposite result. I would quote a high retainer and the highest hourly rate in the county, thinking that would discourage business, but instead it actually increased business: "He must be good because he charges more than anyone else." I found that my reputation suddenly improved again.

Next, I limited new appointments. I scheduled in advance a set number of new clients that I would see each week, so that I could still have ample time to give good representation to existing clients. Otherwise I would see 15 new clients a week. A three-week wait for an appointment with me was not unusual. Again, waiting for appointments only enhanced my local reputation. I continued to tread water.

Finally, in the late 1990s I was able to recruit three associates to assist me. They were individuals who were returning to the area where they had grown up. Although they are associates, we work as partners and they have input in hiring and firing. I find myself seeing more clients again as the chief rainmaker, but now I have associates who can do the large part of the work, while I supervise and review it. We now are the largest firm in the county, but we know that we could use another associate or two, along with more support staff, if we had more physical space.

Technology helped me when there was too much rain, but we're still looking for a permanent solution to the problem: A thunderstorm is right around the corner. Long live the two lawyers in their 80s who maintain full-time practices, because their absence may create a cloudburst that we can't handle. By any chance, is there anyone reading this who wants to come to a 5,000-person town that now proudly contains both a movie theater and a McDonald's . . . and a Burger King?

# §1.6 The Fine Art of Turning Clients Away

*Lonny H. Dolin*

You have done it. Your marketing efforts have paid off. You worked hard to build your practice and your good work produced more work, which in turn begat more work. As a result, you now face a new "problem." Your office phone is ringing off the hook with calls from people who want you to represent them.

When this first happened, you did what you needed to do to maximize your office's ability to efficiently handle more work. You let your staff screen your phone calls. You hired independent contractors, temporary help, or lawyer-service organizations to perform many of the time-consuming nonbillable services you or your already overworked staff used to perform: court filings, multiple signature collection, messenger deliveries, large copying projects, etc. You even hired on an associate or brought in a partner or paralegal. Because you learned to manage your office more efficiently, for a year or two you were able to personally attend the initial consultation with every potential client who called your office. If the case was good, you were able to represent the new client. Things are now out of control again. You no longer can meet every potential client, and if you continue to represent new clients at the current pace, you will be unable to give your existing clients the comprehensive aggressive representation they have hired you to provide. As a result, you have no choice but to turn potential new clients away.

You may be thinking, "How difficult can it be to say no to a potential client?" What is the problem with just telling the people, "Sorry, we are not taking new cases right now"? Unfortunately, this approach creates a horrible impression of you and your office, eroding the good reputation you have spent years building in the community. Such an approach also enhances the likelihood that you may throw away the biggest potential case of your career and minimizes your ability to continue to attract the clients you want. Through the years I have learned that saying "no" the right way to most of the 200 potential clients who contact our offices each month is a fine art.

## Set Up a Screening Process

In my practice, which focuses on employment law, we found it cost-effective over the long run to hire sufficient staff so that each person who calls for representation has direct contact with a pleasant, competent individual. Within a day of the phone call, intake paralegals first do a conflict check on each potential client. Once conflicts are cleared, each intake is told that only a few of the hundreds of individuals who call our office seeking representation each month actually become clients. The paralegal then explains the steps the intake will go through before we can agree to represent him or her. First, potential clients must answer a short series of basic questions about who they are, who their employer is, and what employment-related concern they want to review with me. If the matter is something I am not able to or interested in handling, I will immediately send the intake one of the numerous carefully crafted letters I have drafted detailing, with regret, the reasons I am not currently in a position to take his other case. For example, the case may not be in my area of expertise, the case may be beyond the applicable statute of limitations, I may be unable to take the case on a contingent fee basis as requested, or I may be

so busy at the moment that it would jeopardize my ability to competently handle my existing clients' matters if I currently took on the case.

If the intake's case appears to have merit and value, I will include in the rejection letter the names of competent lawyers who might be able to handle the case. If the intake appears to be weak on liability or damages, I will simply provide the intake with the phone number of our County Bar Association's lawyer referral number. Your reputation and goodwill in the legal community will suffer if you deliberately refer bad cases to another lawyer. Finally, if relevant, my preconsultation rejection letter advises the intake about the short statute of limitations for dealing with employment matters and gives contact information for the Equal Employment Opportunity Commission and the State Division of Human Rights.

By taking the time necessary to personalize your rejection and to provide the intake with relevant important information, you will preserve your reputation as a competent, professional lawyer who cares about clients. You cannot maintain that reputation by abruptly advising potential clients that you are too busy to have any contact with them. It's also important that you put each potential client through the initial intake process as quickly as possible. Your goal is to not further anger an already distressed person, who will be upset by your unwillingness to even meet with him before you decide you won't represent him.

## Questionnaires

Another successful technique used by offices inundated with telephone calls from individuals seeking representation is to screen potential clients through the use of a questionnaire. This technique requires you to send each person who calls your office seeking representation a detailed questionnaire by mail or e-mail. The questionnaire asks for basic information, including a written description of the events causing the potential client to seek legal representation. The general rule of thumb is that there is no charge for this review.

If the questionnaire is returned, it is reviewed by a lawyer. A letter is immediately sent to anyone the lawyer is unable or not interested in representing. If the lawyer does want to proceed further and interview the potential client, he or she is advised that a consultation fee is first required. The consultation fee will cover the time previously spent reviewing the intake's questionnaire and narrative and will also cover one hour of interview time. The intake is advised that if the interview exceeds an hour, he or she will be billed at the lawyer's hourly rate. Prior to the interview and payment of the consultation fee, the intake is advised in writing that an interview is not a guarantee that the lawyer will take the case.

Make it clear that you cannot give any legal advice until you receive and review the intake's materials. Also, make sure you advise intakes that they are to keep the original of all the materials they send you; if you do not take their case, you will not be returning the materials they send to you. In my field, it is also important to remind intakes that they must fill out the questionnaire as soon as possible to ensure that they don't miss the short time limit for pursuing employment claims.

## Postconsultation Rejections

We agree to represent only about ten percent of the handful of clients we interview each month. At the end of our consultation, if we know that it would not be prudent for us to agree to represent the intake, we advise the intake of that fact immediately. We have learned that you can smooth over the rejection in person much better than if you simply decline representation in a letter. Moreover, we have learned that significant false expectations and subsequent ill will are created when you delay telling an intake you will not represent him or her.

Even if you orally tell an intake you interviewed that you are declining representation, it's imperative to also send a carefully crafted closing letter. This closing letter must make it clear that you are declining representation and that your declination is not to be viewed as an opinion on the merits of the intake's case. Encourage the intake to consult another lawyer and provide the intake with names of other lawyers (if the case seems to have merit) or the phone number of the lawyer referral service in your jurisdiction. When it is called for, take an active role in finding another lawyer for an intake you would like to represent but cannot. If your rejection has not been taken well by an intake whose anger may be problematic, you may want to follow up to make sure the intake was able to secure representation.

# §1.7 Networking for Fun and Profit
### *Jeffrey Allen*

The more people that know you and respect you, the more people that may either call upon you to represent them or refer someone that they know to you for legal advice. The simple and undeniable truth of that statement makes it axiomatic to the process of developing a legal practice.

The more people that know and respect you, the greater your universe of potential clients.

If you accept the importance of this premise, then you understand the need to establish networking patterns early in your practice and to continue them as long as you remain actively in practice and seek new client referrals. While we can look at networking from the simplistic perspective of trying to get as many people as possible to know our name, that we practice law and that we have become pretty good at it, we should look beyond that to other aspects of networking as well.

Properly and effectively employed, networking can provide us with new clients and additional work; but it can also give us a mechanism to better serve our client's needs. It can also help us to practice law more efficiently and more effectively.

It should come as no secret to you that over the last 50 years, the nature of the practice of law has changed dramatically. I have practiced for over 30 years. During that time, I have seen many changes in the practice of law. Many of those changes have resulted in improved service to clients; some have made things worse. When I started practicing, my mentor and employer (later partner) had just shy of 38 years of practice experience.

The complexity of legal practice has caused lawyers to focus their practices.

As a young lawyer, he entertained and educated me with stories of the evolution of the practice during his lifetime.

Over the last 50 years, more and more lawyers have focused their practice on narrower and narrower areas. While such an approach enables a lawyer to develop significant knowledge and skill in a limited area, it concurrently limits their expertise in other areas. While focusing one's practice may prove generally helpful, there sometimes comes a point when it reaches the point of silliness. The best example I can give you of such a development is a true story from my own practice. A number of years ago, I represented a client in a dispute with the other shareholder of a closely held corporation. The individuals had managed to develop a great deal of personal animosity towards each other and each felt the other was taking advantage. A large law firm represented the other shareholder. During the early stages of the litigation I dealt with a partner in the other firm whose entire practice consisted of litigation matters. During the course of discovery (but relatively early in that phase of the matter, as I wanted to try to save the clients some money), I suggested a meeting to discuss the possibility of resolving the matter. I met with the lawyer in a conference room in his office.

We talked preliminarily about resolving some scheduling matters relating to discovery, and then I broached the topic of settlement. As soon as I broached the topic of settlement, my counterpart interrupted me to tell me that he had to get someone else in on the conversation. As he explained it, he only did litigation. He did not handle settlement negotiations. He informed me that he had to bring his negotiating partner to handle the settlement discussions. He brought his partner in and remained himself. I soon

A few words about my own practice, as I think they will help you understand some of what I have to say in this section. During law school I spent one summer working for the federal government and a second summer clerking for a medium-size law firm in the financial district of San Francisco. Those experiences convinced me that I did not want to work for the government and that I really did not like the idea of being the junior lawyer in a larger law firm. As a result, I got a job clerking for a small law firm during my third year of law school and found that I felt more comfortable in that environment. When I graduated from law school, I declined opportunities to clerk for a judge and to work for a large law firm and chose to work for a smaller firm. The firm I worked for had three partners and three associates at the time. I became the fourth partner within a year. I practiced in law partnerships (evolutions of the original firm I joined out of law school) until the beginning of 1996. My then partners and I decided to split the sheets, so to speak, and as of March 1, 1996, I no longer had partners, but I did have one lawyer who worked for me. When I first started practicing, I did litigation of all sorts: business, real property, personal injury, dissolutions, bankruptcy, etc. As time went on, I started doing more and more transactional matters and providing business advice and counseling to businesspeople. Eventually, my practice evolved to the point that I did primarily real estate and business matters. Within real estate, I handled most matters including litigation, transactional, lending, insurance, title, construction, and joint ownership. On the business side, my practice included contract litigation, transactional work, business entity formation, and providing legal advice and counsel to startup and ongoing businesses.

understood why. As I started explaining the costs associated with
the continuation of the discovery in the case, the negotiating partner turned to the litigating partner for verification of the legitimacy
of the expenses, as the negotiation partner appeared to have little
concept of what litigation actually involved.

As general practitioners, we pride ourselves in our ability to
do a multiplicity of things for our clients. In truth, however, most
of us realize that we cannot successfully master every area of the
law and have learned that we do some things better than others
and that there are some things we don't enjoy doing or, for other
reasons, really don't do at all.

Larger law firms have often claimed an advantage over small
firms and solo practitioners in representing clients due to the fact
that they have lawyers with different abilities and emphases in
their practices housed under the same roof, thereby enabling them
to provide "full service" to clients. On its face, the claim of more
complete service appears legitimate. In reality, however, a clever
general-practice lawyer can likely provide better and more efficient service to a client through well-developed networking.

While focus on a particular area facilitates the development
of expertise in that area, it also fosters certain myopia. The lawyer
may see issues in his or her field of expertise with acute, perhaps
microscopic, clarity and detail, but that same lawyer may miss
related issues in other fields due to the bias of his or her
perspective.

Conversely, a more broadly grounded lawyer may lack the
expertise of the focus-practice lawyer in the field of focus, but
may prove a better diagnostician of the problems that the client

> Networking with other lawyers offers great advantages to small firms and solo practice lawyers.

must address. The general-practice lawyer's advantage comes from experience in multiple areas, which enables the lawyer to more easily identify problems and issues in a variety of areas.

It may be highly likely that a lawyer with a highly restricted focus in his or her practice will know that area better than lawyers who do not have that particular emphasis in their practice. For that reason, it may prove prudent for the general-practice lawyer to refer parts of the representation to other lawyers who have expertise in certain fields. I have often advised a client to take such an approach. In order to ensure that the client remains comfortable with the representation, however, I have developed a group of lawyers with whom I work and who have expertise in areas that I feel will likely prove useful to my clients over time. Some of the lawyers on that list have general practices but emphasize areas other than those that I emphasize. Some are certified specialists in particular fields (California officially recognizes a handful of specialties for lawyers).

I have known and worked with each of these lawyers for some time. I am confident in them and in their work. Otherwise, I would never refer clients to them.

When I call in one of the lawyers on my list, I often remain in the picture directly to ensure my client's comfort with the situation and because I am doing a service for the client. I have found that my clients generally prefer such an approach.

Because the lawyers on my list have practices focused differently from mine, they also refer clients to me when their clients have issues within my areas of emphasis.

Sometimes your client's interests and/or your ethical duties require you to refer a case out.

Develop a list of reliable referral lawyers.

This form of networking enables a solo practitioner or small-firm lawyer to effectively provide full service to clients, even though the expertise does not always lie within his or her own office. Such a procedure can have some advantages over the large firm version of full-service representation. For example, the large-firm lawyer will probably refer a tax matter to a tax partner in the same firm, even if lawyers in other firms have better qualifications or, for other reasons, may more effectively deal with the problem. Since I don't have any partners, I don't have to worry about whether my partners have full workloads; I am free to bring in the best tax person for the job, either from my list or not.

The size and nature of the list you develop will relate directly to the nature of your own practice and the needs of your clients (present and future). I have found it helpful to include a marital relations lawyer, a tax lawyer (certified specialist), a labor lawyer, a criminal lawyer, and a personal injury lawyer on my list.

You can easily expand the networking concept beyond other lawyers into other professions and services as well. Give some thought to what other professional services your clients will likely need. Determine which, if any, you feel comfortable working with and look for competent providers of those services. For example, as I work in real estate, my clients often have need for escrow services, title insurance, and real estate brokerage services. My real estate and my business clients also often need the assistance of a certified public accountant. By developing a list of providers of those services, I have the ability to provide my clients with referrals that I have confidence in and with whom I have well-established working relationships.

Potential advantages compared to large firm practices . . .

As with lawyers, each of the providers of other related services that I have added to my list has clients that may from time to time require legal services of the type and nature I provide. As a matter of fact, the most consistent sources of my referral business over the years include a lawyer who works in an office that handles only marital or family law matters, a CPA, and two escrow officers. It just so happens that I have represented the lawyer, the CPA, and both of the escrow agents personally in various matters over the time that I have known them. Accordingly, when they recommend me to a potential client, they can do so not just as a result of my reputation and experience, but also on the basis of their personal knowledge of the way I work with and try to protect my clients.

As an additional benefit from establishing such relationships, you now have a source of information if you need a quick answer about an issue that relates to an area of expertise of one of the people on your list. On the other hand, expect to get some questions from others relating to your areas of expertise as part of the arrangement.

While this approach can prove very helpful to your efforts to build a practice, it carries with it some risks with which you should concern yourself. In some places you can incur liability for making a negligent referral. Whether or not you live or work in such a place notwithstanding, you would not want to make your clients unhappy by making a poor referral. Accordingly, if you want to use this technique to help grow your practice, be very careful about who makes it onto your referral list. You will want to make sure that the list includes only individuals whose work you trust enough to have them represent you.

Think about your clients' other professional needs.

If you think you have found someone that you want to work with this way, spend some time talking to the person about it. Find out how they feel about it. I suggest that you not approach it as a trade. I have never tried to bargain with respect to referrals. I have met with them, told them what I had in mind, and explained that I would like to use them on a referral basis. In some cases the person I talked to was already referring business to me; in other cases, they recognized the value of the approach I proposed and inquired on their own whether I had any interest in referrals from them.

As a further precaution, you should send a letter to your client confirming that he or she asked you to make a referral and that you did so; that while you based the referral on the best information available to you and your personal acquaintance with whomever you have referred the client, the referral maintains a separate practice (or does not practice law); and that should your client have any disagreement or unhappiness with the referral, you will willingly assist in trying to resolve the problem, but that you cannot accept responsibility for the problem or for the actions of anyone not a part of your own practice.

Building referral relationships . . .

# §1.8 Cold Calls and Marketing
### *Carolyn Elefant*

Lawyers rarely agree on anything. But ask most lawyers for their opinion on cold-calling for business, and you're likely to find a unanimously negative reaction. "Tacky!" some lawyers might haughtily exclaim. "Won't I appear desperate?" others might ask. Guaranteed, all will ultimately dismiss cold calls as a marketing technique that's beneath them.

Which is too bad. For those lawyers who have the vision to split from the herd mentality or the nerve (and it does take plenty) to pick up the phone and call a stranger, cold-calling offers a cheap and effective way of making contacts and finding work.

## What Are Cold Calls— and Why Make Them?

A cold call is what the name implies: a phone call to a potential source of business with whom you have had only minimal contact in the past or perhaps none at all. Related to the cold call is the cold contact, which takes the form of a written communication to the business source. Cold contacts differ from mass mailings, however. With cold contacts, each pitch is specifically targeted to the potential business source—usually a particular individual—whereas with mass mailings, the information provided is more general in nature.

So, why engage in cold-calling? First and most compelling, cold calls are one of the cheapest and least time-consuming forms of marketing. For example, consider a new lawyer who's just started a practice and wants to make appearances on a per diem basis for busy lawyers. Within a half hour, the lawyer can open up the county bar association directory and call about ten lawyers—or a total of 30 if the lawyer makes a half hour's worth of calls three days that week. Of that group of 30, only two may have work while a few others might ask for follow-up information like a résumé to keep on file. But that's not a bad return for an hour and a half of marketing that doesn't involve any out-of-pocket expenditure.

By contrast, say that same lawyer had decided to send a mass mailing to 30 lawyers instead of making cold calls. First, he'd have to draft and proof a letter, taking the time to make it general enough to apply to all 30 target subjects. He'd then have to type up 30 addresses for a mail merge, print and sign 30 letters, and then print out 30 envelopes. That task involves a minimum of three hours of time, not to mention $11 in postage. And most of the letters would likely wind up at the bottom of the trashcan.

And that's the second benefit of cold-calling: It allows for instant gratification. The recipient of a call can't put off giving some kind of response—either yes, there's an immediate need or no thanks. With mass mailings, it's all too easy for a recipient to put the letter aside and never respond.

Additionally, because cold calls involve direct contact, there's an opportunity for interaction. For example, that lawyer cold-calling for per diem work might reach a contact who doesn't have any such work available at the moment. But during the course of the conversation, the contact might recall that she'd just declined a small litigation matter because of scheduling conflicts and might refer the entire matter out to you. In many cases, if you can keep your cold contacts talking, they may have other ideas to offer—something that doesn't happen when you engage in more passive forms of communication, like mass mailings or ads, which don't require any interaction with the intended recipient.

Finally, cold-calling can give lawyers a marketing edge because the calls are unexpected. So few lawyers make cold calls that those who do will find limited competition. Thus, cold calls can set you apart from other lawyers.

## Limitations on Cold Calls

Before embarking on a cold-calling campaign, it's important to consult your bar's ethical rules or place a call to bar counsel. While there are no limitations on cold-calling other lawyers, most jurisdictions' respective professional codes ban direct solicitation of clients. Thus, for example, in most states, a lawyer who sees an article about several railroad workers injured on the job would be precluded from calling their spouses and offering to represent them in a personal injury action. However, the rules don't apply as stringently for more sophisticated clients. I know of many lawyers (myself included) who, for example, may learn of an administrative action that is adverse to a regulated business and contact that entity, by phone or e-mail, to offer ideas for appealing the decision.

Similarly, lawyers might learn about new government regulations and might call affected entities to explain the changes and to see whether they might have a need for assistance with the development or implementation of programs required by those changes. In this type of situation, the cold call is educational in nature in that it conveys general information rather than solicits business with respect to a particular matter. Thus, bar restrictions on solicitation would likely not apply.

## How to Make Cold Calls

The nuts and bolts of making cold calls are fairly simple. Most importantly, you'll want to spend a little time coming up with a short pitch of under a minute if possible so you don't find yourself stammering when the subject comes on the line. The first 20 seconds of the pitch should be devoted to an introduction that includes your name and your firm's name as well as how you obtained the name of the contact. If you've been referred to a contact by a mutual acquaintance, be sure to mention that person's name in your opening remarks because it will make your contact more receptive. But even if you've just pulled a person's name from the bar association phone book, that can work just as well. For example, you might say, "Hello, this is Jane Doe of the Doe Law Firm. I'm a member of the Cook County Bar Association, and I've gotten your phone number from the association's most recent phone book."

Once intros are out of the way, it's important to ask the person you've called whether he or she has a minute to talk. You don't want to launch into your spiel only to find that the person on the other end is in the midst of an important business meeting. If the person is unavailable, discern a better time that you can call back and follow up at that point. Do not leave a number and ask the contact to return your call, because chances are he or she will never follow up.

If your contact is available, you next need to get to the purpose of the call. If you've called a business that might be interested in, for example, your employment law practice, you might briefly describe the service that you have to offer (perhaps a new employee handbook) and ask if you might send it on for the company's review. Once the company receives the material, you can follow up with a second call.

When calling another lawyer for referrals or contract work, you should come right out and ask if there's any available while at the same time explaining the benefit to the potential source. Here's a sample of what you might say:

"The reason that I'm calling is that I have recently become available for referrals in bankruptcy cases and would like you to keep me in mind for future cases. The XYZ firm has referred me several bankruptcy cases and their clients were satisfied with the results and happy that the XYZ firm could direct them right to me so that they could avoid the trouble of finding another law firm."

Most importantly, you want to avoid an appearance of desperation. Even if you have no other work and feel like the biggest loser, you must always keep in mind that you are offering a valuable service that another lawyer or business entity should be grateful to receive. So rather than mention that you're looking for work because business is slow, say that you're actively pursuing a particular area.

The wrong approach: "I just started my law practice, and I'm having trouble finding clients. So perhaps I could do some contract work for you to fill in the gaps until my business picks up."

In this situation, the contact will wonder what's wrong with you and may also be concerned that if he or she sends work your way, you'll give it short shrift when your own cases start coming through the door.

A better approach: "The reason for my call is that I would like to know whether you have a need for a lawyer to draft motions or briefs on a contract basis. I recently started providing research and writing services on a contract basis to other lawyers, and I really enjoy this aspect of practice and am actively pursuing more of this type of work."

After you've made the pitch, try to gauge the reaction. If the subject gives a terse reply, it's best to say thank you for his or her time and terminate the call. But if your subject seems friendly or interested—if he or she asks questions about your practice or background—try to engage in further conversation. Perhaps the contact might not have work available, but could introduce you to someone else who might. If you're a new lawyer, perhaps the contact might be willing to meet to talk a little bit about law practice. Even a call that won't generate immediate business can lead to work down the line.

### A Checklist for Cold Calling

Ready to start cold calling? Here's a quick checklist to get organized.

#### 1. Get the Names Together

First, compile a list of ten to 30 lawyers to call. Gather names from your own contact list and tips from colleagues. If you're still short, consult a bar directory.

#### 2. Figure out a Format

If you're really organized, you can use an Excel spread sheet, with columns for lawyer's names, the source of the contact, response, and needed follow-up. Paper and pen will work too—just be sure to save your list for follow-up.

#### 3. Prepare Your Speech

Jot down your speech and practice it a couple of times.

#### 4. Set Aside a Time

Set aside a time, preferably 10 to 11 AM or 3 to 4 PM, when lawyers are most likely to be in the office. Then shut off any other phone lines so you won't be interrupted. And be sure it's quiet—no crying babies or barking dogs in the background.

#### 5. Take a Deep Breath and Think Positive

If you're nervous and worried about business, it will show in your voice. So psyche yourself into good humor to make the calls.

#### 6. Go To It

Just start calling, checking people off your list as you go. Be sure to make a note of any needed follow-up.

#### 7. Don't Quit

Almost immediately, you will receive rejections. Don't stop or take a break. Your armor will harden as you work through the list.

#### 8. Set Aside Time for Follow Up

Be sure to follow up, that day if possible, with writing samples or other materials you promised to send. And note which lawyers were not available so you can try them again.

## How to Handle Rejection

No doubt, when you cold-call, you will receive countless rejections. When I have cold-called, responses have ranged from the "I'll keep you in mind" to a curt "No, thank you" or even exclamations like "I guess business is as slow for you as it is for me." The rejection can be embarrassing and often demoralizing until you remind yourself: If you don't have the guts to sell yourself, how can you sell your client's case?

## Try It at Least Once

Cold-calling requires little investment and can ultimately result in a decent payoff. I've found a couple of clients and work through cold calls, but it also helped me locate terrific office space and meet other lawyers who've become friends. Most of all, whether your cold calls are successful or not, the confidence you gain from cold-calling can help make you a better lawyer—and that alone makes it worth a try.

# 2

# Your Rainmaking Team

# §2.1  A Blueprint for Marketing with Staff
## *Robert A. Kraft*

Marketing a law practice still is a tricky concept for many lawyers, full of questions that have no easy black-and-white answers: How much is too much? How slick is too slick? What about all those brochures sitting in the storeroom from our last foray into self-promotion?

My practice, a small personal injury and Social Security disability firm in Texas, eliminated a lot of the nettlesome questions that arise when setting up new ventures by deciding to put our marketing efforts into something we already had: ourselves and our staff. We do not have a separate marketing department, and I routinely remind our employees that we're all in marketing. In a small firm, everyone must contribute to the effort.

Texas has strict rules prohibiting solicitation of injury claims, so we face constraints not encountered by law firms pitching their services to corporations. Our in-house marketing efforts focus more on keeping existing clients satisfied and receiving word-of-mouth referrals than on bringing in new cases from outside sources.

We advertise on television, in the Yellow Pages, by e-mail newsletter—we even have a billboard. But no matter how much advertising we do, the bulk of our business always comes from former clients and their referrals. If you do a good job for people, they will return, and they will refer their friends to you. Naturally, you want to give them a reason to do so, and we've found our staff can be an invaluable tool in encouraging that.

## Hire the Right People

Marketing with staff begins with having the right employees. For a consumer-oriented law firm, this means outgoing people with a professional attitude. Clients obviously want their lawyer and staff to be competent, but they equally want their legal team to be caring, understanding, and friendly.

A simple guideline is to hire good people, train them properly, pay them well, and keep them happy. Note that good pay doesn't necessarily guarantee happy employees. We try to show our appreciation to employees in many ways, including little perks. All employees have a business card with name and job title, and we encourage them to be liberal in handing them out. In addition to the individual cards, we keep at the front desk a stack of generic cards that have a list of practice areas printed on the back to remind visitors of the types of cases we handle.

Staff in general must be competent in their jobs, or no amount of marketing will overcome the negative impression your clients will have of your firm. Employees should be intelligent enough to make decisions on their own and motivated enough to return phone calls and e-mails promptly. If you give your employees authority to make at least some decisions, your clients will be happier because they won't have to wait as long to get answers or action. Obviously, prohibitions regarding employees' giving legal advice must be heeded, but space for autonomy does exist.

Staff continuity also is an important part of marketing. We have 20 full-time employees, and half of them have worked here more than 12 years. Clients develop a great sense of confidence when they deal with the same employees throughout the course of a case, and this consideration is even more important for firms that handle long-term matters for clients rather than typically brief personal injury claims.

## Opening a Case

The new client procedure in our firm begins with the receptionist. Ours is very good at fielding many calls yet still making the callers feel unhurried. She keeps our client database open on her computer, which allows her to quickly look up names and direct calls to the proper employee.

For new case calls, the receptionist determines the type of case, gets a phone number in the event of an accidental disconnect, then forwards the call to an employee in the appropriate department. Every employee is authorized to take information from a new case call, so we never have to tell a caller that no one is available to talk. We try to let the callers talk for a short while before jumping in with "just the facts" questions. This lets callers know we're interested in their problems, not just in taking down the information.

If the caller's problem is obviously something we don't handle, the receptionist gives the call to a specific employee whose main job is to field such matters. This employee gets the pertinent information—we have interview sheets for various types of new case inquiries so we don't forget to ask an important question—and explains why we can't represent the caller. We average more than 40 new case calls per day. Unfortunately, about 90 percent of these are for cases we can't accept, but we still want to make a good impression on callers in the event they someday have a case we can handle.

If we don't accept a case, we make a real effort to refer the caller to a lawyer or government agency that can help. We keep a frequently updated referral list on our intranet that includes lawyers who handle cases outside our practice areas, governmental agencies, and charitable organizations. We have brochures on different legal subjects that we offer to mail; some of them are written by us and some are obtained from other sources. By spending a few minutes on the phone, providing a bit of free information, and pointing potential clients in the right direction, we let them know we do care about their problems, even if we won't be making a fee from them. This extra work takes quite a bit of staff time and may not always appear to directly benefit the firm. Some of the effort is made simply because we feel it is the right thing to do, but some clearly cultivates a potential client base.

We send a "sorry" letter to every caller we can't represent, stating we are not accepting the case and explaining any applicable statute of limitations. Again, we have form letters already drafted for various types of cases. The letter also encourages potential clients to refer friends and family to us for any legal questions and directs them to our Web site for helpful legal articles. We add all such callers to our mailing list, and we send birthday cards, calendars, and newsletters. Many clients come back to us years later, explaining that although we couldn't help them with the original matter, they now want to hire us on a different matter. It pays to show potential clients you care about them, and it pays to keep in touch with occasional mailings.

If a new case call does sound promising, we set up an appointment at which the client meets first with a new case clerk, who enters basic information into our case management program, and then with a legal assistant, who fleshes out the details of the claim and answers most of the client's questions. The client then meets with a lawyer, who can answer any remaining questions. (All these meetings take place in a single room, with the various staff members meeting the prospective client one after another; we offer the client soft drinks and refreshments, as the visit can be lengthy.)

Immediately after opening a case, we send clients an initial letter thanking them for hiring us and reminding them of important information discussed in person. The letter also mentions that we would be happy to talk with the client's friends or family members who have unrelated legal questions, whatever they may be. I pen a short note at the bottom of each letter to personally thank the client for choosing our firm.

A few days later, we call again, thank them for hiring us, verify address and telephone information, and ask whether they forgot to tell us anything in the initial interview or have additional questions. Thirty days after signing up the case, we send another thank-you letter and a questionnaire regarding medical treatment, witnesses, and other items. We also ask whether they're satisfied with our services to date. The point of all this is to let the clients know that we really do appreciate their business and to assure them we're actively working on their cases.

## Teamwork

As is obvious throughout this process, our philosophy has always been to "move work downhill" when possible. If a lawyer doesn't have to do it, let a legal assistant handle it; if the legal assistant is better used elsewhere, move the task to a legal secretary, and so on. We are scrupulous about having all work supervised by a lawyer and very careful not to let employees give legal advice or make legal decisions.

We occasionally receive client letters addressed to "Attorney Smith" although Ms. Smith is not a lawyer. We immediately send the client a letter explaining Ms. Smith's job title and stressing that she is not a lawyer. We do everything possible to avoid the trap of allowing a client to believe a staff member is a lawyer (which is one reason staff have business cards but, if not lawyers, are not listed on firm letterhead).

We take a team approach to handling files, and we encourage new clients to meet all various members of the team. This helps build rapport with the clients and eliminates the "just a voice on the line" feeling when they call us. We include photos and biographical sketches of all employees on our Web site (http://www.kraftlaw.com), and we use employees in some of our television and print advertising. The goal is to personalize the firm in the client's mind. We're proud of each of our employees, and we want our clients to know that.

Clients want lawyers and staff who communicate with them and care about their cases. In a way, our client management software allows us to show clients we care. The program we use,

LawBase by Synaptec, allows us to make unlimited "activity notes" each time we take any action on a file. Whenever a client calls, the person talking with the client can see at a glance what was done on the file recently and by whom, which gives the impression that the client's file is always uppermost in our minds. (I print out all the day's activity notes and read them each evening, which lets me monitor file activity without having to pull files for a physical review.)

A vital part of showing clients you care is listening to them when they complain. But a surprising number of people don't complain when they're unhappy—they just suffer in silence and then never return or make referrals. We try to make it very easy for clients to tell us when they're not happy with our work. We keep a stack of comment cards in our waiting room, and the receptionist also hands one to each client who visits the office. The card asks simply whether the client has any comments. It may be signed or unsigned, given directly to the receptionist or anonymously left in a box in the waiting room.

When we receive signed comment cards, we send letters thanking the client for a compliment or for pointing out a problem with our services. We call if it sounds serious. We send three questionnaires to clients during their case, and each has space for comments regarding our services. We know we can answer any complaints clients may have—the trick more often is getting them actually to complain!

We try to take every opportunity to encourage existing clients to refer friends and family to us. Surprisingly, even clients who are pleased with your services may not realize they should refer their friends. Some think you're too busy to accept new clients or a small matter. Others may not realize you also handle other practice areas. Train your staff to give short cross-selling pitches to existing clients about all types of work your firm handles. (This may be especially important in a firm like ours, where some employees do nothing but Social Security work and others do nothing but personal injury work.) Make sure each employee has at least a basic knowledge of the full range of services you offer.

We maintain a short list of former clients who were especially pleasant to work with or who expressed a particular interest in referring their friends. We occasionally send them postcards asking them to give us a call just so we can find out how they're doing. I created an interview form for those calls so the staff remembers to verify contact information, give news about our firm, and ask whether they have suggestions for improving our services.

The impression your staff makes is important. We can't all be young and beautiful, but we can all be clean and neatly dressed. Our firm requires a coat and tie for men and the equivalent for women, except on casual Fridays. We like the impression of professionalism this gives clients, but we do have one exception: Our dress code incorporates a marketing tool—shirts with our firm logo on them—that may be worn with casual pants any day. Aside from keeping the firm name in front of office visitors, we also get free advertising when employees go out to lunch or run errands.

Most of the "marketing" our staff does is really just being friendly, whether to potential clients, current clients, or employees at insurance companies and government agencies. We don't use high-pressure techniques, and we try to keep clients from noticing that we're marketing at all. Be competent, act nice, and make sure your clients know you want more business: That's marketing in a nutshell.

## Magic Numbers

We get many comments about our firm's telephone numbers: (214) 999-9999 and (817) 999-9999. (The area codes are for Dallas and Fort Worth, respectively.)

We got the 214 telephone number about 12 years ago when a local personal injury lawyer was closing his practice and leaving Texas. We made a deal to purchase his telephone number and his advertising space on the back cover of the Dallas Yellow Pages. (We also had to agree to take over the files he couldn't get anyone else to accept.) The 999 prefix is not in our office's geographic location, so we have to pay mileage charges each month for use of that number.

Obtaining the 817 number was a little more difficult. It was a mobile number used by the telephone company so repairpersons could check phone lines. It took quite a bit of convincing to get them to transfer the number to us. We still pay mobile phone charges for calls to that number.

We feature the phone numbers prominently in our advertising and have had many clients tell us they called because our number was easy to remember. When employees have to give their work number to a store clerk, they always get an odd look, which gives them a chance to mention our firm name.

The only real drawback to the numbers came before ten-digit dialing was required in Dallas and Fort Worth. Every day we would get dozens of calls from little kids who were just punching phone buttons. Now that everyone has to dial an area code even for local calls, that problem has disappeared.

Our Texas toll-free number is (800) 989-9999. I would love to have (800) 999-9999, but it's used by Covenant House, an international service agency for runaway youth. I sent a nice letter to them a few years ago and asked if they would consider selling us their telephone number. I received a rather curt reply saying my request would be passed along to Sister Mary Rose but it was doubtful she'd be interested. Apparently she wasn't, because I've heard nothing further.

# §2.2 Mining Your Own Client Resources
## *Jeffrey Allen*

Experienced lawyers have many means of attracting potential clients. The one method most often overlooked, however, has proven the most effective in my practice. I have found that my existing clients are generally my best source of new clients. Keep this rule in mind: A satisfied client makes the best source of referrals and new business.

The logic of that rule seems fairly difficult to attack. Put yourself in the position of a prospective client. Assume you have a legal problem and have decided you need a lawyer, but that you don't know a lawyer who does the kind of work you need done. On the other hand, you do know Mr. and Ms. Smith, your neighbors, who had a similar problem last year. In a conversation with the Smiths, you tell them of your plight. They immediately respond by telling you that you need to go see lawyer Weiss. Attorney Weiss, they tell you, represented them in a similar matter last year and did a great job for them. The Smiths are friends of yours. Will you

A. Ignore the Smiths' recommendation and look for a lawyer in the Yellow Pages?
B. Ignore the Smiths' recommendation and conduct an Internet search for lawyers?
C. Ignore the Smiths' recommendation and call the lawyer you saw advertising on the late show last night?
D. Accept the Smiths' recommendation?

> Satisfied clients are a great source of referrals and new business.

In my experience, most prospective clients would opt for choice "D," take the Smiths' recommendation, and call lawyer Weiss.

Depending on how well you impressed your clients and upon their own personalities, you may even find their efforts on your behalf more aggressive than Mr. and Mrs. Smith's. For example, I have regularly had all of the following occur in my practice:

- Prospective clients call and describe themselves as friends of clients of mine that had recommended me to them.
- Prospective clients call and tell me that so and so (a client of mine) told them that they really needed a lawyer to help them with a particular problem and that I was the one they should see.
- Prospective clients call and tell me they heard from someone that I never heard of that I was very good in a particular area; I later find out that the person they heard that rumor from knew a client of mine, or knew someone who knew a client of mine.
- Existing clients call me to ask if I would accept a friend/ co-worker/colleague/neighbor/relative of theirs as a client.
- Existing clients bring a prospective client to my office to introduce to me.
- Existing clients call to tell me that they referred a prospective client to me because the prospective client is in deep trouble and needs my help.

Now, in all truth, I don't know a single lawyer who will admit to not wanting to have satisfied clients. That said, we all know that

- Some lawyers do better work than other lawyers.

- Some lawyers do a better job with client management than others.
- Some lawyers do a better job with client relations than others.

So, if we assume that satisfied clients will refer other work to our practice, we have another strong motivation to develop systems in our practice to ensure that we have satisfied clients. Simply stated, we can keep clients happy without tremendous effort and often without regard to the success we achieve for them in any particular matter (although common sense tells you that if you win, you have an easier job of producing a satisfied client).

Satisfied clients will refer their friends and colleagues to you.

## Introduce Yourself and Your Practice

When a prospective client comes into my office, I make it a point to tell them a little (maybe a lot) about my practice and myself during the initial discussion about their situation. I do that on the theory that they have not yet made their mind up about whether to hire my firm and that providing them with such information may help them decide to hire us. If you have a firm brochure, this is a good time to give it to the prospective client.

Tell your clients the type of work you handle.

I also give the client that information because the client may have other matters in other areas that requires legal assistance. If I don't tell the client that we do that work, the client will not likely think we do. By letting the client know what type of work you do beyond the matter presently under consideration, you open the door to additional work and even to the possibility that the client does not hire the firm on the first matter, but hires the firm on another matter as a result of that discussion.

In a similar vein, consider what you hang on the walls of your office. The choice you make represents you. I have seen many offices in which lawyers hang their diplomas and their bar admission certificates on the wall. I have never done that and have never had a client question whether I graduated from law school or was admitted to practice. I have a collection of lithographs that hangs in my office. I selected a well-known artist and a collection of pieces that showed locations from all over the world. In my personal office, I chose images that convey power and strength, such as a steamship and a locomotive. I generally meet with clients in our library/conference room. In that room, I hung a number of certificates of commendation from the local courts for work in connection with alternative dispute resolution. I have also hung in that room awards and acknowledgements I have received for my public service activities. I have had a number of comments from clients and prospective clients about those awards. I think that the acknowledgments from the courts help give the clients a good feeling about me as a lawyer. I think that the public service acknowledgements help the client feel comfortable with me as a person. I believe that many clients perceive both as important to their decision-making process.

> Your office decor reflects on you; make the reflection positive.

## Convey Your Interest in Prospective Clients and Their Problems

People generally come to see lawyers for one of two reasons. Some want to avoid a problem by getting legal help to assist them in acting in compliance with applicable law. Others have a problem now because they didn't seek prior legal advice or assistance. Whichever of those conditions brings potential clients to your office, the clients will want to feel that you are concerned about them and their problems. It always amazes me when I talk to potential clients who tell me that they seek replacement counsel because their current lawyer (1) doesn't really seem to have time for their matter; (2) won't tell them about the status of the case; (3) won't respond to telephone calls or letters. Often such conduct causes clients to think the lawyer simply doesn't like them or that their lawyer does not believe in their case. Such beliefs never help a lawyer retain a client.

## Make Sure the Prospective Client Knows You Work to Satisfy Your Clients

In the course of my first meeting with prospective clients, I generally let them know that while we do help our clients solve problems after they reach crisis proportions, we believe that generally we can help clients the most by providing advice to keep them out of trouble in the first place. That point may not relate to the current situation, but it opens the door to other representation in the future.

Explain to your clients how you will work with them.

I think that clients want and need to know that you will work with them to solve their problems. They want to have some say in the outcome of your work. Explaining to a client that you will provide them with information on a regular basis and that they will play a major part in the decision-making process relating to their case often makes them feel much more at ease.

I have a number of clients that I have represented for many years. Prospective clients often perceive that as a recommendation.

The fact that those clients have chosen to remain with me for prolonged time periods suggests strongly that they have been pleased with my work on their behalf.

## Don't Create Unreasonable Expectations

Do not oversell yourself when you meet prospective clients. Do not allow (and certainly do not help) them to oversell themselves on their case. If you encourage a client to believe you can magically turn their sow's ear of a case into a silk purse filled with cash, they will not easily accept less. You make your case more difficult to settle as a result of such expectations. You also make it harder on yourself to succeed. If you do a great job and get your clients more than they had any reasonable basis to expect, you may still come up the goat if they expected more than they got. On the other hand, if your clients understand the problems and risks associated with their case, they will more likely settle on a reasonable basis; and if the case does not settle, but you get them near the top of the reasonable range of expectations, you come up the hero. Hero or goat, which do you prefer? I always prefer playing hero to playing goat.

*Don't create unreasonable client expectations.*

## Communicate, Communicate, and Communicate

Over the last several years, malpractice insurance carriers have become more and more interested in providing loss prevention information to their insureds. The carriers have correctly perceived

*The key to good client relations: COMMUNICATE, COMMUNICATE, COMMUNICATE (and do good work).*

that if they assist lawyers in bettering their relationships with their clients, the clients will not as readily sue their lawyers. A reduction in lawsuits against insured lawyers reduces the carrier's claims administration costs, defense costs, and settlement costs. That can go right to the carrier's bottom line. For a number of years, our malpractice carrier has sent us memoranda saying, in effect, that research has confirmed that lawyers who fail to respond to their clients in a timely manner generally have unhappy clients and that unhappy clients are more likely to sue a lawyer than happy clients are.

The flip side of that coin is that maintaining good and timely communications with your clients will help keep them happy. Clients do not like to feel that you are ignoring them or even not paying a sufficient amount of attention to them. It does not take a substantial leap to get from a perceived failure to pay sufficient attention to a client to a perceived failure to pay sufficient attention to the client's case. These rules respecting communications with clients have always worked well for me:

- Always send the client a copy of every pleading.
- Always send the client copies of discovery you receive.

- Always send the client a copy of significant correspondence to opposing counsel and, when necessary for perspective or otherwise appropriate, copies of correspondence from opposing counsel.
- Always give your client plenty of notice of any date on which the client must appear somewhere. Clients will see your concern for their calendar as a courtesy.
- Always give your client plenty of notice of any date by which the client must do something or provide something to you.
- Respond to client phone calls the same day you get them, if possible, or at the latest by the next business day. If you cannot get back to the client directly, have your secretary call to explain why you are not available and when you will get back to them.
- Remember that the case belongs to the client. Include the client in the decision-making process with respect to strategy and economics. Document discussions, agreements, and instructions in a confirming letter to protect yourself and decrease the likelihood of misunderstanding or miscommunications.
- Make sure that your bills explain what you did for the client.

- If your client has a question about a bill, make sure you let the client know that you will not charge for your time in addressing the issue.
- If you become aware of a significant event in your client's life (marriage, birth of a child, promotion, new house purchase), send an appropriate message. They will appreciate your thoughtfulness. You may find it helpful to send all of your clients season's greetings cards at the end of each year. It will serve to remind those you have not seen for a while that you are still around.
- If you help a client set up a business entity and don't hear from the client for a while, consider calling the client to see how the business is going. In talking to clients about their business activities, you may discover areas where your services could help them (such as in reviewing contracts or leases or in setting up form agreements for the client to use).
- When you set up a corporation for a client, send the client a letter outlining those things that the client must do on a regular basis. As it comes time for the annual meeting, send the client a reminder notice; ask if the client would like to have you prepare and send out the notice to the shareholders and/or prepare minutes of the meeting.

## Show Patience and Support for Your Client

Your clients consider their work very important, even if it is a small matter compared to others you handle or one that does not present many complexities. In any disputed matter, as their lawyer you are their knight in shining armor. The one that stands up for them, that defends them and advances their position. Some clients will show more anxiety than others. When they do, they need you to hold their hand and let them know you are on their side. Show them patience. Do not get testy with them when they call over and again to check on the same thing. Help them, be supportive, and let them gently know that you are concerned that their bill will be higher than you would like because of all of the time going over the same thing. Consider suggesting that the client send questions by e-mail so that you can respond to them more thoughtfully. They will appreciate that effort and it may save you much time.

## *Let Your Clients Know You Are Willing to Take on More Work*

In the course of your relationship, you can casually let your clients know that you can accommodate more work or that you would like to get a particular type of work. It plants the seed with them that they could recommend you to a friend, colleague, or neighbor. Keep lots of your business cards around and pass them out freely to your clients. If they have more than they need, they just might pass them out to a prospective client for you.

# §2.3 How to "Partner" with Other Lawyers

### Joseph A. DeWoskin

After almost nine years on active duty with the U.S. Army Judge Advocate General's Corps, I found myself at a crossroads in my legal career. Opting to take a road not often traveled by the friends I had made in the military, I decided to leave active military service and work at a law firm, enjoying all the job safety and financial protection that come with a big firm.

Of course I flooded the local area with résumés, targeting all types of firms. I interviewed with some, was offered employment by some, and then, as I was mulling over what to do, a friend of mine presented me with an interesting opportunity: "Come and open your own practice in our office. If you're willing and able to take a chance, it will be the best opportunity to practice law you could ever have."

The best opportunity I could ever have? I had to find out more. "Well," my friend said, "it's an office-share situation. We're all partners, but not in the traditional sense of the word. We're solo practitioners who run our own practices—a few have an associate—but we have the comfort and security of other lawyers to share expenses, discuss cases, and refer cases outside our practice areas."

The primary question for me was whether I could afford to take this chance and open my own law practice. Looking back, the question really should have been how could I *not* afford such an autonomous yet supportive opportunity. My biggest problem at first was explaining to people how I am a solo practitioner but work at a law firm, although the concept of sharing my office with other lawyers is pretty simple to grasp. Being a "partner" by office sharing is a combination of the best of being a solo and being in a law firm. A few years ago, an acquaintance of mine decided to open his own law practice as a solo; within a year he decided the sense of isolation was not worth the advantage of being on his own. He also struggled to find new clients and to cover the various areas of law his cases encompassed. He missed human contact and mentoring.

## Basic Considerations

Before entering an office-sharing relationship, review the groundwork so you're certain about what you're getting into.

## Structure

How is the business legally structured? Are the lawyers separate entities (Law Office of Joseph A. DeWoskin, Law Office of John Smith), or do they present themselves as a firm (DeWoskin, Smith & Jones, A Partnership Including Professional Corporations)? This affects legal liability and potential ethical issues and determines what should be covered in the lease agreement. At my office we are separate but present ourselves to the public as a firm.

## Written Agreement

This may be made with either the primary "partner" or with the other lawyers in the suite. (Discussing everything in the agreement could result in an entire article; here we'll concentrate on general items to cover in the setup agreement. Also, be sure to verify that the agreement does not violate state ethical rules.)

One of the most essential facts to cover is what is included in rent and overhead: a receptionist who answers a central phone line and greets clients, local and long-distance telephone service, fax machine, basic office supplies (pens, paper, letterhead, file folders, Post-its, postage), Internet access, online legal research, legal malpractice insurance, and so on. These items can be tailored to meet the needs of your specific group.

Issues that arise in a true partnership—profit sharing, for example—are not a factor in office sharing; there is no profit sharing with lawyers who do not participate in your case. If you do enter into a traditional partnership, the agreement must make very clear who is responsible for making decisions and addressing other issues that may arise.

My agreement provides a receptionist, firm letterhead, office supplies, a copy machine, a fax, and metered postage for my use.

## Benefits

Lawyers in my office concentrate on different areas of the law, with only some overlap, which allows us to "partner" with one another on cases we otherwise might not take and to learn a new area of law with a more experienced mentor/lawyer. "Partnering" also provides both formal and informal opportunities to brainstorm with the other lawyers in the office. And, unlike the reality in large firms, here a less experienced lawyer can easily find a mentor to answer questions as they arise.

Being your own boss allows a type of flexibility that a structured law firm environment does not provide. You can set your own hours. You can choose the cases you want to take. Most of all, you are responsible only to yourself—and your clients—for your actions and decisions.

Your "partners" also have an interest in your success, which reflects on their prosperity, ensures that the "partnership" remains in effect, and guarantees no empty offices and a constant stream of clients coming through the doors. Finding clients when partnering with other lawyers is easier than trying to obtain clients on your own; you have a ready-made referral network, and cold calls to the office will be referred as well.

Another benefit is fee splitting with other lawyers. If your "partnership" is like mine and presents itself as a law firm, you don't need to address ethical concerns about fee-splitting arrangements when other lawyers work on a case. (Nevertheless, check your state's ethical rules to confirm you're not in violation.)

## Potential Trouble Spots

Although I'm a major advocate of the benefits of office-share arrangements, every silver lining has a cloud, and anticipating potential difficulties is a good idea. Here are a few of the more common quagmires:

- Too many lawyers practicing in the same area of law can affect the inherent referral potential of office sharing.
- Lawyers have an ethical duty to inform clients who is part of the law firm and who will be working on the client's case. In an office-sharing partnership, clients also must be informed that the lawyers in the office are not part of your practice and will have no knowledge of their case. As extra insurance, my client agreement clearly states that I am responsible for the client's case, that I "office share" with the law firm, and that I am authorized to retain additional counsel.
- Client conflicts, although addressed by individual state ethical rules, may arise for lawyers who "partner" in an office share. A thorough, workable conflict system must be implemented to protect all parties. Review your state ethics rules and other guidelines that address this issue.
- A system to address potential legal malpractice claims and bar complaints should be in place. Discuss this issue with your malpractice insurer for guidance on how to structure these concerns.

Additional possible hot spots—such as whether or not you may sue a client to recover fees—should be resolved as they come up if not covered in the original agreement.

The biggest area of potential conflict—in a category all its own—is cash flow and meeting monthly overhead, and how these are affected by keeping and retaining clients. It is up to you to make sure you can meet your overhead and that you take enough cases to remain in a positive cash flow. Developing a good business plan, plugging into referral networks (bar associations, local military installation referral lists and other referral lists), and "partnering" with other lawyers in an office-share will go a long way to ensure that you have a successful practice. "Partnering" through an office-share is like a marriage: Issues need to be addressed as they arise to ensure a successful long-term relationship.

# §2.4  The Virtual Law Firm

## Patrick W. Begos

The idea of the virtual law firm took root early in the now-forgotten history of the Internet, say four or five years ago. The virtual firm was envisioned as a group of independent lawyers located throughout a state, a country, or the world and linked via the Net. A lawyer who needed assistance in a far-off locale could contact one of the virtual partners, and together they could satisfy the client's needs. Groups of lawyers would assemble as needed and disband once the project was finished. It would revolutionize the practice of law. It never happened.

In order for a group of independent lawyers to raise the tide of business, and everyone's boat in the process, you need some things you can't get in a purely Net-based relationship. A group of lawyers in Westport, Connecticut, believed they uncovered the keys to a "real" virtual firm. Of course, like anything these days, there was first a beta version.

## The Beta

In the mid-1990s, several professionals (most of them lawyers) leased space in a Westport office building. It was essentially a real estate deal not much different from a typical office-suite rental arrangement, but relations among all parties were typically very collegial, and the space "felt" like a law firm. Still, there was nothing about it that hasn't been replicated dozens of times.

What is interesting is what happened next. A subset of the lawyers in the suite began to do a lot of business together. It was haphazard but lucrative. Lawyers with complementary practice areas who passed one another every day in the hallway and bounced questions back and forth began to see their suitemates as sources and destinations for referrals. A real estate lawyer whose client called about a litigation matter could refer it to the litigator down the hall; when one of the litigator's cases ended in bankruptcy, he could turn to the bankruptcy lawyer. In addition, the group had a unique member who was a non-lawyer specializing in turnarounds of failing businesses. At one point the turnaround specialist was retained to take over operation of a bankrupt company, and he subsequently hired three lawyers from the group to represent the company in various capacities.

## Lessons Learned

The core group learned a lot from this experience, and they decided to start a new office to put the lessons into practice. This virtual firm, called River-Side West, started with the following principles:

### All business is local.

Having a local client walk in with a legal problem in a faraway locale is the exception rather than the rule. More likely is that a local client will walk in with a local problem outside your practice area. A network of lawyers in the same jurisdiction who can cover most major practice areas is more likely to generate real business.

### Face time is vital.

Regularly passing another lawyer in the hallway plays a significant, though hard to quantify, part in business generation. You are more likely to think of someone you see every day when a real estate matter shows up at the door of your family law practice. Face time allows lawyers to develop a comfort level with one another because they see firsthand how the other lawyers handle their clients and their work.

### Team with different specialists.

Being in the same office allows multiple lawyers to play roles in the same transaction.

A lawyer can be brought in to assist on a particular issue, to cover a specific appearance or meeting, or to participate as cocounsel in a large litigation or transaction. When an existing or potential client walks in the door with a complex problem including issues outside your expertise, you're much more likely to get retained if you can walk next door and ask a colleague with expertise in that area to sit in.

### All for one, not us versus them.

A virtual firm needs a better foundation than a landlord-tenant agreement. The virtual firm should organize along the lines of a cooperative association in which major decisions are shared among the whole group.

### Quality counts.

You have to be comfortable with the idea of one of your "partners" performing services for your best client. Like a true partnership, you can't let just anyone join.

### Think outside the lawyer box.

A virtual firm allows lawyers to work with non-lawyers in ethical and mutually beneficial ways. What might an accountant or public relations specialist add to the office? You benefit from their contacts and expertise, and they benefit from yours. Obviously, lawyer members must take special care to ensure that their relationship with nonlawyer professionals satisfies ethical rules, which will require, among other things, not splitting fees with them.

**Don't hide your light.**

After going through the expense and effort of assembling your virtual firm, capitalize on its marketing and public relations potential. Let people know how your group's unique structure can help them. Use the infrastructure for marketing the group to market the individual practices as well.

The founders of RiverSide West believe they have a model that offers the best of both solo and big-firm practice. Because members are not partners, there's no fighting over how to split the annual profits. Members can work as hard or as easy as they like. But every lawyer has the option to offer clients a full menu of legal services. A full-service firm without partners? Talk about having your cake and eating it, too.

# §2.5 Collaborative Marketing on the Web: The QuiTamOnline.com Experience

## Robin Page West

Anacondas are solitary, slow-moving creatures that hunt for food under the camouflage of rivers and bogs. When the anaconda finally does manage to have a meal, it's often a large one: The snake is capable of swallowing a grown man whole.

I was once a member of a small personal injury law firm. I was the only lawyer there who litigated complex products cases involving toxic chemicals, fires, defective products, and the like. The other lawyers did auto tort and worker's compensation and settled cases daily. They were not favorably impressed by how long things took me, even if my eventual verdicts and settlements were big. This was where I first heard someone compare me to an anaconda.

It's not easy partnering with people used to eating three meals a day when you eat only once every few years. Where could a creature like me find kinship with other like-minded souls?

On the Internet, of course!

Today I'm still the only anaconda in a four-lawyer firm, and I'm still handling an unconventional caseload that moves very slowly. The difference is, I'm no longer alone. Now I participate in a Web site with three other anacondas hanging out in rivers and bogs in other parts of the country, who operate the same way I do.

My Web site collaborators and I all have the same niche practice—*qui tam*—which is geared to a select clientele: people who know about, and want to blow the whistle on, specific instances of fraud against the federal government.

*Qui tam* is an abbreviation of a Latin phrase that means "he who sues on behalf of the king and himself." The Civil False Claims Act (31 U.S.C. §§ 3729–3733) contains *qui tam* provisions that allow private individuals to sue on behalf of the government for fraud committed against it. Examples of such fraud include knowingly billing Medicare for doctor visits not actually performed, purposely billing the military for more food than actually delivered, or deliberately making false statements to mislead the government into awarding a research grant. Ideally, a successful *qui tam* suit not only stops the fraud and deters similar conduct by others, but also results in the whistleblower's receipt of as much as 30 percent of the total amount recovered for the government in the lawsuit. The False Claims Act also allows those who have been discriminated against, harassed, or retaliated against at work as a result of lawful acts they took in furtherance of the *qui tam* action to sue for double damages, back pay, interest on the back pay, reinstatement, and lawyers' fees.

While not all the other members of our respective law firms share our interest in the *qui tam* practice area, all the collaborators on the Web site, http://www.QuiTamOnline.com, do.

## Why Qui Tam?

Motivational speaker Tony Robbins says there are ten basic human needs: love, success, freedom, intimacy, security, adventure, power, passion, comfort, and health. Every person has all these needs, he counsels, but what defines us as individuals is the relative importance we each attach to these needs. While we may not realize it consciously, how we rank each of these needs drives every decision we make about how to live our lives.

*Qui tam* practitioners seem to rank passion and adventure at the top of the list. We live to ferret out fraud, rat it out to the government, draw maps of buildings the FBI will raid for fraudulent billing records, wait years for investigations to be completed, and top it off with front-page news coverage of a vindicated, if exhausted, client making plans to visit Disney World. Nothing gives us as much pleasure as wearing the white hat, exposing

My Web site collaborators and I all have the same niche practice—*qui tam*—which is geared to a select clientele: people who know about, and want to blow the whistle on, fraud against the federal government.

Nothing gives us as much pleasure as getting a reward for our clients—clients who, by the way, are quite intelligent, tenacious, and sophisticated to have figured out the fraud and to have found their way to us so we can bring it to the attention of the government.

How people rank the ten basic human needs—love, success, freedom, intimacy, security, adventure, power, passion, comfort, and health—drives every decision we make about how to live our lives.

Others suggest I might be better off concentrating more on billable work so I would at least know where my next meal is coming from, and when.

fraud, replenishing the taxpayers' money, and getting a reward for our clients—clients who, by the way, are quite intelligent, tenacious, and sophisticated to have figured out the fraud and to have found us to bring it to the attention of the government for them.

Colleagues at my office in Baltimore, where we focus primarily on estates and trusts and corporate law and litigation, tend to rank security and comfort higher than I do. They find my passion for *qui tam* a little strange and wonder about my attraction for such unpredictable cases that take so long to resolve. They ask, "Wouldn't you be better off concentrating more on your billable work so you will know where your next meal is coming from, and when?" Contrast this with my collaborators at QuiTamOnline.com, who are simpatico with the search for adventure and passion. Once we found each other, we resonated, and a force bigger than all of us drove us to develop a joint project involving our niche practice area and our affinity for technology.

## *Purpose of the Collaboration*

Perhaps as a result of what needs we rank highest, my Web site collaborators and I knew in our gut we wanted to create a Web site together. Once we acknowledged that, we started looking for a rational purpose to give our work structure. The obvious one was to generate business by publicizing ourselves. We realized we could create a national presence by positioning our collaboration as a network of lawyers spanning the country from the East Coast

Because *qui tam* is an esoteric, specialized area, when a lawyer gets a *qui tam* case he or she often wants to associate with a lawyer who has expertise in it. We explain on our Web site how we work with referring counsel on cases, and we describe some of the ways *qui tam* litigation differs from traditional litigation to underscore the need for expertise like ours.

all the way to Hawaii. We said goodbye to our images as sole and small-firm practitioners and set to work on building a national network of independent, boutique lawyers.

A second purpose for creating our Web site was to save time by giving potential clients information about the False Claims Act before speaking with them. Because our practice area is very specialized and often misunderstood, we were finding ourselves investing significant time on a regular basis interviewing potential clients only to learn that they were in need of a lawyer in a different practice area, or that they wanted to blow the whistle on something that was either not covered by the False Claims Act or was excluded from it. For example, the False Claims Act excludes claims arising out of a violation of the Internal Revenue Code, so we wanted to weed out tax-fraud whistleblowers before they wound up in our office for an interview.

We had also found that our initial client interviews often lacked focus and took longer than necessary because the potential clients did not know what facts were relevant to our inquiry and came to the meeting without the necessary information and documents. We wanted to eliminate this time sink, and wanted the Web site to educate our potential clients about the False Claims Act and tell them what facts and documents we would need to evaluate their potential case.

We took a two-pronged approach to this challenge. First, we would provide an online narrative explanation of the False Claims Act to give potential clients a basic understanding of what the law does and does not cover. Next, we would post a questionnaire consisting of all the questions we routinely ask at the initial client interview. If potential clients were to provide us with the answers to the questionnaire before we interviewed them, the interview would be much more productive: We would understand the basic facts without having to ferret them out, and the clients would already be focused on the issues and information germane to their potential cases.

Since implementing the pre-interview questionnaire, we have observed yet another benefit: valuable insight into clients' personalities. Those who balk at the hard work of answering the questions may not be the easiest clients to work with. On the other hand, those who order their answers to correspond with the questions, and who attach documents to support their answers, will more likely be the kind of clients we can work with effectively over the long haul.

Even though we initially intended to reach out to potential clients with our Web site, we realized while developing it that other lawyers would also likely be reading it. Because *qui tam* is an esoteric, specialized area not usually taught in law school or continuing legal education courses, a lawyer with a *qui tam* case often wants to associate with a lawyer who has expertise in the area. We explain on our Web site how we work with referring counsel on cases, and we describe some of the ways *qui tam* litigation differs from traditional litigation to underscore the need for expertise in this area.

## Some Caveats

When I left the security of a large firm to start my solo practice over 15 years ago, I shared space with two other new solos. At that time, space sharing was controversial. Bar associations pondered such questions as, How can client confidences be preserved in a space-sharing environment? Won't clients be misled about who their lawyer is if everyone is sharing the same conference room? Can you share a fee with your space-mate even though you are not in the same firm? These questions seem silly today in the world of temporary lawyers and business incubator suites, but back then, the mainstream legal establishment looked askance at space-sharing arrangements.

The most important thing to remember about disclaimers is that you must not mislead people into thinking they have obtained legal advice or representation when all they've done is read your Web site.

In similar fashion, when we were forming QuiTamOnline.com six years ago, Internet marketing was controversial, uncharted territory and everyone was asking the same questions. We knew we could not market ourselves as a firm if we were not a firm, but was there more to it than that? The first thing we did was to research the rules of professional conduct state by state to determine the prohibitions and requirements pertaining to Internet marketing for lawyers. Some jurisdictions did not speak specifically about Internet marketing but had constraints on advertising in general; others had special requirements for Web sites, such as a requirement to name a designated responsible person; some required disclaimers.

We then collected all the law firm Web site disclaimers we could find, with particular attention to those on the Web sites of the largest law firms, who we hoped had also researched this uncharted territory extensively, and then proceeded to draft the most comprehensive one possible in an effort to be compliant with all the prohibitions and requirements we found. The most important thing to remember about disclaimers is that you must not mislead a person into thinking he or she has obtained legal advice or representation when all he or she has done is read your Web site. We also contacted our respective malpractice carriers to apprise them of our intentions and to ascertain whether a collaborative marketing project might jeopardize our coverage. Some of them requested a copy of the text of the Web site before giving us the go-ahead.

We had a series of conference calls to determine the site organization and content.

We drafted site maps and refined them until we were satisfied. Then we divided up the job of writing the copy. Throughout the drafting process, our guiding principle was that we were providing legal information, not legal advice. For example, we gave information about the False Claims Act and we gave examples of fraud against the government. We did not give any advice or opinions. Once we finished our individual parts, we exchanged copy and edited each other's work until we were all satisfied. At that point we were ready to pass the copy to the Web designer to be fit into the design she had developed especially for us to accommodate the criteria we provided her.

We also brainstormed potential domain names and assigned the task of researching available names to one collaborator who reported back to the group on availability until we reached consensus.

## Fees

Fees were not an issue we had to spend much time on. At first, we considered whether, if a client found us through the Web site, we should all share in the fees from that client. We quickly decided that would not work, primarily because of the restrictions in many jurisdictions on sharing fees with lawyers not in the same firm. We ultimately decided that the lawyer with whom the client enters into a fee agreement is entitled to the entire fee. We do not share fees unless we share the responsibility for a case. Sometimes this will happen, for example, when a client comes to the Maryland lawyer with a case in Hawaii, and both lawyers work on the case. In that situation, the Maryland and Hawaii lawyers share the fee according to the terms of the specific fee agreement for that particular case. By treating fees this way, we do not need to determine how the client found us or who originated the case, or whether the client came to the lawyer through his or her law firm Web site or through the *qui tam* Web site. Because the source of the client is irrelevant to the distribution of fees, we have no issues, no disputes, and no hard feelings over the source of the business.

As a practical matter, since we are so evenly spaced throughout the country, the members of the network are not competing with each other. Rather, we find ourselves working together on matters and using each other as a sounding board. We give each other advice and support, and now and then we send a client each other's way. We figure what goes around comes around, and we don't obsess over who's ahead. Working on the cases, getting to know our clients and what makes them tick, and bringing the cases to fruition is as much a reward for us as the dollar recovery. To us, being a part of the process is as important as the monetary result.

QuiTamOnline.com has been invaluable to me in the client interview process. When a new client or potential referring

When a new client or potential referring counsel has a bunch of basic questions or wants to know what information I need in order to evaluate a potential case, I may refer them to the Web site rather than spend half an hour on the phone.

Because the source of the client is irrelevant to the distribution of fees, we have no issues, no disputes, and no hard feelings over the source of the business.

We give each other advice and support, and now and then we send a client each other's way. We figure what goes around comes around, and we don't obsess over who's ahead. Working on the cases, getting to know our clients and what makes them tick, and bringing the cases to fruition is as much a reward for us as the dollar recovery. To us, being a part of the process is as important as the monetary result.

counsel has a bunch of basic questions or wants to know what information I need in order to evaluate a potential case, rather than spending half an hour on the phone, I may refer them to the Web site. As far as the site's value as a tool to generate business, we keep statistics on hits and sometimes we try to analyze this compli- cated question. But, like the faux-ivory religious icon poised on the fuzzy dash mat of my friend's daily driver, no one quite knows whether QuiTamOnline.com is fulfilling its intended purpose. But we sure don't want to get rid of it only to find out it was.

## §2.6  Bar Service: More Than Just Referrals
### *William H. Wilhoit*

Undoubtedly, any lawyer who devotes some time to bar service has been asked by a partner or associate, or maybe even himself, "Why do you serve in the bar association?" This is never a simple answer, and there is not just one answer to the question. The answers will vary from individual to individual, and may differ with the same person because there are many reasons to devote your time to the bar association.

The most altruistic of reasons is that service to the bar association is a service to our profession. The bar association stands for professionalism in our field. The goal of the bar association is to promote a better quality of legal representation to the public. This may take the form of providing continuing legal education so that lawyers may stay abreast of modern trends in the legal practice. The association educates its members as to ethical considerations. It also offers practical advice for law practice management, so to make the business more efficient.
It should be noted that the bar association also sponsors public service projects to benefit the underprivileged and less fortunate. The organized bar has a noble cause.

While sharing these altruistic ideas, however, partners in your firm (or yourself in a solo practice) must be concerned about the bottom line. Yes, the bar association does wonderful things for the profession as a whole and to the community, but does service in the bar association generate the business needed to justify the time commitment to such an enterprise? One of the most famous of Abraham Lincoln's sayings was, "A lawyer's time and advice are his stock in trade." By investing time in bar association activities, the lawyer is investing the stock in his trade to that service. Is this an investment or merely a charitable contribution?

Our service in the bar association is an investment. The dividends reaped from bar service are diverse and profitable. Obviously, the first dividend that comes to mind is the referral of business from other members of the association. However, there are other dividends that accumulate from bar service.

The first thing that should be pointed out is that bar "service" does not mean just attending meetings. Obviously attending conferences and conventions for the continuing legal education requirements is beneficial to the lawyer. The American Bar Association puts on some of the highest quality CLE programs in the country. It pulls from a diverse group of highly experienced lawyers from across the nation to enlighten and educate others on the modern trends of practicing law. The biggest names in the legal profession can be found at American Bar Association meetings, where they are speakers or moderators at sessions involving their particular field of expertise. Attendees go home with more knowledge about the particular area of law in which they practice than they had when they arrived. This translates into a more educated representation of their clients, which should help business.

However, when we talk about bar service, we mean "service." This means actively participating in a particular section (or sections) and committees of the bar association. Service means not merely being on the receiving end, but putting something into the process. So, how does this service generate business?

No lawyer should underestimate the value of reputation. Standing in the community is the lifeblood of a lawyer. A client comes to your office because of your character for being a competent lawyer. This reputation comes from the perception that your colleagues and community have toward your ability to represent your clients.

A chief marketing tool for a law practice is to enhance its reputation in the community and with your contemporaries.

Officers and committee chairs of the bar association, whether it be national or state, are typically some of the most respected members of the bar in their particular communities. Lawyers know that bar service requires time and devotion to the profession. Bar service requires some organizational skills (or the lawyer will not last long either in bar service or in the practice of law). By extended bar service over a course of several years, the lawyer develops a reputation and respect among his or her colleagues.

Bill Robinson, elected treasurer of the American Bar Association in 2004, was the youngest lawyer ever to be president of the Kentucky Bar Association. His entire professional career has included service in both the Kentucky and American Bar Associations. His reputation is legendary, especially in dealing with others and resolving conflicts. He attributes his success to the organized bar:

> As virtue is its own reward, volunteer work in the organized bar enhances our profession, as well as the career of the lawyer who recognizes that personal and professional growth is most efficiently and meaningfully found in the service of others. Enhanced relationships with

other lawyers and members of the judiciary through volunteer service in the organized bar will not infrequently help facilitate the resolution of issues and controversies in the professional arena, in part because of the credibility earned in the organized bar.

It is akin to the proverb of casting your bread upon the water. You give up some bread for the little fish to eat. For one day, you may catch that well-fed fish that has now grown into a much bigger fish. Your service will more than likely not go unnoticed, and may pay bigger dividends further down the stream of your career.

However, you need to be sure that your community knows of your good work. When appointed or elected to a particular position in the bar association, send out a press release to the area newspapers. This informs the community of your devotion to professionalism in the legal practice. This type of publicity can do nothing but increase your reputation and respect in the community. Lay people may not understand the extent of the service given to the bar association, but they probably do understand the character that such service demands. The service demonstrates the type of character that they would want in their lawyer.

By increasing your reputation with your colleagues and in your community through bar service, you increase your publicity as a competent lawyer. Obviously, the community's perception can equate to more business for your particular practice.

However, perceptions can be deceiving, especially when it comes to perceived reputation as a good lawyer. Therefore, it is important to follow through. As previously mentioned, the bar association provides quality continuing legal education. Bar service provides the lawyer to be on the ground floor of that instruction: not just attending the CLE program, but actually being instrumental in the publication of the materials and putting on the program itself. It is one thing to watch a program and another thing to actually help in the production of that program. Whether it be editing the pamphlets or discussing the topics to be covered, bar service gives a unique insight into the education provided to its members. This unique insight is more valuable than mere attendance.

For example, somebody can show you how to put together a model car. However, you are more likely to remember the details if you actually participated in the building of that model car. Even more educational is assisting in the drafting of the written instructions to building that model car. Likewise, because of your participation in the process, the quality of education of bar service is more educational than just mere attendance can provide.

Typically, in producing these programs, the bar member must associate with an expert in that field. The speaker in the CLE has special knowledge on the topic of the class. What could be more beneficial than working with this person in his or her field of expertise?

It has been said that it is not *what* you know but *whom* you know. In law school I had the opportunity to clerk for one of the top law firms in Kentucky. I said then and still say today that law school got in the way of my education. I learned more by listening to, watching, and assisting those lawyers as they put together a case for trial than I learned in three years of law school.

Similarly, bar service puts you in a position to be associated with some of the greatest legal minds in our country. Bar service allows you not only to interact with these individuals in a social setting but also to "pick their brain" on issues that may present itself to you in your practice. The greatest legal minds in our country may have thought of some particular issue that you had not considered in the case you are handling. This interaction can also provide better representation to your clients. Your contemporaries may be amazed that you seemed to have come up with

this novel issue in representing your client. (Reputation building, again.)

However, the brilliant minds in the bar association may not be the ones that actually help your business. There are regular people that provide service to the bar association. (Just ask those who know me.) This is when the referrals come into play.

If you have gone to one or two bar association meetings and met a few people, you will probably say that you never have received a referral from anybody that you have met at the bar association. However, if you actually devote your time to bar service for more than just a couple of years, your name will get around.

Referrals come through networking. Networking requires more than just talking to another lawyer at a cocktail reception. Referrals come from those lawyers whom you have impressed through your work and your knowledge of bar service and the legal profession. It is surprising the number of referrals that can come through an office from bar service.

It is a big country, yet it is a small world. Service in the American Bar Association puts you in contact with lawyers from across this great nation of ours. You may only see them a handful of times a year, but the friendships that are formed are bonds that can last forever. Some of the people I respect most are those I have met in the bar association. Though they are scattered across the country, it is still a small world. How many referrals could a small one-horse-town lawyer from eastern Kentucky receive? More than I could imagine. It is amazing how lawyers from all corners of the United States end up having some legal development in Kentucky. Who do they call? They call someone they know and respect as having a good reputation for bar service and quality representation in the legal field. (If they cannot reach that person, they call me.)

The referrals may not be in the area of your practice or may be in another part of your particular state. However, by receiving the referral, you get the opportunity to refer the cases that you cannot handle to other lawyers who can deal with the situation. The lawyer on the receiving end is typically quite grateful for the referral and is likely to reciprocate in the future. You could say that referrals of referrals beget more referrals.

Even in-house counsels benefit from contacts in the bar association. Justin Goldstein, in-house counsel for a national bank in Pittsburg, has been involved in both the Pennsylvania and American Bar Associations. He receives a referral at least once a month, which he passes on to his friends in the private practice, fostering good will and increasing his reputation. It has also allowed him to make inroads with lawyers whose clients may need the services his bank provides. All of which increases his reputation at his bank.

Furthermore, bar service within your state gives you the opportunity to meet and get to know lawyers throughout your state. This provides opportunities for referrals within your state, but it also provides a valuable resource. These lawyers may know the judges in areas unfamiliar to you. They can give you insight as to practice procedures and local rules before that judge, which can benefit you in your representation of your client. Likewise, they can give you insight into your opposing counsel. Knowing whom you are up against is one of the most important factors to be considered in representation. "It is not what you know, but who you know."

It is clear that business generated from bar service is not one-dimensional. It is not based solely on referrals from people that you meet at conventions. It is as multidimensional as the individuals themselves. Bar service and the educational experience that comes with it increases your reputation in the community and with your colleagues. They will stand up and take notice of your time commitment and organizational skills. As Bill

Robinson says, "It is doing well by doing good." This not only generates business from referrals, but it makes you a better lawyer. As everyone knows, the better lawyers get the better cases. The better cases generate the better business.

Bar service will produce more business in your practice. This business will be high-quality business because that is what is expected of such a well-respected lawyer. However, you will find that bar service will not only increase your business and make you a better lawyer, it will also make you a better person.

# §2.7 Can the Rainmaker and the IRS Be Business Partners?

## *Dennis Jacknewitz and Patrick E. Stark*

Rainmakers: individual lawyers who, blessed with personality, expertise, or that certain pizzazz, have the uncanny ability to recruit and maintain business clients or obtain business client referrals for their law practice. Even when the reality of their wining and dining is more like a cup of coffee and a bagel, rainmakers incur a number of business expenses while keeping current clients happy, obtaining new clients, and mining contacts and referral sources. This inevitably leads to involvement with the Internal Revenue Service (IRS) and its complex guidelines regarding allowable deductions. Believe it or not, if a rainmaker doesn't overreach, the IRS can be the rainmaker's most productive business partner.

Although rainmakers can take clients to Hawaii or Las Vegas or wherever to develop business relationships, how the trips are structured will go far to determine whether the expenses are deductible on personal income tax returns or, preferably, business entity tax returns. By planning ahead, the rainmaker can enjoy entertainment or other activities and the IRS underwriting of such activities. Major categories of typical expenses are explored in this section.

## In-Town Transportation

Normal commuting expenses to and from home or office generally are not tax deductible. But stopping by a client's office en route turns the very same nondeductible commuting expense into one that is tax deductible. Both the mileage from your office to the client's business and the mileage from the client's office to your home are then deductible.

To compute such expenses, should you take actual expenses or standard mileage rates published by the IRS? Whichever you decide, be consistent. For actual expense deductions, keep track of gas expenses, oil, repairs, insurance, depreciation, car clean-up expenses, and so on; multiply the total of the expenses by the percentage of business use for the vehicle to obtain the proper deduction. For example, if you use your car strictly for business affairs 80 percent of the time, you can deduct 80 percent of all costs associated with maintaining the car. But you must keep track of the costs with receipts or a manual or computer log.

Most people will opt for the less cumbersome option of keeping track of business miles incurred.

However, you still must document parking costs, tolls, and cleaning costs on a regular basis if you want the tax deduction. The IRS-approved mileage rate for tax year 2004 is 37.5 cents per mile for owned or leased vehicles.

## Auto Lease versus Purchase

Will you come out better tax-wise leasing or purchasing a company auto? This depends on a number of variables, including the residual value of the vehicle at the end of the lease period, the percentage of business use of the vehicle, and the tax bracket of the lessor. You can use an online financial calculator to help with this decision (one example is http://www.dinkytown.net). Leasing is probably easier than owning a vehicle in terms of record keeping, because you can deduct the business percentage of the lease payments and don't have to calculate depreciation and such on a leased vehicle. For luxury vehicles, the deduction for the actual lease payments is reduced to approximate the depreciation limits on purchased vehicles.

Want to get a faster write-off on that new vehicle? One way to get around the depreciation limits is to purchase a sport utility vehicle (SUV) rated at more than 6,000 pounds gross weight.

These vehicles are often quite luxurious, and because they are not considered "luxury autos" under IRS regulations, these vehicles can be written off more quickly than non-SUV vehicles can. For example, if you purchased a $40,000 SUV in 2003 and used it 80 percent for business, you could expense $32,000 under section 179 of the Code the first year.

The 2003 tax act allows you to expense up to $100,000 of qualifying depreciable property, plus you can deduct first-year bonus depreciation of 50 percent on any other qualifying assets (generally machinery, office equipment, off-the-shelf computer software, and some leasehold improvements).

## Travel and Lodging

You do not have to be away from home for more than 24 hours for a business trip to be considered out of town. However, you do have to be away overnight, or long enough to require securing lodging to sleep or rest. Your travel agent may advise you that staying over Saturday night can save on airfare. If the additional cost of staying Saturday night is less than the original plane fare, lodging and meal expenses for the extra day are tax deductible. For example, if you can save $400 on airfare by staying Saturday night, and your additional lodging and meals cost $325, you can deduct the $325 in expenses even if the business part of your trip ended on Friday—courtesy of your business partner the IRS. (Unfortunately, the IRS will not let you deduct travel expenses for investment seminars or stockholders' meetings.)

## Entertainment

The IRS believes abuses in the area of entertainment expenses do occur and therefore has set limits on allowable deductions. The result is that entertainment is deductible only if the expense passes either the "directly related to" or "associated with" tests established by the IRS. The directly related test requires more than a general expectation of receiving income or a business benefit at some point in the future from the expense. The main purpose of the entertainment expense must be the active conduct of business—you must initiate a business discussion with the entertained party during the entertainment period. To meet the associated-with test, the entertainment must be associated with the active conduct of your trade or business (the business of practicing law) and take place either before or after a substantial business discussion.

Many types of entertainment expenses are allowable, including visits to nightclubs, theaters, and sporting events, if the circumstances meet one of the above tests. Additional restrictions are imposed by the IRS for activities such as entertaining on a yacht, during a fishing or hunting trip, or at a vacation spot. For these types of activities, the cost of renting or maintaining an entertainment facility such as a hunting lodge is not deductible under IRS regulations, but the out-of-pocket expenses like beverages, food, and so forth are deductible.

Recreational or social activities for employees, including holiday parties or golf outings, do not have to meet the directly related or associated-with tests to be tax deductible. The deduction includes the expense for renting a facility such as a ballroom or swimming pool. Expenses for employees of the law firm also are not subject to the 50 percent reduction in meals and entertainment deduction that usually applies, so long as the entertainment is primarily for rank-and-file employees, although it may also include highly compensated employees.

Country club dues and similar membership fees for venues for recreational or other social purposes are no longer deductible under current IRS guidelines. Only civic or professional association dues are exempt from this disallowance. If you entertain clients at home, however, costs associated with meals, drinks, a pianist or string quartet, and similar types of entertainment are deductible if the primary purpose is business and not social.

When purchasing tickets for a sporting event or stadium concert, only the face value of the ticket is tax deductible, not the fees paid to a ticket agent or scalper. If a skybox is involved, the IRS imposes even more restrictions: The skybox must be leased for more than one event to be deductible. In order to determine the deduction, the face value of the highest priced non-luxury box ticket is used and multiplied by the number of seats in the rented space. For example, if there are 12 seats in the luxury box and the most expensive regular box seat costs $40, the deduction is limited to $480, even if the box cost $2,500. Food and beverage costs are deductible if they are separately stated on the bill.

The IRS disallows expenses it determines to be lavish or extravagant. But that doesn't mean you can't stay in a first-class hotel or entertain at a five-star restaurant; to qualify as a deduction,

the expense must be reasonable considering the facts and circumstances, such as the position of the person claiming the deduction and the person being entertained. A luxury suite at a hotel may be reasonable when used to meet with or entertain clients or prospects for business.

## Controversial Areas

Combining business with pleasure will cause the IRS to examine your expenses very closely. If the primary purpose of the trip is business, the entire cost of transportation to and from the destination is deductible, even if you add a short personal side trip (of course, your personal expenses are not deductible). On the other hand, if the primary purpose of the trip is deemed personal, no transportation expenses are deductible, and only expenses directly related to the business, such as meals and lodging once you are at your destination, should be claimed.

If the primary purpose of your trip is business but you want to take your spouse along, your spouse's expenses may be deducted only if the spouse serves a bona fide business purpose and is an employee or officer of the corporation, LLC,

LLP, or other law business entity. Participating in social functions generally is not considered a business purpose, although the tax courts have allowed such expenses in certain circumstances.[1] If the law firm pays for your spouse but the expenses ultimately do not qualify for a business deduction, the amount expended on the spouse will be included in your gross income for that particular year and taxed accordingly.

Suppose you find yourself in one of those situations where your client only now remembers some "other" information she should have shared before you accepted the case. You lease a jet to fly cross-country to converse with your client rather than use a commercial flight. Is this a legitimate deduction? Possibly—the rule is that the business portion of the cost is deductible if the airplane is used primarily for business and if commercial flights are inconvenient or unavailable. If the costs associated with the private plane are unreasonable, the IRS may limit the expense to the price of a first-class commercial airline ticket.

---

1. *See, e.g.,* Disney v. United States (CA9 1969), 24 AFTR 2d 69-5123, 69-2, USTC 9494.

## Exotic Expenses

You want to attend that convention in London, and you want the IRS to pay all or part of the bill. Will it work? Generally you can deduct travel expenses for attending a convention if you can show that your attendance benefits your trade or business. In order to take a deduction for a convention held outside North America, you must be able to prove that it is as reasonable for the meeting to be held outside the United States as it is to hold the meeting here; for example, if the convention was held in England so attendees could study the British court system firsthand and discuss it with barristers.

What about that really great CLE course given on the Mediterranean cruise ship? If you meet the very strict IRS reporting requirements, including a statement from the seminar sponsor verifying days and hours of business meetings, up to $2,000 per year of expenses for attending conventions, seminars, or similar meetings on cruise ships can be deducted. Forget the Mediterranean, however—the ship must be registered in the United States and visit ports of calls only in the United States or its possessions.

## Good Deals That Still Exist

Despite IRS limitations on business deductions, some deductions you might have thought obsolete may still exist:

- Travel from home to a temporary work site (such as a client's office).
- Total cost of traveling to and from a foreign location, if the trip is primarily for business and lasts one week or less (even if more than 25 percent of your time is spent on personal activities).
- Total cost of noncommercial employer-provided vacation flights for employees, as long as the employees include the value of the flight under the Standard Industry Fare Level rates as part of their income, even if the actual cost was higher. (Standard Industry fares generally equal the cost of a first-class commercial airline ticket.)
- A noncommercial flight taken by an employee not flying primarily for business can be valued at zero if at least half the regular seating capacity is occupied by employees whose flights primarily are for business. This applies to both current and retired employees, but not to directors or independent contractors.

- New 401(k) rules allow a self-employed individual or single-employee law firm to create an individual retirement plan and defer up to $12,000 of income for the year. For individuals over age 50, that deferral increases to $14,000. Additionally, the law firm can contribute to the plan and deduct 25 percent of the individual's salary for that year. The two amounts combined cannot exceed $40,000 per year.

## Employer versus Employee Expenses

Is it better for the company law firm or the employee personally to claim the business-related tax deduction? Generally it makes more sense for the company to take the deduction, especially under a "nonaccountable plan." A nonaccountable plan includes reimbursements in employees' taxable wages. The employee can claim the expense as an itemized deduction, but the deductions are reduced by 2 percent of the employee's adjusted gross income and are further reduced as the employee's income increases. Not such a good deal for the employee.

An "accountable plan" makes much more sense for the company and the employee but does require that the employee substantiate expenses to the employer. The employee also must return to the business any funds in excess of substantiated expenses.

The company can pay a fixed amount per day (per diem) instead of reimbursing actual expenses. A list of allowable per diems based on locality and date is available at http://www .policyworks.gov/perdiem. You could also use optional high/low per-diem rates based on high or low expense areas. Even when using per diems, the employee must still substantiate the business purpose of the meeting, time, and place to the employer.

Rainmaking can be expensive, but by making the IRS into a partner, the rainmaker can benefit the business by entertaining clients in a nontraditional luxury environment and save tax dollars while making a great impression on clients and prospects.

## Charitable Rainmaking

Serving on the board of directors of a nonprofit or community organization such as the local symphony or art museum board can be a great way for a rainmaker to network with wealthy and influential contacts and receive applicable tax deductions for the activity. Mileage and out-of-pocket expenses are deductible as charitable expenses on itemized tax returns. Underwriting a fund-raising event may be deductible as a public relations expense—in addition to being a great advertisement for the lawyer or firm.

# 3

# Rainmaking with the Client in Mind

*Find your niche, and market your practice to target audiences.*

# §3.1 Niche Marketing: The Inside Track to Client Development

## David Leffler

You read a lot of advice on how to get clients, but deep down inside you just wish that there was something that could give you a leg up on the whole client acquisition thing—like an uncle who could hand you all the business you need from the mega corporation that he just happens to own.

Well, I can't provide that uncle to you (if I had him I'd keep him for myself), but I do have something that I can share with you that will give you a leg up when you go out there trying to convince people to hire you as their lawyer.

Niche marketing is not just some kind of fancy term thrown around by consultants. It's something that you actually can do even if you don't have a big marketing budget or a lot of time to develop a marketing plan.

Merriam-Webster's dictionary has several definitions for "niche." One is "a specialized market." But better than the definition is the etymology of the word "niche." According to Merriam-Webster, the word "niche" comes from the Latin word *nidus*, which means "nest." Developing a niche market law practice is like building a nest—a specially designed nest for a particular kind of client. But instead of twigs and leaves, the nest you build is made out of the expertise and services that you develop in a particular area of the law.

By the time you finish reading this section you should have a pretty good idea of why niche marketing is so valuable and how you can develop a successful niche in your own law practice.

**Developing Your Niche**

- Identify your skills, talents, and passions.
- Don't eliminate a niche idea too quickly because it seems too impractical.
- Get whatever training you might need to fill any knowledge gaps.

**Marketing Your Niche**

- Participate in business organizations in your niche.
- Write for publications in your niche.
- Get quoted in print, television, and radio about your specialty.
- Form relationships with prominent people in your field.

## A Niche Is Born

I fell into my niche completely by accident. The year was 1990. The economy was in the dumps. The firm in which I had recently become a partner had closed its doors. Since I didn't have a sufficiently significant book of business to be a partner in another firm and I was too far along in my legal career to be hired as associate, I opened my own practice.

Someone recommended that I volunteer at a local not-for-profit organization that provided counseling and training to women business owners as a way to generate legal business. My visit to the organization was the beginning of a 14-year relationship, ending only when it closed its doors in the summer of 2004.

I began by teaching a business law course and conducting one-on-one counseling sessions. While helping women getting out of constrained economic situations by taking a business idea from a dream to reality was a rewarding experience, the size of the their businesses were not large enough to justify the cost of a lawyer.

What this experience did do was expose me to a whole sector of the legal market that was not particularly well recognized at the time. There are elements that distinguish the woman business owner from their male counterparts. Often the women I came across had fewer resources, fewer connections, and less training than men in business. Yet this did not lessen their determination.

Women also received far less support from their families and friends. While men were expected to go out into the world to make their fortunes and their whole social network supported them in their endeavors, women often were responsible for child care and household duties in addition to the demands of their entrepreneurial activities.

Finally, women often did more and asked for less for their labors than their male counterparts. They didn't seem to have the confidence to ask to be paid what they were worth, whether it was for their services or their products.

This knowledge and experience led to my developing a roster of women business owner clients. How did I do it? When I met a women business owner I was able to communicate in a way that let the woman know that I understood her concerns. I was able to do more than simply draft a contract or review a lease; I also could give advice about the development of her businesses that addressed her unique concerns, even before they were expressed.

I became aware of other organizations for women business owners and became involved in them. And over the years, the women that I was counseling at the not-for-profit organization were growing their businesses to a level where they could be valued clients in my law practice.

One great aspect to building a niche client base is that while you are doing it, you don't have to give up all of the other areas of practice that you have before establishing a good base of niche clients. In fact, you can have a niche practice and still practice in other areas, depending on how much work flow you receive from your niche. Even today, women business owners compose only a portion of my business law practice, albeit an important one.

## Creating Your Own Niche Market

I fell into my niche market totally by chance. But how can you discover and develop your own niche market to kick your client acquisition program into high gear?

First, figure out your skills and talents. I am a business lawyer, so representing business owners made a lot of sense. I have good communications skills and do not intimidate clients, which is important for those women who are breaking into an arena that up to recently was largely male dominated. Most importantly, I have a sincere interest in supporting women business owners.

A good place for you to start your discovery process is to think of what your interests are. This is a good clue to your talents, and will also point toward what you like to do. Whatever niche you develop should not be based solely upon "where the money is." If you don't have a real interest in it you will not make a success at it, or if you do, you will be miserable. We all only have one shot to go through this world; you might as well spend your time doing something you like. Besides, your natural enthusiasm for an area that you do enjoy will make the whole process a lot easier.

Sailing might thrill you. Perhaps you can design a practice around some aspect of maritime law, provided you live near a coastal town with an active port. There are many lawyers who love sports and have gone into sports law. If the Internet fascinates you, you could bone up on intellectual property law and develop an Internet law niche. There are an enormous number of possibilities.

Do not eliminate a possibility too quickly because it does not seem practical. I am aware of one lawyer who, because of his passion for cycling, developed a specialty in bicycle law, dealing solely with personal injury cycling cases and other matters related to cycling.

Try doing an Internet search to see if there are other lawyers who already have a specialty in the area in which you are interested. One Internet search that might bring up relevant Web sites is the name of your niche plus the words "law" or "lawyer" or "attorney." Get other resources to explore possible niches from your law school's job placement office.

Once you decide what niche is best for you, do everything that you need to do to serve this niche. Here is where you gather the twigs and leaves to build your nest. This includes making sure that you are up to date on the relevant law and even perhaps structuring the billing and other aspects of your firm's practice to fit with this particular client base.

## On Becoming an Expert

Now comes the fun part—the marketing. Am I serious? Most definitely. Why is the marketing fun? Because when you are marketing to a niche market, things tend to go a lot better than when you are marketing to "everyone" as part of a general practice. You are an "expert" in your niche—people will feel much more inclined to hire you because of your recognized expertise.

But wait, you say, you are not recognized for your expertise. Well, who is that up to You guessed it; it's up to you. What, you thought that as long as you worked hard in a particular field that the law fairy would one day alight on your shoulder, tap you gently with her magic wand, and declare you to be an expert? As loath as I am to shatter any long-cherished beliefs, I'm here to tell you that there is no law fairy.

For the most part, those lawyers that you have heard about who are experts in one field or another did not become experts by accident; it's usually only after a long and directed effort on their parts that they are recognized in their field as having special knowledge that makes them an "expert."

So what do lawyers do to become recognized as experts? There are a number of things, all of which you can do, and all of which fall under the category of communications in one form or another.

First, find business organizations that fall within your niche. Find out if you can give a talk regarding legal aspects of their business. For instance, instead of giving a talk to a group of business owners as a business lawyer, if you are developing an Internet law niche you can give a talk to members of an online business association. Think of how much more successful you can be if you hold yourself out as a lawyer that does "Internet law" to a group of business owners that are constantly having to deal with this very subject, rather than speaking to a mix of business owners on a topic that may or may not interest them.

Next, find publications in your area of law, both in print and online, for which you can write articles. An article about maritime law in a sailing magazine or Web site will get you a lot more business than a legal article published in a general circulation magazine or Web site.

Contact local newspapers and radio and television stations to offer yourself as a source for comments whenever there are news reports where your area of law is relevant. If you feel that this sort of publicity is vital to promoting your practice, consider hiring a public relations firm to get your name out there.

Join business organizations within your niche and participate in their activities. Trade organizations often like having a lawyer as a member as a way to get access to some free expertise. Participation is a good way to spread the word about your niche practice and meet potential clients.

When you find people prominent in your field, try to get to know them. See if you can stop by their office or meet for coffee one morning for a short chat. Your immediate purpose here is not to get business but to establish a relationship with someone key in your industry. This way you can introduce these key industry people to others, which will enhance your stature in your industry. Also, they might refer business to you sometime in the future.

When meeting these people, keep in mind that some people you will click with and some you will not. Pay a lot of attention to those with whom you do click. There is great potential there for a long and mutually rewarding relationship. For those that seem not to be interested, don't fret about it, no matter how important a person he or she may be. You can make some further follow-up attempts, but don't wear yourself out trying to cement a relationship where there just isn't the right mix.

Finally, keep in mind that your state's lawyer ethics laws may prevent you from referring to yourself as an "expert" or "specializing in" a particular area of law because it implies that you have received some form of certification. While you may not be able to say that you are an expert in Internet law, it would most likely be acceptable to say that you either limit your practice to Internet law or that a portion of your practice focuses on Internet law. Check your state's ethics laws to see what restrictions apply.

## *Gather Those Twigs and Leaves!*

A reputation is built one step at a time. What you need is determination and the ability to stick it out over the period of years that it will take to get the recognition that you are seeking. But if you stick with it and keep your focus, you will achieve your goal of being a recognized legal expert in your niche, and have a much more effective way to build your client base.

# §3.2 Five Practical Ways to Market a Real Estate Law Firm

### *Yolanda Williams-Favors*

There is a saying that no product sells itself. This is true in the field of law, just as any other business. The reason any law firm markets is to get clients. In the real estate field, it is difficult to develop loyalty in clients. Real estate agents, mortgage brokers, lenders, and builders are usually professionals and knowledgeable about the real estate business. They do not see lawyers as laypersons do—in awe of our knowledge and ability to pass the bar. Our clients merely see lawyers as a means to an end—getting a check. They do not care about mounting title exam bills, difficult title issues, following closing instructions, having funds wired before disbursing, or mortgage fraud. They just want their check. If you cannot get it to them fast enough, they go on to the next lawyer. To succeed in this climate, your real estate firm needs a well thought-out marketing plan.

Here are time-proven tips that other real estate lawyers and I have used. Some will work for you, some will not. You must decide what you want to accomplish in your business and develop strategies to reach your particular goals.

## Write an Article

Writing an article shows that you are knowledgeable and an authority in your field. However, you cannot just sit down and put pencil to paper. Here are some ways to help ensure that (1) your article will be accepted and published and (2) your article is relevant and helpful to your clients:

- The article should be relevant to real estate law; however, do not limit yourself to this area. An article on the preparation of a will or power of attorney would be useful to real estate agents when conversing with purchasers about protecting their homes.
- The article should specifically discuss recent developments in the chosen subject. This clarifies that your research is up to date and reliable.
- If your reader is a layperson, narrow your subject matter and keep complex legal terminology to a minimum, to prevent confusion.
- The first readers of your article should be your clients! They will appreciate the information and think of you whenever they have

a question on the subject. Print the article in your newsletter or simply e-mail (or regular mail, if that is still used) to your clients, along with a note stating that you thought they might appreciate the information.

- Next, contact as many publications as time allows, to get your article read by as many people as possible. Take advantage of the increase in organizational and corporate newsletters and contact any company (profit or nonprofit) that may be interested in an article written by an authority. Trade publications, general business magazines, and community newspapers are desperate for interesting materials, as are small businesses, nonprofit organizations, churches, real estate companies, and government agencies. You can also try your local bar association committee for your area or practice group.
- Once you find interest in your article, it is important to meet your deadline, even if it is your own deadline for your newsletter. While it is difficult to practice law (because we lawyers are so busy running the law firm as a business), it is important to schedule time for marketing that business. Further, you want to be known as a person of your word and not as someone who is undependable.

## Get a Booth and Give Stuff Away

It is a great marketing strategy to place you in a scenario surrounded by a concentrated pool of successful target clients. However, nothing is more disenchanting than paying your left foot for a booth and either no one comes to your table or everyone comes for the for giveaways. In either event, you have wasted a lot of money and time. A conference for your local National Association of Professional Mortgage Women, Mortgage Brokers Association, or National Builders Association sounds like heaven on earth, and can be. However, you must plan your booth and giveaways so that the attendees visit because they are attracted to your services, not just to the freebies.

- Do not have gifts that are consumable on the spot. The purpose of the gift is for the attendee to see your name over and over again. Once the consumable is gone, so is your logo.
- Have a gift or activity that will not interest a "freebie fanatic" (who will not use your services anyway), but will pique the interest of a real potential client. Not everyone will stand in line for a free mortgage calculator, but a mortgage broker will.

- Do not place the gifts on the table for all to come and snatch. The items should be handed out personally, after your workers obtain qualifying and contact information. Speak to each attendee individually. Ask questions to develop a rapport and a subject for a later discussion. Try to remember something particular about each attendee to bring up when you contact him or her later.

- Ensure that you have printed promotional information on your company to hand out with the freebies. You need more than just a logo.

## Learn to Network a Room

It is very difficult for most lawyers to network. However, real estate lawyers must learn to sell themselves to be successful. I think of myself as a professional offering my expertise to solve someone's problems. This makes it easier for me to self-promote. While attending a function, you must learn to "work a room." This is a learned skill. You simply have to create a plan of action and set goals of how you are going to work the event prior to attending. Here are some tips for doing just that:

- Have *up-to-date* business cards.
- Before the event, obtain a list of attendees and become familiar with potential networking "victims." If you know one of the attendees, call him or her ahead of time to arrange lunch.
- Decide whom you want to meet and practice how you will introduce yourself. Your introduction should be less than 25 seconds, stating your name and that you are a real estate lawyer. Memorize a "memory hook"—a short, catchy phrase that helps people visualize what you do. I sometime use, "We have 'real' solutions to 'real estate' problems."
- Once you arrive, do not concentrate on people you know unless they can introduce you to someone you want to meet.
- Ask for cards before giving yours. Take time to really look at their card. My father, the Reverend Hosea Williams, always wrote something on the back of a card to help him remember something specific about that person. Let the attendee know that you are noting something on the back of the card that will help you refer clients to them.
- When speaking with someone, make eye contact and avoid interrupting them. Resist the temptation to talk so much about yourself.

Repeat what is said during the conversation to show that you are listening. Try to find something in common with that person.

- Concentrate on developing the relationship and leave selling yourself to a later time.
- Do not complain. You never know with whom you are speaking.
- Follow the advice of one networking guru: "When you enter a group, listen for three minutes and avoid striking up the conversation."
- If you need to end the conversation, simply say, "Excuse me, I need to use the phone (or say hello to someone)."
- Always send a follow-up letter within a week. Include something about your prior conversation and, perhaps, one of your articles.

## Market to Your Present Clientele

One of the most ignored marketing tools is to market to your present clientele to retain them. Even more, real estate is one of the few areas of law in which the lawyer auditions before potential clients. For example, if your mortgage broker client sends a purchaser, you audition before two real estate agents during the closing. We all know how important customer service is; when you are auditioning before potential clients, it is more important than ever.

- Return all telephone calls promptly. If you cannot, have an assistant do so.
- In your voice mail message, give the caller the option of speaking with an assistant since you are not available.
- Check voice mail and e-mail regularly during the day.
- Notify clients of unexpected closing expenses prior to closing.
- Notify clients of unexpected title problems as soon as they arise.
- Send a preprinted form to the listing agent upon receipt of the title order requesting payoff and seller information. We fax or e-mail the form and retain the confirmation in the event of future discrepancies.
- Notify the selling agent or your client if you are unable to contact the listing agent or seller.
- Give clients the option of receiving title binders via e-mail.
- Give clients the option of ordering titles online. If you do not have a Web site, you are working in the dark ages. Larger firms give clients passwords to the Web site, so they can review

private information about their loans, such as the sales contract and scheduled closing time. This is costly for small firms; however, ordering titles online is as easy as e-mail.

- Give clients the option of receiving copies of closing documents via e-mail or compact disk. My clients love this. You will need Adobe Acrobat 6.0; however, since I bought this, I use it more than sliced bread anyway.

- Have a copy machine that faxes, scans, copies, and prints. Also, configure your computer to do the same from your desktop. This saves hours of time in my office and allows us to service our clients more quickly.

- Offer free or reduced services for borrowers who close with you. For instance, we sometimes offer a free simple will with every purchase. Real estate agents love this.

- One lawyer friend offered a free bottle of champagne, with his logo on it, to all purchasers. Sometimes he opened a large bottle of carbonated grape juice at the closing with plastic champagne glasses to celebrate.

- Offer a gift basket of new home goodies for purchasers, such as gardening tools or fix-it stuff from a home improvement store. We once gave away flower arrangements with live fish in the bottom of the vase. A customer

kept that fish for over a year! She remembered us.

- Keep your clients informed of seminars, articles, and other educational programs, whether or not sponsored by your firm. Invite them to attend events of interest to both of you.

- Be ready to close at the scheduled time. Nothing irritates potential clients more than waiting in your lobby for two hours to close a loan, regardless of the reason. Their lawyer could always do it better. When it comes to the point of closing, any delay appears to be the fault of the closing lawyer.

- Nothing makes you look better than to issue checks at the closing. Some firms cut checks while preparing the closing package. Your closing secretary can make changes later. While difficult in this age of the lender requiring all executed documents to be faxed prior to wiring the funds, have all required documents signed first and fax them while completing the closing to speed up the process.

- Do not be afraid to give a little free legal advice. I give my clients perks of free legal advice on simple matters. It takes only a few minutes of my time and I make up the difference with increased closings because of it.

- Be as accessible as possible to your clients.

My clients often reflect their amazement at how quickly I pick up a call from them, rather than turn them over to a secretary. They voice their appreciation often.

## Do Your Part to Prevent Mortgage Fraud

A home is the biggest investment most people will ever purchase. I often wonder why anyone would sell or purchase such an asset without the assistance of a real estate lawyer. Although real estate agents are knowledgeable about the subject, they are not qualified to analyze the complex legal documentation that can enter into a real estate transaction. They cannot provide legal advice. They are not qualified to answer questions regarding the recent changes in federal and state laws involving mortgage transactions.

Now more than ever, buyers and sellers must be mindful of the growing trend of mortgage fraud and their involvement therein. I know of innocent people who thought they were involved in simple investment opportunities, but instead were taken advantage of by criminals. Unknowingly, they broke federal and state laws and eventually were indicted on federal mortgage fraud charges. At the very least, buyers or sellers can have their credit ruined and funds stolen. Had a lawyer represented these people, they would have been protected.

Marketing materials geared toward representing buyers and sellers at closings, and alerting them of these issues, is not only a good marketing tactic, but is a public service. The new area is sometimes referred to as mortgage law.

Run advertisements that state, "Why would you purchase your largest asset without a lawyer?" Write articles, give speeches, and tell all who will listen that though real estate is a good investment device, it can be a dangerous business if you do not protect yourself. Offer to represent buyers from the time they submit a loan application to the time of closing. Offer to represent the sellers from the time they put the house on the market. Note that real estate agents get the house sold. Mortgage lawyers protect your legal rights.

# §3.3 How to Attract Business Clients
## *David Leffler*

I often get the question, "Where do you get your clients?" I'm often tempted to answer, "On the southeast corner of 53rd Street and Third Avenue."

If only finding clients was that easy. As a business lawyer, I typically do not have clients who provide me with recurring business month after month, year after year. My clients have times when they need my services, but once those services are completed it could be a while before they need me again. So I need a steady source of new client matters.

Thankfully, after over 20 years of being a lawyer, I have a client base that comes up with enough new matters and referrals that I am rarely without anything to do. However, I still am required to go out and renew this base from time to time. In this section I will reveal some of my more useful methods of doing so. However, I won't require you to sign any confidentiality or noncompetition agreements.

## *Getting Started*

The first thing you should do is to get out there and meet people. But don't attend meetings with other lawyers for this purpose. True, you may get some referral work. But the biggest payoff comes from attending meetings of business owners, or

### Attracting/Keeping Business Clients

- Attend public speaking events geared toward business owners.
- In the Q&A at a speaking event, volunteer early and first announce your name and profession.
- Write articles that provide solutions to business problems.
- Make your Web site clear and easily understood, and provide at least one area that is updated regularly.
- Maintain good communication with your clients.
- Have a genuine interest in your clients' businesses.
- Attempt to provide concise and easily understood solutions to business problems.

at least those business people that make the decision on hiring lawyers. It may be a meeting of your local Chamber of Commerce, a trade association meeting, or a business lecture.

Which of these meetings should you attend? Attend talks given on business topics that will attract the top people from the companies that you want to represent. There are likely to be potential business clients at a talk entitled "How to Grow Your Business."

In addition to the topic of the talk, two other indicators of whether or not there will be valuable leads are the quality of the speakers and the sponsor of the talk. High-level speakers tend to attract high-level executives. A sponsor is important because different sponsors tend to attract different kinds of crowds. The U.S. Small Business Administration sponsors many seminars for businesses, but very often the businesses are so small that they either don't have any significant legal needs or cannot afford the legal services they do need. Seminars sponsored by accounting firms, securities firms, or business publications attract a much higher quality of attendees.

If you have a specific area of business that you want to develop, such as high-technology clients, attend conferences given for the personal computer industry or for biotechs, or even more specific topics such as the latest developments of multimedia on the Internet.

## A Marketing Secret Revealed

Here, revealed for the first time in print, is my best method for generating clients when attending a talk where questions are permitted from the audience. It is a method that almost guarantees an introduction to at least one business owner needing a lawyer.

First, try being one of the first people to ask a question. Sometimes, rather than picking a raised hand from the audience, a microphone is set up in front of the room for people to line up to ask questions. Then you want to be the first up because once one or two people break the ice by stepping up to the microphone, a big crowd usually follows, making for a long line, and everyone may not get a chance to speak due to time constraints.

Whichever method is used, the audience tends to pay more attention to the first couple of questions asked, and then rapidly loses interest. You want as many people as possible to be paying attention to you, so try to be first up.

Now the important part of this technique is not only to come up with a good question that shows that you are intelligent, but also, when you begin to speak, to first introduce yourself and identify your profession. For example: "Hello, I'm David Leffler, a business lawyer here in Manhattan." Then ask your question. This will let everyone in the room know that you are a business lawyer. Free advertising!

One or more prospects always approach me afterwards. The reason this works so well is because of something very few lawyers ever realize: There are people looking to hire lawyers all the time, but they just don't know where to look for them. Your biggest task in marketing is simply to make yourself known to them. The odds are very good that if you announce that you are a business lawyer to an auditorium full of people attending a lecture on business issues, several people there will be looking for a business lawyer and at least one of them will approach you.

I am sure many of you dread getting up to speak in front of a room full of people, especially when you have just a few minutes to come up with a question that is both relevant to the talk you have just heard and insightful. I enjoy speaking in front of people, but even my heart races a bit as I am waiting to be called upon. But the effectiveness of this technique makes it worth overcoming any fears of public speaking.

Once again, by choosing a business lecture with quality speakers, you allow the sponsors of the talk to do the hard work of getting a crowd of mostly business owners, your target market, in the room. It is then up to you to make yourself known to this crowd rich with potential clients.

## Writing Articles That Generate Business

To attract clients through publication, you must write articles that business people will want to read and that create a compelling reason to hire you. You can write an article on a legal aspect of operating a business, but if it isn't something that a business owner will feel is important to his or her business, then you are not being effective in creating a marketing tool from your writing.

So how do you find a topic that will be interesting to the owners of the businesses that you want as clients? More important, how do you write an article that will create a compelling reason to hire you?

Business people have all kinds of worries. Worries about making sales, worries about competition, and worries about cash flow.

Some of their worries are legal in nature, and it's your job to find out what some of those worries are and to be able to present a solution to them.

For example, something high on the radar of most business owners right now is the concern about employee lawsuits related to wrongful termination of employment, sexual harassment, and a host of other issues. Imagine a business owner's relief upon reading an article you've written that addresses this problem and provides useful advice.

Writing such an article shows the businessperson two things about you. First, you were interested and perceptive enough to be aware of *their* concerns. Second, you were smart enough to find a useful solution.

The solution, by the way, should be something that is cost effective and easily implemented. For instance, if the potential client's business is in an area where protection of trade secrets is important, you could suggest the implementation of confidentiality agreements and perhaps discuss other methods, such as patent protection.

You've impressed the potential client with your perception and smarts. Now, how do you get them to hire you?

The emotion that motivates people into action more than any other is fear. So, rather than write an article entitled "How to be in Compliance with Employment Laws," write an article entitled "How to Avoid Employee Lawsuits." This will get your prospects' attention *and* provide them with a compelling reason to hire you.

## Advertising

Advertising is not as valuable a marketing tool for business lawyers as it is for lawyers practicing consumer law, such as divorce or personal injury. While someone might look in the Yellow Pages for a personal injury lawyer, it much less likely that they would look there for a lawyer to represent their business. (Don't forget to check with your state's ethics laws on advertising if you do decide to do any advertising.)

People are more likely to find their business lawyer from an introduction by a friend or a chance encounter at a meeting. Web sites are good for people to get a better idea of your expertise after they have met you, but it is mostly person-to-person contact that will get you business. I say "mostly" because you can and will get business from a well designed Web site, but I don't recommend relying principally on this method of generating new clients.

You can read the many articles that exist that will tell you what makes a good Web site for your law practice, but let me say that the key elements are

- Good, easily understood content that is useful to your target audience and explains what your practice is about.
- A simple design that allows people to navigate with ease and find what they are looking for.
- A reason for viewers to come back, which means regularly changing content.

An example of this last item is a regular column on legal concerns of a particular industry that comes out on a monthly basis. Also, you might consider placing a stock market ticker or other business indicator on your Web site that appeals to your target business owner. Such items are readily available for your use from various Web sites.

Another aspect of Web site marketing is what is called search engine optimization, though there are certain hazards involved with this. Search engine optimization refers to changes that can be made to your Web site, some visible and some not, that will make it more likely that you will show up near the top of a search engine's result for various terms.

The technically inclined can implement some of these changes themselves. There are also search engine optimization (SEO) companies that promise to do this for you. However, be very careful whom you hire for this, because some of these SEO companies employ techniques that violate rules set out by Google, the most popular search engine. If Google discovers you using these techniques, it will take you out of its Web site index, which means you will find your law firm Web site locked out of the most popular search engine on the planet.

Lastly, create a firm brochure prepared that includes your firm's mission statement, a description of your practice, your bio, and a description of some of the matters that you have handled. You can also print copies of your articles to include in materials handed out to potential clients.

## You've Got the Business Client— How Do You Keep the Business?

There are certain qualities that a business client appreciates in a lawyer:

### Communication skills

Being easy to talk to encompasses two qualities. First, you should be approachable, not distant in your manner. If you have a professional demeanor that is intimidating, business clients are much less likely to feel comfortable asking you questions. Second, you should provide direct answers to questions. Nothing drives a client crazy like a lawyer giving a 15-minute answer that the client can't understand and that doesn't answer the question asked.

### Your interest in their business

Asking a simple question like, "How is business?" makes clients feel like you have an interest in them beyond your hourly rate. You should attempt to have a genuine interest; otherwise your questions about their business might seem artificial. I happen to have a real interest in what is going on in my clients' businesses, so this works well for me. I also provide contacts that can help their business and introductions for new business.

### Solutions that are easily quantifiable, not open-ended

Business people are usually very busy, with not enough time in the day to get everything done.

If they have a legal problem, they are not interested in arcane theories of law. They want the easiest, quickest, and least costly solution possible, whether it's a legal problem or a shipping problem. True, it is not always easy to come up with a quick solution to every legal problem, but you should attempt to solve their problems with this concern in mind, and this attitude will show when you deal with your client.

## And Finally . . .

You will get better and better at attracting business clients as you get more experience in dealing with them and their concerns. What impressed your law professor is unlikely to impress your business client, who is mostly interested in results, not your eloquent exposition on legal theory.

Who knows? You may become so attuned to the business world that you might decide to leave the law and become a businessperson yourself. You certainly wouldn't be the first lawyer to do so.

# §3.4 How to Attract Probate and Estate Planning Clients
## *Ronald A. Jones*

Wills can be a tough sell. Folk wisdom is that if you die without a will, "the state gets everything," and nearly anyone you ask will sagely nod his or her head and say, "Everyone needs a will." In fact, my local pastor, preaching to a largely elderly congregation, has repeatedly noted from the pulpit that part of good stewardship in caring for your spouse and family involves having a will. In spite of this, at least half of Americans do not have a will. As lawyers, we understand the necessity of having a will, naming a guardian for minor children, ensuring that spouses are taken care of, naming a responsible executor, and minimizing the costs of probate. And, doubtless, the public could be much better educated on why wills are needed. I have yet to figure out a way to convince people that they should have a will, but what I can figure out is why they should hire me to draft the will once they have decided they need one.

First, while some people may be able to make a living focusing exclusively on estate planning and probate, for most solo and small firm practitioners, estate planning and probate are going to be a major practice area but not an exclusive one. This is not necessarily a bad thing; you can do some cross-pollination between practice areas. It is not unusual for people for whom I have drawn up estate planning documents to return to me about other legal matters, ranging from real estate to family law to personal injury. Likewise, if I have someone contacting me about any other sort

**Help the Clients Come to You**

- Use wills to cross-market other areas of your practice.
- Locate your office near the potential clients.
- Set fees competitively.
- Impress clients with your efficiency.
- Make sure the heirs know how to find you.

of legal matter, I will make a point of asking them at the final interview or contact, "Oh, by the way, do you have a will"? Frequently they do not, and typically they will ask then and there to set an interview date. Also, quite a few past or current clients will refer you to other potential clients.

Second, considering that the majority of Americans do not have wills, you should ask, "Who does, in fact, draw up wills?" Although it is arguable that a young married couple with minor children actually needs a will more than an elderly empty-nest couple, it has been my experience that elderly individuals are much more likely to feel at ease setting out their final wishes. In seven years of practice, I have drawn up over 400 wills; I can count on two hands the number of couples under the age of 50 who have had me draw up wills. My typical will client is over 63, drawing Social Security and a pension. While senior citizens and retirees can be found everywhere, they are concentrated in particular communities. Personally, I belong to the Willie Sutton school of law office location: You put your office where the clients are. Being near a retirement center is enormously helpful in selling wills. If you are in a county with a large retirement community, you are better off locating near those clients, rather than downtown near the courthouse as many lawyers would prefer. Many elderly clients are uncomfortable driving for long distances, and may be afraid of parking and walking in downtown areas. An office located near their communities, with adequate parking, is likely to make them more comfortable in traveling to your office.

Clients are more likely to use you if you are close to them. Lawyers who locate their office near the courthouse are putting their convenience over the clients; lawyers who put their office near the clients are more likely to draw those clients than a lawyer with an office downtown. This is particularly true for elderly clients, many of whom don't like to drive.

The third factor to consider is how to set your fees. In the past, wills have been a loss leader; lawyers would deliberately underprice their wills in the expectation that they would make fees off of the probate of the will. Many of the wills drafted by a lawyer may wind up being probated by that same lawyer, but given the increasingly competitive market for lawyers, resulting in lower revenue for legal services, and the increased mobility of citizens, there is no particular guarantee that a lawyer will wind up seeing any probate fees off of a particular will. Estate planning has to stand on its own two feet in order to make it worthwhile. The key to setting your fees is to be competitive—you don't necessarily have to be the cheapest available, but if you do set your fees too high, you are not likely to get very many clients. Personally, I do a lot of "flat fee" estate planning; for a nontaxable estate, with no special needs trusts, I can interview the client, prepare and send the documents, and conduct the execution of a typical will in an hour or less; I deliberately set my fee so that I am making more, on the average will, than I would make charging an hourly rate. Now, your ability to do this sort of flat-fee estate planning is going to depend on several factors: the complexity of the estate plan and your efficiency in interviewing clients and drafting and executing the documents.

Flat-fee estate planning is not likely to pay off for complex estates; if the case involves a potentially taxable estate or a noncitizen spouse, you are better off doing this on an hourly basis. The first few interviews, drafts, and executions are going to take you quite a while, but you will become more efficient with experience. The best way to minimize time spent on actually drafting a will is by efficient use of forms; there are will-drafting packages available. I use the Florida Will and Trust Manual published by the Florida Bar; it has separate wills for married individuals and single individuals, with minor children, with adult children, and with no children; as well as wills and trusts for nontaxable estates and taxable estates. Such a system requires minimal changes to complete the document; if I have an elderly couple with adult children, I already have a will that makes reference to a spouse and children; if it is a single person without children, I have a form that is already set up without such references. Efficiency is essential if you are going to be doing a large number of wills. This allows you to make a profit while keeping your costs, and fees to the client, down. All other things being equal, larger fees will equal larger profits, but things are rarely equal; in order to become efficient, you have to conduct a lot of will interviews and draft a lot of wills, and you are unlikely to do that if you have priced yourself out of the market. Understand that there are some people who will buy entirely on price; the lawyer who competes strictly on price is going to have a tough time making a living. The key is to price competitively—somewhere in the middle of the fees charged locally for the same type of work.

Another advantage of being efficient at drafting wills is that you can quickly respond to potential clients. Frankly, too many lawyers take too long to have the client come to the interview, take too long to draft the wills, and take too long to set the will signing. If you can do a will interview in 30 minutes, and draft the documents in 10 or 15 minutes, when the client calls and asks what a will costs, and how long it will take, the client is much more likely to choose you if you are competitively priced and can see them within a reasonable time; the client is also likely to be impressed if he receives the draft documents within a day or two of the interview. A client who has to wait two weeks for an interview, and then wait up to month to get the draft documents, is unlikely to be impressed and is not likely to recommend you to anyone else.

During the interview, ask if the client is interested in other documents; typically I will recommend a durable power of attorney, a health care surrogacy, a living will, and a preneed guardianship. If you are in a state where living trusts are useful, you may recommend those as well. The client may have some questions about the usefulness of those documents, and if you can cogently and succinctly explain their importance, you will nearly always be able to sell the documents. Once again, as far as pricing goes, price competitively. Odds are that it will not take you much longer to get the information needed to draft the documents, and if you have a good forms package, you should not take much longer to draft the additional documents.

Clients are convinced that probate is expensive, and there is a cottage industry in "avoiding probate." Many lawyers, and some nonlawyers, market living trusts to clients. And lawyers have differing opinions on the value of living trusts. Personally, I am less than thrilled with them for most individuals, but still, people want to avoid probate. I am making use of "Ladybird Deeds" or "enhanced life estate deeds," which essentially allow the grantor to retain a life estate with full powers to mortgage, give, transfer, or sell the property without joinder by the remainderman, and allow the grantor to retain all proceeds. If these are allowed in your state, they can be very profitable; and they can be sold to the client in addition to the standard will package.

The fourth consideration, advertising, is a dirty word to many lawyers as well as to many state bars, but if you want clients, you are going to have to let them know you are out there. Many people rely on Yellow Pages advertising, and the American Bar Association has done several studies on effective Yellow Pages advertising. Newspapers can be quite useful, but in order to be cost-effective you should ideally reach all of your target audience, but not pay for advertising to anyone who is not likely to use your services. In fact, that is the ideal for all advertising: reaching only those likely to buy what you are selling. Although there is no perfect method for precisely targeting your potential clients, things to consider include the circulation of the publication; if you draw from a relatively small geographic area it is a waste of money to spend for advertising over a much larger metropolitan area. If you have a local weekly or monthly paper that circulates primarily in your targeted community, it may be more cost-efficient to advertise in that rather than a large metropolitan daily. Also, when advertising, tell the clients what you do, not the areas of law that you practice in; lawyers may know what "estate planning" is, but the client is looking for some-one to draft a will. Don't advertise "Estate Planning"; tell them you do "Wills, Trusts, Powers of Attorney, Probate." Likewise, "Elder Law" is a mystery to many people; "Guardianships and Medicaid Planning" is much more likely to tell them what they want to know.

While drafting a will does not guarantee that you will be contacted to handle the probate, chances are that if the survivors know you drafted the will, you will be the one who winds up probating the estate. It is absolutely essential that your name, address, and phone number appear on the documents. I use commercially available will envelopes and will covers, printed with "Last Will and Testament of" and blank spaces for the testator's name. It takes a little experimentation, but you can easily develop a template through your word processing program to print the testator's name and date of will, followed by "Prepared by [your name, with your address and phone number]" in prominent lettering and grind the documents through your laser printer. Your name and address should go on both the will cover and will envelope. If the survivors can't find you, they aren't going to hire you.

# §3.5 How to Market an Alternative Dispute Resolution Practice
## *Andrea Goldman*

When I attended my first mediation training, in 1996, the session began with an ominous message, "Don't quit your day job!" Needless to say, this was a fairly discouraging way to begin my entry into the world of alternative dispute resolution (ADR). Although in many ways, the message presented was accurate, it is possible for a small firm or solo practitioner to make a foray into the world of ADR and develop an additional practice area, or even switch over entirely.

The first thing to consider when thinking about ADR is which type of practice interests you. There are many titles out there these days, including arbitrator, mediator, facilitator, conciliator, and even collaborative lawyer. Each of these positions has its own "spin," and not all are suited to every practitioner. Dispute resolution occurs along a spectrum and can be defined as follows:

Negotiation → Collaborative Law → Facilitation → Conciliation → Mediation → Mediation/Arbitration → Arbitration → Litigation

Negotiation occurs informally between parties without the aid of a third party. Collaborative law is a relatively new field in which advocates agree to work cooperatively together without resorting to litigation. Facilitation involves trying to resolve disputes with the aid of a neutral facilitator who helps move the discussion along. A facilitator frequently works with a group. A conciliator is generally associated with a court program and will help parties try to settle a case. Mediators act as third-party neutrals as well, but their goal is to try to help the parties reach an agreement that is generated by the participants' efforts. The mediator does not impose his or her own solution, but helps to generate options that will hopefully result in a resolution of the matter. In mediation/arbitration, the process starts out as a mediation, but if a settlement cannot be worked out, the mediator switches hats and becomes an arbitrator. The arbitrator acts as a private judge and makes a ruling regarding the case. Arbitration can be binding or nonbinding, and frequently there is a limited basis for appeal. Finally, matters are usually litigated if no other solution can be found.

A little soul-searching is in order when you are thinking about an alternative dispute resolution practice. Law school trains us to work as advocates for our clients. Some of us are more confrontational than others, but the ethical rules demand that we zealously represent our clients. Making the transition to ADR requires a transition in mindset. Some lawyers find it easier to look at both sides of an issue and maintain a neutral stance. Others form opinions and prefer sitting in the decision-making position. Neither personality is better than the other. It is important, however, to recognize one's strengths and choose an area of dispute resolution that is suitable.

After choosing an area of alternative dispute resolution to pursue, it is necessary to seek out the appropriate training. In Massachusetts, there is still no certification required for

**Mediation Defined**

1. Voluntary (in most cases)
2. Cooperative model driven by the parties
3. Confidential—privatizes disputes
4. Agreement created by the parties
   a. Higher rate of compliance
   b. Enforceable
5. Defuses the adversarial nature of litigation—turns back the clock
6. Cost effective—can be cheaper than litigation
7. Efficient—tends to be quicker than litigation

mediators or arbitrators unless they participate in court-connected dispute resolution. It is hard to believe that anyone can hang out a shingle as a mediator without credentials, but that is the current situation. Any practitioner worth his salt, however, is going to seek out the best training possible. In most states, community mediation programs offer the best training for mediation. State mediation associations or the Association for Conflict Resolution (http://www.acrnet.org) are likely to have lists of available programs.

The most important feature of any training is the opportunity to acquire mediation experience once the training is completed. The reason for this is that the best mediation training comes from court-connected programs (usually small claims court), and most programs will not place you on their panels if you have not trained with them. To avoid this Catch 22, it is therefore imperative to find out if one is guaranteed an internship of some sort in the courts. In addition, it is important to ask if there is a formalized program involved in the internship, and if it costs extra. One should also make sure that the training offers the requisite number of hours as required by your state statute. Massachusetts has adopted the Uniform Rules on Dispute Resolution requiring more than 30 hours of training in order to participate in court-sponsored programs. In pertinent part:

1. **Training Requirement.** A mediator shall successfully complete a basic mediation training course of at least thirty hours and a court orientation. . . .
2. **Mentoring and Evaluation Requirement.** A mediator shall complete the mentoring and evaluation requirements contained in the Guidelines. . . .
3. **Continuing Education.** A mediator shall participate in any continuing education required by the approved program with which he or she is affiliated or by the court department in which he or she is providing services.
4. **Continuing Evaluation.** A mediator shall participate in regular evaluation. . . .

In most programs, the new mediator starts out by observing a number of mediation sessions. He or she is then given the opportunity to co-mediate with a more experienced neutral. Finally, the new mediator mediates solo while being observed.

Once the training is completed, the next step is to attempt to join mediation panels. Your training program will hopefully offer you a place on their roster, and that is a great place to start. The federal district court in your state may also have a mediation program. Other entities that have mediation panels include state government, the United States Post Office, the World Bank, and the National Association of Securities Dealers. Mediation panels are generally quite restrictive and are frequently closed for long periods of time. It requires persistence and patience to be listed on panels.

Arbitration trainings are given by agencies that offer arbitration services. Probably the best-known arbitration organization is the American Arbitration Association. If one is lucky enough to have the kind of background and experience that AAA finds attractive, this organization will provide excellent training in the arbitration process. The National Association of Securities Dealers also has an arbitration program and requires participation in their training. It takes a long time to develop either a mediation or arbitration practice, and one should expect that it might be quite some time before receiving that first case.

Once the credentials are acquired, it is time to think about how to market your ADR practice. As with marketing any business, it is best to start with what you know. Although there are people who study ADR and then go directly into the business, they are few and far between. Most solo or small firm practitioners already have some areas of expertise and an established clientele. The ADR practice should be a natural outgrowth of these areas. Employment lawyers should consider employment mediation and look into agencies that deal with employment issues (in Massachusetts, there is mediation at the Massachusetts Commis-

**Stages of a Mediation**

1. Introduction—setting the stage
   a. Tone
   b. Rules
   c. Relaxing the parties
   d. Establishing mediator's authority
   e. Seating the parties side-by-side
2. Fact finding—learning perspectives
3. Issue/interest identification and clarification
   a. Joint sessions
   b. Private sessions
4. Generating/prioritizing options
5. Creating the agreement

sion Against Discrimination). Labor mediators or arbitrators can affiliate with government agencies that handle labor disputes. Construction lawyers are frequently used as arbitrators and mediators. Personal injury lawyers engage in mediation as well. The rule is, start with what you know, and let everyone you know become aware that you are now an arbitrator and/or mediator.

Another way to attract clients is to join private mediation/arbitration panels. The biggest alternative dispute resolution companies are the American Arbitration Association (http://www.adr.org) and JAMS® (http://www.jamsadr.com), but there are also a number of smaller panels out there. One example of an alternative dispute resolution company in Massachusetts is ADR/Equimar (http://www.adr-equimar .com). There are 90 dispute resolution professionals listed on ADR/Equimar's panels, which include personal injury, employment, construction, and commercial. These professionals are currently handling approximately 800 cases per year, divided among personal injury (70 percent), business (15 percent), employment (5 percent), construction (5 percent) and other (5 percent). Their caseload is 80 percent arbitration and 20 percent mediation. When asked how lawyers are chosen for their panels, Brian King, a case manager for ADR/Equimar,

stated, "We choose our panelists by looking at their background and making sure that they have done both plaintiff and defense work. We also listen very carefully to our clients' suggestions on who they have used in the past."

JAMS has over 200 neutrals on its panel who arbitrate and mediate cases full-time. On average JAMS hears approximately 10,000 cases a year, but that number has increased dramatically in recent years due to large class actions. Many of these cases include thousands of hearings. The vast majority of their matters are in the practice areas of business and commercial, class actions, construction, employment, environment, insurance, and intellectual property. Seventy percent of JAMS's revenue is generated from mediation and 30 percent from arbitration.

"Panelists come to JAMS in a variety of ways," said Steve Price, JAMS president and CEO. "Many times mediators and arbitrators are familiar with JAMS because their colleagues from the bench or bar are with JAMS. Each of our neutrals brings considerable dispute resolution experience to JAMS when he or she joins the organization."

In 2003, 174,895 cases were filed with the American Arbitration Association (AAA). AAA has approximately 7,800 total panelists. There are approximately 780 mediators on their mediation panel. In 2003, approximately 80 percent of their cases were insurance cases, 9 percent commercial cases, 8 percent labor cases, and 4 percent accident and other cases. Of the 174,895 cases that were filed, 64,511 were mediations/conciliations. AAA actively promotes ADR in the community, and recently completed an objective study that demonstrates that businesses save enormous amounts of money by pursuing alternative dispute resolution instead of litigation.

Being placed on a panel is just the beginning of the process, however. One still has to market oneself in order to receive cases. The best marketing is usually networking with other lawyers. They understand ADR and its role in and outside the litigation process. Writing an article for a legal journal or newspaper, giving a CLE course, or speaking at a bar association meeting are all excellent ways to gain recognition as a mediator and/or arbitrator.

What about the lay public? In my experience, a talk or article about "mediation," or "alternative forms of dispute resolution," does not attract a large audience. It is far better to speak about a substantive subject, such as "how to resolve a neighbor dispute," "dealing with home contractors," "what to do when the dry cleaner ruins your favorite outfit," or "what landlords need to know," and include information about ADR as part of your talk. For most people, their introduction to ADR occurs as a result of making contact with a lawyer about a problem, and consequently, they become involved in mediation or arbitration.

Hopefully, with the training period completed, all that hard work at marketing will start to pay off, and those mediation and/or arbitration cases will start coming in. How should one charge for these services? Typically, parties split the cost of an ADR professional. This is not always the case, however, as sometimes mediation or arbitration clauses in contracts make these processes mandatory, and the "contractor" will pay for all the costs, since the "contractee" has no choice in the matter.

Some mediators charge their regular hourly legal rate, and require a minimum half-day or three-hour fee for setting the time aside for a mediation. Others charge by the half or full day. Keep in mind, however, that in many jurisdictions lawyer mediators are competing with nonlawyer mediators whose rates may be lower. Before advertising one's rates, it is a good idea to do some market research. The Massachusetts legal newspaper conducts and publishes an annual survey of ADR professionals, including rates. One can also look at Web sites and advertisements for arbitrators and mediators.

Another issue is preparation time and follow-up. Are you going to request preliminary memoranda? Will you charge for reviewing these and other documents? Who will write up the agreement if one is reached? As an arbitrator, will you make a simple ruling, or prepare a reasoned decision?

Speaking with other ADR professionals will help you in making these decisions. It is an excellent idea to observe as many other mediators and arbitrators as one can. It will help you develop your "style" and determine what makes for a skilled mediator. Getting involved in ADR organizations and reading journals also helps to improve skills and keeps one in touch with the profession. Obtaining referrals through these ADR networks is generally not very successful, however. Most programs are working quite hard just to sustain themselves. Overflow cases are not common, and people tend not to give cases away. Given the fact that many organizations make most of their money through training, in certain states there are many more ADR professionals than there is work to support them.

Marketing an alternative dispute resolution practice can work if one maintains realistic expectations and goes about it the right way. The process can take quite a long time unless one has a preestablished client base, so it is necessary to start the journey with one's eyes open. Get proper training, seize every available opportunity to practice your newfound skills, and try to be placed on panels. Once you know the ropes, try to market in your area of expertise and experience. Network with other lawyers, and make sure you tell everyone you know about your new practice. Do not try to market to other ADR professionals; it is usually just a frustrating exercise. Observe other mediators and arbitrators so you can develop your style and keep improving your skills. Finally, determine how your practice will be divided between alternative dispute resolution and legal advocacy, and use your new skills in both areas of your practice.

# §3.6  How to Market to Ethnic Communities
## *Victoria Tran Sood*

### *It's a Small World After All*

The world is getting smaller and more mobile. More citizens from around the world are immigrating to the United States, either temporarily for work or permanently. They no longer concentrate in large cities and have begun to establish themselves in small towns. They become members of the community and are subject to the same legal system and laws. They are therefore prospective clients to lawyers practicing in the community. *A lawyer's success with an ethnic community is dependent upon the lawyer's appreciation and understanding of the ethnic community's culture and legal needs.* Only with such foundation can marketing efforts be fruitful.

One or more ethnic communities, in addition to many smaller ones, probably dominate each locality. I enjoy eating very much, so I will use food to illustrate the point. Within the 15-mile drive from my home to the office, the ethnic foods that are available to my choosing are lumpia and pansit (Filipino), samosa and paratha (Indian), dim sum and won ton noodle (Chinese), and pho (Vietnamese). If you are clueless about the items on this menu, then find out if there are ethnic communities in your locality that serve those wonderful and delicious dishes. Not every locality is as diverse as Northern California. But your locality has probably at least one ethnic community that is already established or is

Mrs. Victoria Tran Sood is a Vietnamese lawyer in San Jose, California. She practices probate and trust dispute, probate, estate planning, and international tax. She thanks all the lawyers who shared their experience and ideas on marketing to the Vietnamese community in the San Jose area.

http://www.ailf.org/ipc/policy_reports_2004_newtrends.asp. *New Trends in Immigration: Immigrants in the Heartland of America.* Rachel Rubinstein of Haverford College. The American Immigration Law Foundation.

Ethnic communities are undiscovered jewels. Find yours and be profitable.

establishing itself, and this growing ethnic community is in need of your legal expertise.

## Ideas Create Ideas

This section will guide you through the process of finding facts that are relevant to your target ethnic community so that you can execute a marketing plan that is effective and cost-efficient. This section, however, is not a step-by-step marketing guide for each ethnic community in your locality. The steps suggested in this section will open the door to your target ethnic community. Do not stop until your target ethnic community invites you inside and, better yet, asks you to stay for food. With persistence and patience, you can be successful in your target ethnic community.

## Ethnic Lawyers and Nonethnic Lawyers

For this discussion, let us divide lawyers servicing an ethnic community into two groups, "ethnic lawyers" and "nonethnic lawyers." Ethnic lawyers are lawyers whose ethnicities are that of the target ethnic community; for example, a Vietnamese lawyer like myself would be considered an ethnic lawyer. Nonethnic lawyers are lawyers whose ethnicities are different from the target ethnic community; an example is a Caucasian lawyer servicing the Vietnamese community.

Competency is the No. 1 consideration in retaining a lawyer.

Competency and quality of the service are the primary considerations of prospective ethnic clients when they engage a lawyer.

Everything else is secondary, including a lawyer's ethnicity or fluency in the foreign language. But everything being equal, most ethnic clients prefer ethnic lawyers because of their understanding of the culture. As a result, these ethnic clients assume, rightly or wrongly, that ethnic lawyers will be empathic and understanding to their circumstances and thus will be more effective in resolving their legal issues. Another reason ethnic clients prefer ethnic lawyers is the ethnic clients' preference to communicate in their native languages, even if they are bilingual. Nonethnic lawyers, however, should not despair.

Nonethnic lawyers have their own advantages when practicing in an ethnic community. Some ethnic clients prefer nonethnic lawyers. Privacy and false assumption of competency are the main factors influencing ethnic clients to engage nonethnic lawyers. Ethnic clients assume, rightly or wrongly, that their matters will not be a topic of gossip in the ethnic community if they engage nonethnic lawyers, who are not a part of a networking grapevine. Moreover, some ethnic clients sincerely believe that Caucasian lawyers are more competent than ethnic lawyers.

Although foreign language capability and cultural understanding are not the controlling factors in engaging a nonethnic lawyer, an ethnic client is likely to engage a nonethnic lawyer who has an interest in the language and culture. In the Vietnamese community in San Jose, a few Caucasian lawyers speak Vietnamese, and Vietnamese clients favor them over nonethnic lawyers who do not speak the language.

Ethnic lawyers are favored for their sensitivity to the culture and fluency in the language,

Nonethnic lawyers are perceived as more competent.

## Practice Areas

Legal services surrounding issues affecting individuals and small businesses are commonly demanded in ethnic communities. These areas of practice are family law, criminal defense, personal injury, immigration law, and entity formation. Most lawyers, both ethnic and nonethnic, practicing in an ethnic community consider themselves as general practitioners but emphasize one or two of these practice areas.

The hottest areas of law in ethnic communities include family law, criminal defense, personal injury, and immigration law.

Although the demand in these areas of law remains steady, external political and economical forces also affect the niches of those practice areas. For instance, the Indian community has had a constant need for immigration lawyers. But during the dot.com boom, most of the demand was concentrated in business immigration, petitioning for H-1B temporary work visas and green cards for professionals. When the dot.com bubble burst and preventing terrorist attack took center stage after the September 11 tragedy, the demand for business immigration slid like the stock market, but the demand for deportation (removal) defense skyrocketed like the housing market in the Bay Area. During this period, a new demand was emerging in the Indian community—international tax planning. None of the lawyers in the Indian community had the expertise to handle the matter or knew of anyone who did. These clients were left scrambling for qualified advisers. Had lawyers who practiced deportation defense and international tax in the locality been attuned to these changes, they could have availed their services to the Indian community.

Growing areas include estate planning, civil litigation, and employment law.

The lawyers would have more clients and more income and the needs in the Indian community would be met.

Demand in other areas such as civil litigation, intellectual property, estate planning, tax planning, tax controversy, and employment law is growing to reflect the demographic and generational changes in ethnic communities. Although the need for these services may not be in great demand until a few years from now, lawyers need to be proactive and establish themselves in the community. Ethnic clients are more likely to retain a lawyer whose name is commonly recognized in the ethnic community. Start marketing now to get a head start. But for your marketing to be effective, you need to identify and understand your prospective ethnic clients.

## Identifying Prospective Clients

Knowing the ethnic make-up in the community is the first step to capturing a new market. For instance, certain cities in California are dominated by certain ethnic groups: Vietnamese in San Jose, Garden Grove, and Westminster; Indian in Fremont and Sunnyvale; Filipino in Union City and Newark; and Chinese in Milpitas and Monterey Park. When the target market is identified and understood, only then is the first marketing tool used.

The first place to start determining the presence of ethnic communities in your locality is to browse through the Yellow Page for ethnic restaurants and markets. The number of listings indicates the size of the ethnic community. You will discover that ethnic restaurants and markets are located within proximity of

Dining and shopping in the community are your best marketing research tools.

each other. Now visit them. While there, pick up ethnic newspapers and magazines; many ethnic markets and restaurants have
ethnic magazines or newspapers for a nominal price or for free.

## Networking

The next step is to identify your competitors and/or referral
sources. Most lawyers servicing an ethnic group advertise in
more than one ethnic magazine or newspaper. Browse through
the magazines and newspapers you accumulated from the ethnic
restaurants and markets, focusing on lawyer advertisements. Pay
attention to the lawyers' areas of practice and locations. Most
lawyers situate themselves close to their prospective ethnic clients.
Contact these lawyers and start your networking process.

Your competitors are also your mentors and referral sources.

If you are not comfortable making cold calls to these lawyers,
then network with them through organizational events, such as
ethnic bar associations or ethnic business chambers. You can find
these ethnic organizations on the Internet, in the Yellow Pages,
or through your local bar associations. If your community has an
ethnic bar association or an ethnic business chamber, attend their
networking events and stay in touch with the people you meet
there. For example, the Vietnamese community in northern California has a Vietnamese American Bar Association and a Vietnamese American Chamber of Commerce.

The lawyers you meet are your referral source, whether
or not these lawyers practice the same areas of law as you do.
Lawyers who have practiced in an ethnic community for many
years are familiar with the skills and expertise of their colleagues

www.vabanc.org. For membership information, email membership@vabanc.org.

Vietnamese American Chamber of Commerce of Santa Clara's contact information is 255 North Market Street, Suite 110, San Jose, CA 95110. Telephone: 408-288-7602.

and are often looking for lawyers to refer the matters neither they nor their colleagues handle. These lawyers are your primary and most important source of referral and marketing advice. Networking with these lawyers is the most effective and cost-efficient marketing tool.

## Print Advertisement

Second to networking is print advertisement. Before placing an advertisement in an ethnic magazine or newspaper, you should have talked to and received advice from the lawyers you contacted on the type of publication, price, content, and layout of the advertisement. Your advertisement should be in both English and the language of the ethnic group. Most ethnic publishers do not translate the advertisements, fearing lawsuits resulting from mistranslating technical words. If you have established a good rapport with the lawyers you have met through networking, they will happily review and translate your advertisement. Nonethnic lawyers usually list an assistant who speaks the language of the ethnic group as the contact person.

Use print advertisement for branding.

As with any print advertisements, you have to screen your prospective clients. You will find a few good cases from the many callers seeking free advice or the lowest fees. But once you establish a client base in the ethnic community, you will receive a steady stream of clients from your former and current clients in that community. By then, you no longer need rely on print advertisements to bring in clients, but you should continue to use print advertisement as a medium for name recognition.

## Radio, Television, Internet, and Newsletter Advertisement

Most lawyers servicing ethnic communities do not advertise on the radio or television. Radio and television advertisements are more costly than print advertisement and are less effective. Moreover, Internet and newsletter advertisements are used to a lesser extent than radio and television advertisements. Lawyers, including myself, in marketing to ethnic communities, probably underutilize these tools. These tools should not be dismissed just because they are not commonly used.

Test the waters first before investing in these costly marketing avenues.

## Other Marketing Tools

### Anchoring

Anchoring is a term I use to describe the placing of business cards or promotional materials at various businesses for the public to pick up. Ethnic markets and restaurants often have a bulletin board or designate a specific area, usually by the cash register, where you can leave your business cards and promotional materials. Make sure you ask the business owner's permission before leaving your business cards or promotional items there.

Supplement your marketing at nominal cost.

### Teaching

Teach a course that your prospective clients are interested in. For instance, immigration lawyers should teach a course on preparing for the naturalization exam. Business lawyers should teach a course on selecting an entity for a newly formed business. These courses are usually offered by local community colleges or nonprofit groups, so contact them to inquire about becoming an instructor.

## Conclusion

Ethnic communities are an untapped source of prospective clients. They are also difficult to attract and maintain unless you appreciate and enjoy working with ethnic communities. If you are sincere and ready to service the ethnic communities, you now have the tools to proceed. Marketing does not guarantee client engagement, but relationship development does. Therefore, continue to network and maintain great client relations while you market to ethnic communities.

# §3.7 How to Market a Legal Research and Writing Practice to Other Lawyers

### *Lisa Solomon*

Marketing legal research and writing services to other lawyers presents two main challenges. The first is figuring out what kinds of marketing activities attract the most, and best, prospective clients. The second is convincing those prospective clients of the advantages of outsourcing their legal research and writing projects to you—in other words, convincing them to become your clients.

Since starting my legal research and writing practice in 1996, I have tried almost every type of marketing. Some marketing activities take a lot of time; others require more of a financial commitment. Not all have been equally successful.

First, some general principles. The great thing about being a solo researcher/writer is that, compared with larger firms, you need relatively few clients to be successful. Since every lawyer who has to do a motion, an appeal, or just legal research is potentially a client, concentrating your efforts locally or county-wide is likely to produce a sufficient client base unless you practice in a locale with few other lawyers; conversely, because you can apply your research and writing skills to the law of any jurisdiction (not only the jurisdiction where you are admitted), you have a virtually unlimited pool of potential clients nationwide. Some marketing activities lend themselves to developing a local client base, while others have a broader reach.

## Spread the Words

Like lawyers in more traditional practices, you face the challenge of keeping your name in front of current and potential clients so that when the need to outsource arises, hiring lawyers will remember that you are available to help them. This is a perfect opportunity to get more marketing mileage from your published articles and speaking engagements.

As soon after publication as possible, send reprints of your published articles to everyone on your contacts list, along with a brief cover letter explaining the connection between the article and the contact's needs. E-mail your contacts announcements of your upcoming speaking engagements, and provide a link to the sponsoring organization's Web site to make registration easier. After you present a seminar, send out copies of your seminar materials. With these communications, you combine the benefits of the one-on-one networking that has helped you develop your contacts list with your one-to-many speaking and writing efforts.

One of the obstacles you face in getting work from clients is that their need to send out legal research and writing projects may be sporadic. When the need arises, potential clients might not realize you're out there, and existing clients might not remember you're out there. So it is important to make frequent contact with both potential and existing clients.

In my experience, the single most effective way to market a solo legal research and writing practice is through networking at bar association functions. Even if you are not involved in the leadership of a bar association, regularly attending bar association events gives you an opportunity to meet lots of potential clients. Meeting people face-to-face helps develop trust and also allows you to address at the outset any questions or concerns about outsourcing that a potential client may have.

There are a number of ways to maximize the benefits you derive from networking. One way is to make networking a two-way street: think about what you can do for potential clients, not just about what they can do for you. For example, I know a lawyer who does lawyer coaching and consults with firms on the business aspects of their practices. I recommended him as a speaker for a solo and small firm symposium in New York City, which was organized by a lawyer I know through my local chapter of the Women's Bar Association of the State of New York. In turn, he interviewed me about how a firm can increase its profitability by outsourcing legal research and writing for an "audio magazine" he publishes. After the audio magazine came out, I submitted a notice about the interview for publication in both the local and statewide Women's Bar newsletters, which gave both my interviewer and me additional exposure at no cost to either of us. The speaker referral also helped my colleague from the Women's Bar, who now has a qualified presenter for future programs.

Another way to derive the greatest benefit from networking is to network with people who themselves have many contacts. Get to know the leaders of your bar associations and the folks who just do a lot of schmoozing: they'll have the most opportunities to recommend you to their colleagues. Since law is a personal service business, a recommendation from a respected member of the local bar goes a long way. Similarly, if you decide that you want to broaden your circle of contacts by taking a leadership role in your bar association, try to get involved with a committee that naturally brings you into contact with a wide swath of the local legal community, such as the membership or law practice management committees.

It is also important to go where your potential clients are. For example, instead of (or in addition to) joining the appellate practice section of your state bar association, join the tort law section, or the criminal law section, or the commercial law section. In other words, hang out with litigators!

Other time-intensive marketing activities have not yet been as productive for me as networking. Although marketing gurus encourage professionals to write for publication and give seminars, so far I haven't gotten any clients as a direct result of my efforts in these areas. However, as evidenced by the fact that you are reading this, I am hesitant to give up these marketing activities. The continuing legal education courses I have presented are yet another way to "touch" potential clients and increase my name recognition in the local legal community. The articles I have written expose me to a much wider audience than I can afford to reach by paid advertising. Indeed, everything works together, since the publications are an important component of the package of materials I send out to prospective clients, and the package is a "touch" that reinforces the other contacts.

The time commitment networking, writing, and speaking require can be balanced by other types of marketing that call for more of a financial investment. I have had some success with print advertising, focusing primarily on local bar association newsletters. Advertising locally is much more affordable than advertising in publications with a wider circulation. Local bar newsletters generally come out monthly, so, unlike daily legal newspapers (such as *New York Law Journal*), they generally "hang around" on a prospect's desk for a good long time. Also, many of the people who see my ads have met me in person, making the ad another "touch" to reinforce our meeting; conversely, when I introduce myself to other lawyers at bar association functions, their first response is often, "Oh yeah, I saw your ad in the bar association newsletter."

To further increase my visibility, I recently had some custom notepads printed, with my name, logo, contact information, and tagline ("Comprehensive legal research and writing services for lawyers"). These notepads have a variety of marketing uses. Bar associations are always looking for donated items for convention or golf outing goodie bags. I have focused on getting my notepads distributed in this manner to members of associations to which I belong, since it is likely that they have heard about me, or even met me, before. I also include a notepad in every package I send out to prospective clients. The notepad provides a daily reminder that I'm available to help—at least until all the pages are used up!

Finally, although I have a Web site, very few of my clients first found out about me through my site. Nevertheless, in this day and age, a Web site helps to establish your credibility and permanence in the field. When developing your Web site, remember that it is a prime example of the very product you are selling (i.e., persuasive writing): it should be finely crafted, with no typographical or grammatical errors.

In addition to the "how" of marketing legal research and writing services, there's also a "what." To successfully market your research and writing services, you have to overcome three different hurdles. First, you need to convince potential clients of the benefits of outsourcing their legal research and writing work. Second, you need to convince potential clients of the benefits of hiring a solo practitioner, rather than a large research and writing company, to provide those services. Finally, you need to convince potential clients that they should work with you.

When you meet a prospective client, be prepared to discuss the benefits of outsourcing legal research and writing work. Since one of the primary reasons lawyers consider outsourcing is because they have too much work to do and not enough time to do it, you should focus on the use of outsourcing to free up a lawyer's time and thus to help relieve the stress that accompanies overwork.

Position yourself as a smart alternative to hiring an (or another) associate. Point out that hiring an associate requires a significant long-term investment in both time and money and immediately adds to a firm's fixed expenses, but that when a firm outsources legal research and writing projects, it pays only for the time it takes to complete the project and undertakes no long-term obligations. Remind potential clients that an employee adds to their administrative burdens, especially if they are sole practitioners. Note that hiring an associate will result in increased malpractice rates and subject the client to all the financial and legal responsibilities that accompany "employer" status. Ask your potential client whether he has ready access to the research materials he needs. Does he have the expertise necessary to write an effective appellate brief? Does he like doing research and writing, or does he enjoy "outside" work, such as trials, depositions, and client meetings, more? Probing all of these areas will help you determine which additional selling points are important to the lawyer with whom you are speaking.

A lawyer who has never before hired an outside researcher/writer may have many questions about the process. Cost is likely the most important concern. Here's where you have the opportunity to explain that if he can bill the client for doing the work himself, he can bill for the time you spend doing the work instead; in fact, he can reap additional economic benefits by using your services because he can mark up your time just as he would an associate's time, as long as the total fee to the client remains reasonable. Make sure he understands that, even with a markup, outsourcing can also be cost-effective for his client because your research and writing expertise, familiarity with the available resources, and facility in searching large databases for sometimes elusive answers makes you extremely efficient at accomplishing these tasks.

A potential client may think outsourcing is an all-or-nothing proposition, or he may be uncomfortable delegating work. In these circumstances, ease him into the concept of outsourcing by suggesting that you do the research and send him the cases, and he can draft the brief.

A potential client may be familiar with the concept of outsourcing, but might be more inclined to look to one of the large players in the legal research and writing field than to a solo. Here, if your potential client is another solo or small firm, take advantage of the camaraderie of "solo-ness." With all potential clients, stress the "personal touch" that a solo can provide.

Finally, sell yourself. Make writing samples available on your Web site or offer to e-mail them to prospective clients, and arrange with two or three current clients to serve as references for you. Send potential clients a package of materials about your practice, including (at a minimum) your business card; a letter or brochure describing the different types of projects that can be outsourced, your background, and your substantive areas of expertise; and reprints of your publications (whether written by you or about you). Since getting repeat business requires less marketing effort than developing new clients, once you have landed the client, provide high-quality, responsive service to keep the client coming back. Satisfied clients will also do your marketing work for you by referring their colleagues to you.

# §3.8 Big Game Hunting: The Short Course for High-End Marketing

## *Robert A. Zupkus*

Marketing your legal talents to sophisticated clients has never been a greater challenge. Solo and small firms traditionally have a difficult time successfully reaching corporate or sophisticated clients. Typically, this client group believes it needs service by larger firms.

Traditional client acceptance issues are now compounded by recent economic realities. Every year, law schools turn out more lawyers. The baby boomer lawyers have yet to depart the field. Law firms are embarking on a new round of mergers and acquisitions resulting in global law firms with lawyer populations in the thousands and huge marketing budgets and reach. Simultaneously, there are fewer high-end targets of business opportunity. Corporations continue to go through mergers and acquisitions, shrinking the pool of available clients. Businesses continue to fail or downsize. This further shrinks the reservoir of available clients and legal business. There are no more glorious IPOs creating new business, which need lawyers to represent them.

Darkening this picture is the growing lack of corporate client loyalty. The corporate fiscal problems have spread to the legal service arena. Clients are striving to lower all their costs and contain them with increased certainty. This includes legal services. House counsel and upper management consumers of legal services are busy simply staying afloat themselves. They no longer have the luxury of time to leave the office, mingle and meet with new

Small firms seek unique challenges when marketing to sophisticated clients. These challenges can be met with a well-constructed marketing plan.

Enjoy the intellectual challenge that high-end marketing provides.

potential lawyers, or be open to new ideas concerning their representation. Corporations are becoming more introspective in their personal relationships because of internal upheavals and layoffs.

## Have a Plan

With the changing landscape, now more than ever, marketing cannot be done randomly or haphazardly. Legal marketing has to be well thought out and planned. Legal marketing must be more efficient because it still must not be mistaken for or replace a lawyer's social service within the community. A lawyer still has a major obligation to give back time and effort to the community as a whole.

So much economically rides on marketing that development of an organized plan takes research and time. The American Bar Association and the state and local bar associations publish tremendous marketing materials. This is no time to reinvent the wheel or embark upon marketing alone. Take the thoughts of experts with you. Become familiar with the literature in legal marketing, which was never taught to you at law school. Once you have surveyed the many ways legal talents can be marketed, map out your own particular skill set in terms of what is comfortable and affordable. One cannot be expected to pursue all avenues of legal marketing such as bar or organizational work, speaking, writing, belonging to the rotary club, etc. Your skill set, wallet, and time must fit within the many different marketing strategies. Your ultimate plan must be personally comfortable and affordable to you. Do not attempt to do marketing, which is distasteful to you or creates economic strain.

Do prepare a time and dollar budget for marketing. You still need time and money to manage your own business and service your existing clients. Marketing comes after you take care of the existing essentials. Prepare a specific business plan of who within your firm will do what and for how long a period of time before any effort is objectively appraised as to value.

As part of your marketing plan, you must identify your target legal clients and desired legal work. Are you really interested in serving this type of client and performing this type of legal service? Why are you interested in these target markets? You cannot be all things to all clients. A solo or small firm can produce only modest revenue. If it's only about the money, perhaps marketing within a solo or small framework is not for you.

Your target market must be reasonably set. Speak to lawyers who already practice in this area and find out what their life is like from Monday to Friday. Consider whether you are in the right geographic location for the type of legal services that interest you. For example, it is rare to find a steady stream of work in intellectual property law in middle America, or to find farm and ranching legal work in New York City. This states an obvious, but really think this issue through, and again research it. Through the local bar association or your Chamber of Commerce you can determine the number of lawyers who practice in a particular area and the population of potential clients. This helps you decide whether your hometown will actually support the type of practice you envision for yourself.

## The Product Piece of the Plan

As part of your marketing plan you must determine exactly what it is you sell to your clients. Like every other lawyer, you are essentially selling your time. A lawyer has no definable product that can be plucked off the shelf by a consumer. No less a person than Abraham Lincoln stated that the only stock in trade that a lawyer has is his or her time and advice. Of course, time must be well spent in the service of a client. The lawyer's time serving a client must be accompanied by careful analysis, a defined skill set, integrity, and efficiency.

Knowing that the common product denominator is time, how do you set yourself apart from the competition? You must think through what your clients really want besides a stunning brief on the statute of limitations. Clients need your availability. When you are sick, you want to see the doctor now. You don't want it to be the case that the doctor will finally see you now.

Your clients want thoughtful solutions that work. Clients want efficiency, a prompt response at a reasonable price. The lawyer needs to be completely familiar with the clients' needs. The lawyer must never assume what the client needs; the lawyer must ask.

In a solo or small firm setting, a client most often views the lawyer as a specialist. Typically, the sophisticated client will not turn for help to a small general practice firm. That client instead turns to large firms with many departments or to house counsel for perceived general issues.

## So Just Where Is the Elusive Client?

The lion learns that the herd gathers around the watering hole and that game is not sitting in the midst of the pride. The lawyer must go where the clients are. This means participating in industry trade associations, rotary clubs, private specialty bar associations, or other venues not completely populated by lawyers. Use existing clients to locate new additional clients for you.

Typically, membership in a conventional bar association provides a low referral base. With the development of international, national, and regional law firms, major client work that used to be networked through traditional bar associations is now referred within their own ranks. Corporations tend to develop and cling to their list of lawyers for reasons of their own efficiency. This does not mean that a lawyer should completely avoid bar associations or community work. This still needs to be done. But some of your expectations of client generation need to be revised.

## The Ethics of Marketing

Many ethical considerations surround client generation. First, the lawyer must look to the Model Rules of Professional Conduct on concepts of appropriate solicitation. Additionally important is the code of conduct or ethics of your particular client. Many corporate clients allow no gifts to the point of not even accepting a free lunch. The old days where there was almost no limit to client gift-giving have evaporated.

Yet clients do expect some recognition of their relationship with a law firm. So, the law firm must revise its ideas about spreading cheer and goodwill.

A law firm might still host a general party where many clients and potential clients are invited. A law firm might hold a raffle at such an event to award theater or sporting event tickets. A table at a charity dinner might be purchased, and then clients invited to the charity event.

There are some specific do's and don'ts for legal marketing. Don't spread yourself too thin. Don't market yourself into debt of time or money. Don't advertise to the masses; you are seeking high-end clients. You really must focus your legal services and any direct advertising message. Any advertisement, for example, should be associated with a charity publication (one you truly endorse) or a trade publication.

There are many do's to marketing. Do compile a list of your good deeds and accomplishments for distribution among your clients or potential clients. Do have a Web site. This does not get you new clients but it helps keep the ones you have. They feel your professionalism is validated by the Web site. Do build personal relationships. Do keep your personal relationships alive by frequent contact. Do keep marketing. Clients will come and go through no fault of your own. Clients will need to be replaced. Do have patience. Do have fun!

# §3.9  Five Essential Steps to Rainmaking in a Really Small Town
## *Ted A. Waggoner*

If you have not lived in a small town for a while, let me set the scene. The courthouse is the center of town and is the largest building in town, with county offices on one side and the jail on another. The business district extends from the two other sides with a couple of banks, real estate offices, the local newspaper, and the local radio station all facing the courthouse. All the fast food places are out by the highway, and the best lunch in town is at the back of the drugstore. I live on the outskirts of town and the commute is pretty reasonable. On a good day it takes seven minutes to get to the office, but when both stoplights on my route are against me, the drive can take upto eight minutes.

In this community there are four law firms, and my firm, with three lawyers, is the largest in the county. The judges, full-time prosecutors, and retired lawyers fill in the legal community. The town has 6,000 of the finest people you would want to know, and another 1,000 that keep the police, probation, and welfare departments busy.

We do some rainmaking here, but it is different from that practiced by my friends in larger cities and larger firms. Rainmaking here is thought of as building a book of legal clients with enough legal work that you have to refer the extra to other offices, or finally add to the number of lawyers in the firm.

**Small Town, Big Opportunities**

- Rainmaking is how you improve the quality and quantity of work you do.
- The strength of your relationships with current and potential clients and the value of your reputation to unknown potential clients are critical matters.
- A quality staff is vital to succeeding in the practice of law.
- The average satisfied customer will tell four people of a good customer experience, while the average dissatisfied client will tell eleven people about a bad experience.
- The essence of successful rainmaking is the creation of a high-quality professional relationship with your current and potential clients.

## Benefits of Rainmaking

One of the benefits of rainmaking is improving the quality and quantity of work you do, allowing you to pick the better clients for yourself, while still serving the needs of the remaining potential clients with other lawyers, in the firm or outside. Of course, it remains your responsibility to determine that the referral lawyers are competent to handle the work referred. Making referrals inside the office also forces you to better know and appreciate the practice skills of the others in the office, and to supervise their work for the firm's clients. Most clients will still regard the rainmaker as their primary lawyer and their problems will land on your desk if they occur. Not knowing about the client's case is no excuse to the client, to the malpractice carrier, or to the Bar Disciplinary Committee.

Another benefit of rainmaking is the opportunity to increase the demand for the legal work you do, and produce more income as a result. Greater demand for your services has two tangible benefits: more fees and higher fees. You will earn more as you are busier with less downtime, and both you and your staff will become more productive in the process of meeting the demands for output. You will also be able to move toward higher quality legal work and the higher fees it offers. The requirement to balance client demands with your need for free time for yourself and family will allow and may even force you to increase the fees charged.

Clients are willing to pay higher fees for quality legal work, and by coupling increasing demand with increasing legal quality, you will be able to accept the quality legal work and refer the commodity legal work. As you take on higher quality work, you need to build better relationships with the consumers of your quality work. The more quality work you do, the greater the benefits you achieve.

## Five Skills Needed for Effective Rainmaking in a Small Town

I have identified five primary skills needed to be an effective rainmaker in a small town:

- Reputation
- Relationships
- Staff
- Desire
- Plans for Rainmaking

These five attributes are critical for becoming effective in the practice of rainmaking and in benefiting from the efforts. Success in these steps, and the continued repetition of the steps that create success, will result in your building a stronger practice of law.

## Reputation

In building a professional presence in a small town, you first must establish a reputation for doing good legal work, and doing it well. Most lawyers who are building a practice want a professional reputation of being a high-quality lawyer who is confident and trustworthy. Setting that goal before you each day will help make it possible. The converse is true. If you do not worry about clients' deadlines and getting work done promptly, or about protecting yourself from concerns about your integrity, your clients may recognize this as a lack of professionalism, and that will create serious problems with your professional reputation.

Another difficulty with being a small-town lawyer is that unlike some of the big city lawyers, we cover a variety of legal fields as the needs of our clients change. Many small-town lawyers began practice by handling criminal defense and domestic relations cases with an occasional personal injury case included. Some stay with a litigation practice; a few move into business litigation or occasionally some insurance defense work. Others take on various types of business transactions, or probate and estate planning and administration, and occasionally, if you still have a locally owned bank, some banking law issues.

While the collective memory of the community is generally pretty short, there will be those restaurant owners or mechanics who recall the domestic relations case you handled against them. The zealous and ethical representation of one client may restrict your future practice opportunities. The lawyer must always be aware of the competing interests of current and potential clients, and address them in proper ways not to cause harm to the current client. After our firm hired an associate with some experience in bankruptcy cases, we quickly discovered that the variety of conflicts inherent in the business clientele our firm represents, in the medical community, a large local bank, and a few utilities, precluded most of the bankruptcy cases that the associate might have been able to generate.

## Relationships

The strength of your relationships with current and potential clients, and the value of your reputation to unknown potential clients, are critical matters in your long-term professional success. You need to focus your relationship building on the potential clients you want to serve. If you decide to focus on employment cases for workers, the time spent with union hall leaders will be productive toward your goal. If your focus is personal injury, you need to know the police officers and emergency room personnel.

Building relationships with key community leaders may be easier in a small town than in a larger community. I assume most readers are not returning home to a family's multigenerational law practice, where a number of the relationships are passed on by the earlier generation of lawyers. Small communities generally have few people with professional degrees. Often the smaller community will welcome young lawyers and other professionals as a part of their community improvement drives.

Local service organizations, the Chamber of Commerce, and all of the charity organizations are hungry for new individuals, and those who may be able to understand some of the issues of such organizations are often given quick access to board positions and to leadership roles, which creates an opportunity to deal with the important community leaders.

The ability to practice effective rainmaking calls for you to take advantage of these exposure opportunities with the leaders who will be important in your practice. Some community leaders may be slow to accept new candidates for leadership and may not appreciate the challenge that a young professional brings. Every community has certain ancillary roles that will provide an opportunity to build your reputation as a person who understands issues, can solve problems, and gets the work done on time.

## Staff

The primary purpose of rainmaking is to create more legal work, for more fun and much more profit. Since few lawyers do their own typing and clerical work, a quality staff is critical to succeeding in the practice of law. Associates, paralegals, secretaries, receptionists, and bookkeepers all need to realize that they are in the people business. You are responsible for reminding them of their importance to the clients. It seems the weakest person on the staff is the one who usually gets the opportunity to make the law firm's first impression with a new client. An emergency call, a sick child, or an ill-timed coffee break will disturb all the protective steps you take to put your best staffer up front.

The quality of your legal product is directly tied to the strength of the staff. Correct billings depend on the correct posting of understandable time records (I, for one, make unintelligible time entries, but I expect good staff results—at least after the first week). Lawyer-staff relations are reported to be a weak point in many firms. The lawyer holds unstated expectations, while the staff members are not properly led by whatever form of management exists. In small-town firms, the management structure is usually the lawyer or the partners. The occasional office manager may or may not have the authority, the skills, or the training to lead the rest of the staff.

Adding work to a dysfunctional staff is a problem that must be corrected at the earliest possible opportunity. Failure to build a functional staff means that you are unable to meet your clients' needs promptly and professionally. The costs to a law office from the mistakes made by lawyer or staff error can be staggering. When you add the value of lawyer and staff time needed to fix your error to the costs associated with the loss of rela-

tionship and reputation that follows a client's discovery of the simplest mistake, you often find there is no profit in doing the work twice for one fee.

## Desire

More than any other attribute, a lawyer has to desire the better life that comes from being a rainmaker. Better as in a more productive work life with more financial rewards, and with an appreciation of the relationships and reputation that are built in getting into the position of a rainmaker. The successful rainmakers are respected in their communities. As a respected leader, others will look to you as a problem solver, because of your prior success at solving problems in areas that get you noticed by those affected.

If as a lawyer you do not want to put in the time and efforts needed to succeed in some aspect of the small community you inhabit, that does not make you a bad lawyer, but it does make it hard to qualify as a rainmaker. You may solve equally as difficult a set of problems as the rainmaker, but on a less public stage. As a result there is less notice taken of your solution and of you as a competent lawyer.

To create the professional relationships you want with potential clients, you must get out and meet the potential clients, spend some time with them, let them get to know your thinking and reasoning ability. That takes time, energy, a system, and a commitment to expanding your share of the firm's client base.

The commitment to expanding the client base is not one all lawyers will have, but the rainmaker must have it, and must be supported by the other lawyers and the staff who should be ready to take on the legal work found or created by the rainmaker. Those lawyers receiving the new work from the new clients must be ready to work with and support the rainmaker in the joint representation of the client, by keeping the producer of the client's work involved in and aware of the legal activities of the client's case. The rainmaker must remain aware of the case progress, so when the client sees you on the street, you know enough to discuss the matter and reassure the client of your ongoing involvement in the case.

## Plan

The final essential needed to become an effective rainmaker in a small town is the same as in any community. You must plan for it. An action plan of five to ten steps is critical to getting started. Start by identifying the practice you have, and the one you want to retire with. Is it the same? What steps will take you from here to there? How many years do you have before retirement to get there? Plant the seeds now to work your way to the practice you want. Take that leader you need to work with on the local project to lunch. Yes, he can afford it more than you, but pick up the tab.

## Barriers to Success

We need to identify a couple of barriers you can find in a small town to becoming a successful rainmaker. Small-town lawyers tend to become local celebrities, mostly due to the absence of other more natural celebrities. We have no TV anchors or sports stars (outside of the high school teams). Just moving to town is normally worthy of a front-page story and a picture in the local paper, as well as an interview on the local radio. These are quickly followed by the invitations to join the boards of various local community groups, service clubs, and not-for-profit agencies, which are always looking for warm bodies. Whether to remain a minor celebrity or grow into a major celebrity in the small town is a choice each lawyer has to make over time.

Because of the higher profile that comes with being a professional person in a small town, as a new lawyer you need to quickly discover your personality strengths and weaknesses. You will find that subsequent paths are determined by your personality style. If you are generally a bulldog-litigator type, you are better off to recognize it early and be true to your style.

Many lawyers give the public an inconsistent message between the type of practice they want to build and the type of personality they have. It is hard for you as a lawyer to get away with living a hard-charging and high-profile personal life if your goal is to represent the banks and real estate brokers. Criminal defense work comes easier if your name is associated with a sense of toughness.

One noted social scientist has said that the average satisfied customer will tell four people of a good customer experience, while the average dissatisfied client will tell 11 people about a bad experience. A half dozen angry clients telling 70 people that you are "a lousy lawyer" has far less consequence on the professional reputation you have in a city of 50,000 than in a town of 7,000. Satisfied clients are better for you than dissatisfied clients in either setting, but the smaller the

town, the greater the concentration of bad news and the more damage it can cause.

Celebrity, style, and client satisfaction can be barriers to your success if you do not recognize them as such. Early recognition allows you to use them as opportunities to move into leadership roles, which elevates your ability to succeed as a rainmaker.

## Finding Success

The essence of successful rainmaking is the creation of a high-quality professional relationship with your current and potential clients. They have to hold you in high esteem and trust that you will look out for their legal interests. You can best define when you are achieving success by noting the referrals you receive. It is in the quantity and quality of referrals that success is seen from your efforts at rainmaking.

As a young lawyer, I was honored when a local businessman hired me in the most important legal matter going on in his life at that particular moment—his daughter's divorce. He was vitally interested in seeing that she was well represented. Many divorce referrals did not seem like much of an honor, but when it was apparent how important it was to her and her father, I realized that an important event had occurred in my practice. He would, and did, tell others about my legal efforts on behalf of his daughter and his satisfaction with those efforts.

Rainmaking can be difficult due to the personal nature that professional relationships sometimes have. Small-town residents often expect a friendship familiarity with their lawyer (or doctor or banker). Another aspect of small-town rainmaking is that there are fewer places to hide from the clients who are not satisfied with your legal work. When the client will likely see you or your spouse at the farmer's market on Saturdays, church on Sunday, or the grocery store during the week, such issues tend to take on a more personal meaning. Running into a frustrated client whose real estate closing is now a month overdue from the deadline you promised is a problem if you want to be successful in the eyes of the clients.

## Conclusion

If you want to make rain in a small town, you have to take advantage of the many opportunities.

Noted Indiana lawyer Frank McHale said, "To succeed as a lawyer you need to run for political office. To make good money as a lawyer, run for office only once."

You have already probably taken some of the steps suggested toward being a rainmaker. You may be on the board of a community organization or theater group. Now work at it and make it better. Offer solutions to the problems of the organization; do not just point out problems or potential problems. Build your relationships, and thereby strengthen your reputation. Improve your staff as best you can, by training, education, and working with them to improve their performance.

Increase your desire to be a better lawyer and more productive member of your firm. Then design a plan and carry it out. Next week redesign the plan, based on the failures of this week. Do it every week until it is working. Then work the plan every day. Mark your calendar for a six-month review of the design of the Rainmaking Plan.

Do not waste a lunch sitting at your desk when you can be out building your practice and the firm.

# 4

# Tools for Rainmaking

# §4.1 Isn't It Time to Get a Web Page?

## *Keith B. McLennan*

To answer the threshold question "Is a Web page necessary to the modern law practice?" you might consider only that the Internet is the most useful place to research the topic of Web pages. We asked the same question when overnight delivery, the fax machine, and e-mail became common, and I suspect most agree that even though these items may not be "necessary," prevailing work habits make them indispensable.

Many advocates of Web pages point to easy access to routine procedures and general information as their primary benefit. Yes, you or your secretary can communicate this information by telephone or mail it out, but how many free minutes do you have each day? The more solo and small firm lawyers can streamline basic procedures, the easier it is to survive in this increasingly bottom-line-oriented business climate. A Web site helps you do that.

If you don't have a Web site, potential clients and colleagues alike may consider you something of a second-class citizen. Similarly, without a firm or professional e-mail address, you may be viewed by the more techno-sophisticates among us as not quite up to par. After all, mick&sharon123@aol.com, although fine for your family, will hardly inspire confidence in court. On the other hand, too much of a good thing can easily backfire: The ego factor in lawyer Web sites is sometimes beyond considerable, so keep in mind that a captive audience for your life story is not an acceptable goal.

## Content

Most Web site designers provide a basic framework or idea, usually as a template, but it's up to you to provide the content. At first this may seem easy: name, rank, and serial number—what's so hard about that? Even though Web sites commonly are described as a business card online, a good site that truly functions on your behalf as a promotional tool is much more than that. The sites I find useful contain additional information as well:

- Directions to your office
- Information request forms
- Your areas of practice

- Particular or special achievements and firm résumé
- Blurbs or factoids—gleaned from *Lawyers Weekly,* for example (with appropriate credit, of course)—on items of interest to consumers
- Hyperlinks to useful information sources consistent with your practice areas
- Client intake and/or feedback form

That simple business card is starting to look a little cluttered, isn't it? You will spend a lot of time assembling such critical information, then editing it down to a usable Web format. Your initial page design, however, can be as simple or as complicated as you desire, so keep in mind that it's perfectly acceptable to start with the basics and add flourishes after you're up and running for a while. Of course, like any other tool or marketing device, a Web page requires regular care and feeding to remain effective.

## Decisions, Decisions

Creating a more professional e-mail address was one of the reasons my small firm of lawyers made the initial decision to pursue online options. We wanted to get away from our individual AOL addresses to exhibit a higher level of sophisti-

cation to clients, potential clients, opponents, vendors, and the like. The Web page was a secondary goal that seemed more doable once we reserved our domain name. Currently, our Web page is a fairly bare-bones firm résumé, which makes it easy for visitors to navigate and for us to keep current. (There are few things more frustrating than an out-of-date site or one that is difficult to navigate. You're better off without any Web presence in these instances.)

## Looking over Your Shoulder

One thing to keep in mind is that liability exposure increases for erroneous or infringing information printed on your site. I call this the "looking over your shoulder" phenomenon (which also comes into play with newsletters, pamphlets, and any other marketing vehicles). The electronic medium, however, presents a few unique opportunities for entrapment:

### Copyright infringement

Much as you may want to prevent others from reproducing (or copying) what appears on your site, be sure that material displayed on your site is free of previous copyright restrictions—or obtain permission to use it.

### Images

Because our lives are so densely saturated with images, it's sometimes easy to forget that many images, too, are protected by copyright. Make sure what you use is either original artwork or design or properly licensed for your use.

### Domain names

These must be original and not in conflict with other registered domains, derivatives of other domains, or trademarks. Companies such as Register.com (http://www.register.com) can register your domain name for a small fee.

### Trademarks

Infringement occurs when a party uses a registered mark in a way that creates a likelihood of confusion, mistake, or deception for the consumer. Linking your site to someone else's or using their trade- or service-marked domain name or logo on your site without permission could create confusion about the relationship between your site and the linked business.

### Defamation

Be careful what you put on your Web page, especially statements made about a person or organization that could be considered damaging to their reputation—this could get you sued for defamation. Much as in e-mail, which often is sent off the cuff without fully contemplating its tone, content, and timing, statements hurriedly posted on a Web page are more prone to claims of defamation than a dictated letter you proofed and edited several hours after writing it.

Automation is the trend in the practice of law, as it is in other professions and industries. Efficiency is the game of the future, and, in the end, a good Web page is just another way to maximize time.

## Building Your Web Page

Now that you have decided to take the plunge, follow this formula for successful design and implementation:

- Do an online search for lawyers and simply start reviewing existing Web pages. Narrow the search to your geographic area to check out prevailing standards there.
- Ask staff or family and friends to look at the sites as well. The reactions of nonlawyers can be particularly valuable.

- Gather together all printed information that relates to your law practice—articles, seminars, résumés, newsletters, old brochures, and so on. Some of it may work online, or particular pieces may remind you of details to include on the site.
- If you don't use a professional marketer, contact a local college for a referral to a marketing student who can help you assemble the information that will best promote your firm.
- Unless you're well on your way to geekdom, hire a Web site designer.
- Focus on the areas of practice that are (or will be) most profitable and those that you most want to highlight.
- Prioritize the information in a way that allows you to deliver your message on the very first page.
- Keep graphics to a minimum. Even though broadband and faster downloads are the rage, many people use dial-up services that load slowly. The more graphics, the slower the site—and the more likely a viewer will exit and look elsewhere.
- Be clear about your message or mission; don't try to be all things to all people on your site.
- Sign up for a local Saturday class or a CLE on Web site design to get more familiar with basic Web concepts.

## §4.2 How Technology Can Help You Market Your Practice and Build Client Relationships

### Nerino J. Petro Jr.

Technology as a whole, and legal technology as it applies to lawyers, is a fact of life. Changes and improvements occur on an ever-faster basis and our society is rapidly embracing and adapting them for improved quality of communications, increased work productivity, and improved education as well as improved quality of life. Sadly, too many solo and small firm lawyers are failing to embrace the very technology that has become a part of everyday life for most people and companies.

These lawyers don't consider legal technology to be "mission critical" to the practice and the delivery of legal services to their clients. If they do use some level of technology in their office, they look at it as the electronic equivalent of a legal pad and pen or typewriter. They fail to grasp the possibilities, as well as the opportunities, that legal technology is presenting to them to improve their practice, their quality of life, and their financial bottom line.

But just having a computer isn't enough. Everyone knows a lawyer or firm who only looks to use the bare minimum of technology. They don't purchase legal-specific software such as case and matter management, or time, billing, and accounting forms, or pleading drafting aids. These lawyers are the ones who continue to use computers and technology beyond its useful life span. They paid good money for it five years ago and it still works, so why do they need to spend more money today? And while they are trying to get back the dollars they paid five years ago, they are missing out on the technological improvements that improve ease of use and productivity that they and their staff could be using.

Are improved data sharing and compatibility really all that important? Can profession-specific enhancements really make the lives of lawyers and their staff better? Do clients really care if they can't communicate with their lawyers by e-mail or that their adversary appears in court with laptop computers and professional-looking presentations? The lawyers who answer these questions with a negative are those who don't see the need or value in such "luxuries" as broadband Internet access, owning their own Internet domain and Web site, having more than one e-mail address for the firm, or having e-mail accounts other than AOL, Yahoo, or MSN.

When these lawyers do add technology, they often don't see the value in the legal-specific packages. Instead they try and use an "off the shelf" product because it's less expensive. Then they spend a lot of time, energy, and money reinventing the wheel rather than focusing on what they do best.

Other lawyers do add legal-specific technology, but to them, it is a tool only for the legal portion of their practice—trial presentation, document generation, calendaring, and client information—not the business side. As lawyers, we know that marketing is important, but too often lawyers overlook the benefits that the legal-specific tools they have available can provide. Legal technology isn't just for using in the courtroom or for preparing documents or billing clients: It can help market your practice on an almost daily basis to prospective clients and improve relationships with existing clients. Use the technology available to

- Improve client communications.
- Provide alternative means for clients and prospects to get information faster.
- Allow delivery of services with little or no direct initial interaction with a lawyer.
- Help create a "brand" for your practice.
- Identify profitable areas and clients of your practice.
- Track referrals and provide follow-ups.
- Identify specific practice areas for targeted marketing.
- Identify and capitalize on recurring work such as annual corporate reports and minutes preparation, biannual reviews of estate and trust plans, etc.

The ultimate goal is to use technology to improve efficiency, productivity, and marketing efforts, allowing the lawyer more time to focus on client needs and deliver a higher standard of client services. Experience shows that this should result in happier clients who are more likely to refer the lawyer to others. This increases business, which improves the quality of life and the bottom line for the lawyer. While general-use software can provide some of the benefits of legal-specific technology, it will require many compromises or costly add-ons to provide the same level of usability.

There are more ways that technology can be used. Some specific ideas and examples for using legal and general technology to market your practice include the following.

## Target Information and Marketing Materials

One of the benefits of using a legal-specific matter-management package such as TimeMatters, Practice Master, Amicus, or Abacus is the ability to identify matters by a practice area. You can create lists of matters and then select the clients associated with the practice areas for which you want to send targeted information and marketing materials. Rather than just sending out general information newsletters, you can target clients for newsletters and information that is focused on their specific needs. For your corporate clients, you can send information regarding changes to your state's business corporation act or changes in tax treatment. Clients who rent property can be targeted for information specific to landlord-tenant matters. If you are using a legal-specific time and billing package you can also create detailed reports on the practice area or areas where the majority of your income is coming from, which may surprise you. Using this information, you can further tailor your marketing efforts to those areas that are your most profitable. You can also

- Keep your clients' birth dates in your matter management system; sending birthday cards shows a more personalized level of service than just sending out a holiday card to all of your clients.
- Use the information to provide seminars on practice-specific areas and ask your clients to bring a guest. The guest can be tracked in the matter management system and be placed on the mailing lists for the practice-specific newsletters and marketing materials.

## Track Referrals and Provide Feedback to the Referring Source

Referrals are a terrific source of business, and networking with other professionals is a great way to market your practice. But how do you keep track of the referring source? Do you follow up with a thank you? Can you identify the referring source for prospects that are outside the practice areas you want to service? If referrals are coming from other professionals such as accounting, investment, or insurance sources, how long do you think they will continue to refer potential clients to you if they never know that you in fact received the referral? A matter management program can be used to track how a prospect was referred to your office and allow you to automatically generate a thank-you letter to the referring source. Receiving a thank you for a referral is more important than most lawyers realize. Technology can help you maintain this source of prospective clients and track referrals, as well as providing follow-ups and thank you's to the referring source. It is not unusual for larger firms to send out a note or thank you for a referral; you can leverage technology to provide the same level of service.

## Identify and Capitalize on Recurring Work

Lawyers who represent small corporations, limited liability companies, or other business entities that have annual reporting and record keeping requirements can use matter management system to automate notifying the clients and to generate the necessary documents. Each month you can generate a report for those matters that have anniversary dates approaching. Using this information, you can process the necessary paper or e-mail notifications, including the requests for information to prepare the documents for actions taken over the past year. By doing this you provide the perception that you have harnessed technology to deliver timely services to help your clients meet their legal requirements. Happy clients are more likely to refer you to others. The benefits to your practice are not limited only to business matters; use your technology to identify and remind your estate planning clients to review their estate plans and trusts on a regular basis.

## Use the Internet to Provide Information and Improve Client Communications

The Internet has had a great impact on the information (and misinformation) that is available to your clients. Everyone has visited Web sites that are nothing more than a brochure on a firm or practice and really don't provide anything of value to encourage repeat visits. This is true of small firms and large: They haven't recognized that the Internet is a marketing tool, one that, unlike more traditional marketing mediums, can be changed, updated, or expanded relatively easily and for little ongoing investment after the initial cost of creating the Web site.

Look at your Web site not merely as a brochure on your practice but also as a tool to provide information and services to your clients and prospective clients.

Think about the telephone calls you get from clients and prospects: Are there any common themes or questions that keep coming up? Do you or your staff find yourselves answering the same questions for a particular practice area over and over again? For example, if you do a lot of real estate, do you routinely provide information on your state's property disclosure requirements or information on getting utilities changed? Put this information on your Web site and then let each client know where to find it.

FAQ (Frequently Asked Questions) areas have become standard on most Web sites as companies have found that this can benefit themselves and their customers. Let your clients know that you provide helpful information on your Web site that is available 24/7. Even better, let them know there's no charge for them to use your Web site for this information. If you represent landlords or tenants, you can put up information on the requirements for serving notice for nonpayment of rent, links to statutes, and other resources.

If you find the risk level acceptable, you can take your Web site to the next level: Create client-only areas where clients can obtain simple forms that are used regularly. If your state has specified formats for a landlord's five-day notice to quit, make the form available for download for those that always prepare one on their own. Or you can create a simple page where the client fills in the blanks and then you generate the forms for them. At some firm Web sites, clients can answer a few questions, and the firm will then prepare a simple will or other document for them either at no charge or a reduced fee. Provide your client the option to complete the annual corporate questionnaire you send out online. You can set up your document generation templates to use this information to prevent you or your staff from reentering everything by hand. You can also use your Web site or a Web log (or "blog") to provide regular information valuable to your clients or the public.

E-mail can also improve your client interaction and marketing ability. E-mail can replace traditional paper mail and postage in many instances. This can result in a saving of both time and money. You can attach the e-mails to the client's matter in your matter management system and have all of the communications at your fingertips. You can also use e-mail for distributing your newsletters and targeted information materials to your clients. The informational materials that you e-mail can include reference to your Web site or blog and can also encourage your clients to share the information with others who might be interested. It is much easier for someone to forward an e-mail to a friend or acquaintance than it is to make and mail a photocopy.

Look at the Internet as one more tool in your marketing toolbox to be used with all of your other tools to build your practice.

As the public's level of technology increases, so too will its desire to use those professionals who also embrace technology to provide high-quality services in a cost-effective and timely fashion. As technology increases the pace of everyday life, it also increases the client's demand for easier and quicker access to legal services.

## §4.3  How to Make Your Bills a Rainmaking Tool
### *Natalie R. Thornwell*

Billing for legal services can seem simple when taken at face value. But smart practitioners and technology-savvy firms know that bills are not only the means to getting paid but can also serve as a very important rainmaking tool. When a firm examines the source of its business, many find that previous and existing clients account for the majority of its new business. So exactly how can a firm's bill make rain?

First, the billing statement should look and feel like the firm. If a brand has been developed for marketing purposes, this should be included in all billing statements. Today's automated billing programs allow users to include graphics and other formatting and design options to make the bills look like other firm correspondence. Even if the firm decides not to generate bills on its most expensive stationery, the font styles and header and footer details should match other firm work product. Even the window envelopes or the self-addressed stamped envelopes used by firms can match brand styles. Clients can continue to experience the firm's brand when they get bills, and respond in positive, business-generating ways.

Extending a firm brand to billing statements is just the beginning in making bills a rainmaking tool.

A firm can demonstrate its flexibility in its billing procedures by having the ability to generate bills not only on demand but also in the format desired by the client. For instance, a particular client may require monthly e-bills or periodic bills utilizing the ABA's Litigation Code Set. Other firms may have various formats that accommodate discounts for bills that are paid early. Being able to give clients what they want and not be locked into formats or options that are too rigid can help firms retain clients who recognize the value of working with a firm that has command over its billing data and procedures. A firm should be able to move from hourly billing to flat-fee billing and back to hourly fees for other portions of work without jeopardizing a client's historical billing data. A firm should also not lose a great amount of time or efficiency in accomplishing this.

The tracking of time for fee bills is yet another way to make rain. How so? Clients might be interested in knowing how well the firm has integrated technology into its procedures and that a firm utilizing the latest technology tools is dealing with their business. When an associate or partner is entering time via a handheld device or digitally recording information for generating a later billing statement, the client will likely be impressed, and more likely to return to the firm for services or even recommend the services of the firm to others.

Billing technology for law firms has made it possible to generate bills with just a few mouse clicks. Lawyers utilizing modern billing tools are able to generate reports on billing data quickly and in formats that are helpful in delivering professional and efficient legal service. How much is owed to the firm, how long it has been owed, and what has yet to be billed are important pieces of billing data and should be readily available from any modern billing system. These A/R (accounts receivable), aging, and WIP (work in progress) reports can help firms better command their billing information and directly affect the level of service that can be given to clients. If a firm cannot tell a client how much he or she owes, how can that client have confidence in that firm's service or even recommend the firm's services to others? It is vitally important for firms to

implement adequate systems for billing, and obtain appropriate training for bill management tools.

A good billing system can provide reports about both productivity (Lawyer B and Associate C are generating the most amount of work in a particular practice area and the firm can set obtainable billing goals based on this information) and profitability (the firm can create a special-interest page on its Web site for its work in train wreck cases based on the amount of profit being produced by this practice area). Standard reports like these can be found in most good time-and-billing programs and can be sorted in many different ways, e.g., by "timekeeper" or by "client."

With billing item descriptions that are easy to understand, a firm can convey professionalism and care in demonstrating value to its clients. Descriptions on bills that "tell a story" of service will likely be appreciated and can demonstrate the value of service. For example, "No Charge" items show the client that the firm is not interested in billing for every single little item, a practice that often annoys clients who generate considerable amounts of fee income for a firm.

Bills begin the moment a client comes into existence. Firms should be in the habit of making the billing process simple and straightforward. Including a sample copy of a bill along with the fee agreement can help the client understand how important the process is and also show exactly what is expected of the client. Circle "balance due" areas on the sample and show the client that this is the figure to submit. For clients requiring more sophisticated billing, like large corporate clients, make sure that the billing staff in the firm review and are able to quickly generate reports on billing details in both summary and detailed formats.

Again, anyone from the firm or any of the firms' clients should be able to get to pertinent information about the client matter via the billing statement. When billing statements are effective, clients will again find value in the work of the firm; they will continue to be clients and will tell others about the service they are receiving. By using well-thought-out billing statements, a firm can generate a level of confidence in its service to its clients and continue to make rain as it communicates professionalism via its bills.

# §4.4 Building a Service-Centered Firm

*Matthew W. Homann*

I know this book is about rainmaking. However, no matter how good you are at bringing business through the front door, if you are unable to keep your existing clients happy, their business will just as quickly exit through the back door. Serving your ideal clients exceptionally well is the key to building a successful practice. In this section, I'm going to help you to identify your ideal clients and build your practice around them. I'm also going to show you how one firm (mine) applied these lessons and made our practice better, stronger, more profitable, and more fun!

Lawyer, heal thyself!

Quick, think about the last time you marshaled all of your creative and intellectual energy to help a client out of a particularly sticky legal mess. Now, when was the last time you devoted that same amount of brainpower to think "big picture" thoughts about where your law practice is now, and where you want it to be?

I speak from experience. I was a general practitioner with hundreds of active files in family law, real estate, business, and estate planning. The dozens of weekly deadlines and the pressure to know "the law" in multiple disciplines over-whelmed me. I hated keeping timesheets and routinely lost hundreds of hours per year to sloppy timekeeping and to the guilt of billing financially distressed clients for services I was sure they couldn't afford. On top of that, I struggled with finding time for office administration tasks. Sometimes bills wouldn't go out at all, because I was too busy working for clients to charge them.

I decided that in order to reinvent my practice, I had to take the creative energy I was giving to my clients and save some for myself. At the end of 2003, I took two weeks off and spent that time thinking about the firm I had—and, most importantly—the firm I wanted. What follows are ten steps to help you think critically about where you are, and help you get to where you want to go.

For the next month, take 30 minutes each day to seriously think about your business. Do you enjoy coming into the office every morning? Are you doing the work you like to do? Are you working with clients who respect your efforts? Are you making the money you want to make?

If the answer to any of these questions is "no," read on.

## Step 1: Don't Think Like a Lawyer

Ask a hundred people what businessperson gives them the best customer service, and I'd wager that not one of them will name their lawyer. I've often wondered how we've earned the moniker "professional service providers" when so few of us are truly professionals at providing service!

Instead of learning how to serve your clients from other lawyers, look to how other businesses serve their customers exceptionally well. Who runs the most successful businesses in your town? Who is the best insurance agent? The most popular broker? The busiest florist? The hottest restaurateur? Meet these people. Take them to lunch. Ask them how they've become so successful (they will be flattered you asked) and apply their lessons to your own business.

Oh, and one more thing. Find out how many of them bill by the hour. I'll go double or nothing that not one does!

## Step 2: Find a Niche and Own It

Pick something you could do exceptionally well, and learn to do it better than anyone else. Speak to groups about your expertise. Join trade associations. Write a blog. Whatever you do, make this the one thing, above all others, that defines why someone should become your client.

## Step 3: Identify Your Ideal Client

This one seems like a no-brainer, but it is essential that you build your perfect firm around the clients you most want to serve. It is impossible to consistently deliver exceptional service unless you like the people you work for. Don't believe me, try this:

Pick your least favorite client—you know, the one you hope doesn't call, the one who pays his bill late, berates your staff, and makes outrageous demands on your time—and fire him.

Now, how much better do you feel? Our least favorite clients don't deserve our hard work, and probably aren't getting it anyway. And because we simply can't do our best work for clients we don't like or respect, we must dump them as soon as ethically possible and get on with the business of serving the clients we're most able to help.

Identifying your ideal client is only half of the equation. You must get to know your client as well.

Here is a quick exercise that will help you learn what your ideal client values:

Go to the kind of stores your ideal client frequents, and look around. What draws your perfect client to the stores he or she shops in? Is it price? Is it selection? Is it quality? Is it atmosphere? Go back to your office and compare your office's "look" with the look of your ideal custo-mer's favorite store. Could you make your office more inviting or accommodating? Then think about what you sell (and how you price it). Are you Wal-Mart, Target, or Neiman Marcus? Which one do you want to be?

## Step 4: Give Them Something for Free

Okay, you've become an expert and identified your ideal client. Now it is time to show off. Identify the single legal issue that is keeping your ideal client up at night (or should be) and show her how to solve it. But don't just show one at a time, show them all. Put on an invitation-only seminar that focuses on that single issue. Invite all of your ideal clients.

At the seminar, demonstrate your expertise. Ask your attendees to suggest future topics, and also to suggest others who should get an invitation the next time. Finally, follow up with the atten-dees one on one (in person, if at all possible) to thank them for coming and to ask them if there is anything you can do for them in the future.

## Step 5: Have Something Cool to Sell

Don't think that your expertise and your winning personality are enough to get clients to hire you.

You need to have something cool to sell them. In my firm, I don't bill by the hour. Instead, I offer my clients a variety of "service pricing" plans that include, at a minimum, unlimited tele-phone conferences with me. I also guarantee my service. My clients pay me by the month for all the services included in their plan, and I will quote them a flat fee (before the work is begun) for any extra work they may need. My clients love it, and I have found that "Guaranteed Service" and "Predictable Pricing" are the cool things my clients love to buy.

All of my clients are also part of a unique club. In addition to the seminars I do, I have begun a regular "Saturday School" where I invite others to teach general business principles and to talk on topics of interest. I also have times I've set aside for my clients to "walk in" and chat about whatever they want—at no extra charge.

## Step 6: Don't Sell It to Everybody

Don't let just anybody hire you. Once you have established a base of good clients, tell them that you are limiting the number of new clients you will take to better serve your existing ones. How-ever, suggest to each client that you will still be happy to meet with people they refer to you. Give each of your clients a card (like a coupon or gift certificate) that entitles the bearer to a consultation with you. The more exclusive your client "club" is, the more others will clamor to get in.

## Step 7: Stop Advertising

At my firm, our advertising budget has become our "client appreciation budget." Apart from a single-line listing in the Yellow Pages, we're putting all of our advertising money (for us, nearly $1,000 per month) into improving our client experience. We'll be finding new office space with room for clients to use as a "business center," with free wireless Internet access, coffee, etc.

## Step 8: Ask Your Clients to Point Out Your Faults

An unhappy customer will tell far more people about a single bad experience than a happy customer will about many good ones. Unless you systematically solicit feedback from all of your existing and former clients, you may never know why they left (and what they are telling everyone else). Ask your clients to point out your mistakes and reward them for doing so. Specifically, ask them this one question, "How likely is it that you would recommend my firm to a friend or colleague?"

In my firm, I add a "report card" to every invoice I send. It asks my clients to give me a grade on specific items—like returning telephone calls or keeping promises. I also include a "suggestion box" for them to add any ideas I can implement to make my firm work better. Clients who complete and return the report card with their payment receive a small discount, and I get invaluable insights into my practice and how my clients perceive it.

## Step 9: Simplify Your Client Communications

Every week, pick one of your "standard" forms (like a retainer agreement) and give it to a sixth grader. Ask if he or she understands it. Then rewrite it from scratch. Clients don't like to feel stupid, and every piece of communication they receive from you that makes them that way decreases the likelihood they'll consult with you in the future.

## Step 10: Pay Attention to the Little Things

If you are a matrimonial lawyer with a lot of female clients, does your waiting room have only *Car and Driver, Golf Magazine,* and *Field & Stream*? Can your clients overhear your telephone conversations, or see confidential documents from other client's files? Are you constantly apologizing for the mess in your office? Is your secretary less than pleasant on the telephone?

Ask people who will be honest with you to audit your firm experience. Specifically ask them to pay attention to the little details—your clients do.

## Step 11: Underpromise and Overdeliver

Keep a "promise log" on your desk and keep track of all of the things you promise to do (and when you promised to do them). Share your promise log with your secretary to make sure things don't fall though the cracks. Now, try to overdeliver on each of your promises. For example, in my office, we regularly quote clients a flat fee for the work we do. Every time a client receives a bill that is less (even marginally so) than the quoted price, the client calls to see if there is some mistake. When I say that the project didn't cost as much as I'd anticipated, the client is speechless—and delighted.

Whether you implement all 11 steps at once, or whether you try one at a time, these steps will make a difference in your practice. You'll feel better about the way you deliver services to your clients, you'll enjoy practicing law more, and your clients will give your practice the kind of appreciation it deserves.

# §4.5 How a Branch Office Can Bring in More Business
### Jean Maneke

Are there days when you feel trapped in your office, struggling with all the phone calls and wishing you could just get away for one day? It's possible to do just that and at the same time to cultivate new clients and build your law practice. Just look around you for a second location to open an office.

This may sound impossible if you are carrying heavy overhead in your primary location, but in fact it will cost you less than you think. Some lawyers are fortunate enough to have vacation homes in cities not too distant from their home base; opening an office near your vacation home will not only allow you to spend more time in a setting that you find relaxing, but also will begin to build a practice in a location that you might be considering for retirement.

In other cases, particularly if you live in a large metropolitan area, you should look around you in some of the rural communities that are within an hour or so from town. Many small towns, which as you already know are suffering from a shortage of medical professionals, are also suffering from a shortage of legal professionals. Call some county courthouses and inquire about the number of resident lawyers in the area and you may be surprised to find only one, if that. And in many of these rural counties, there are banks seeking legal assistance, wealthy farmers looking for advice and probate, or criminal matters needing attention.

**Ten Reasons Why a Big-City Lawyer Would Enjoy a Small-Town Practice**

1. The funeral home director leaves you a piece of candy when he drops off the day's funeral announcements as he distributes them to businesses in town.
2. When you walk across the street to the courthouse, you can enjoy being outside for five minutes on nice days without having to skip out on work.
3. Clients know by seeing your car outside your office that you are in town and stop in to tell you about things in their lives that often give you a chance to "sell" them additional legal services.
4. Clients bring you farm produce when they have too much, because you poor city folks don't get good produce at home.
5. You can run to the grocery store on the way home by just walking across the street.
6. When you leave your fountain pen in the courtroom, all the folks in the courthouse know whose it is.
7. You don't have to wear a suit to be taken seriously when you meet with clients.
8. Checks don't bounce.
9. Clients understand when you get interrupted by your kid on the phone.
10. Everybody knows your name.

Starting a rural practice has many benefits. Imagine, if you will, a beautiful fall day when you escape your routine in the city, trading it for a relaxing drive through the fall colors and past the apple orchards and pumpkin patches. Imagine watching the combines gathering the fall bounty as you make your way to the office where rent is cheap, where you need only a modicum of your usual office equipment, where clients know that Tuesday is your day in town and so they are hanging around your door when you arrive. It can be a reality for you.

First, you need to consider where to locate your branch office. Perhaps you want to be in the county seat, so you are close to the courthouse. One benefit of being in the county seat, besides that it is quick to run across the street to the county courthouse when you want to look through a file or if you need a law book that you don't have, is that you can duck over there to make local counsel appearances for all those big-city lawyers who haven't discovered the beauty of taking a day to play in the country. The county seat will also be the location of the county offices, so you can cultivate those potential clients.

Or perhaps it makes more sense to locate your office in the community that has the largest commercial businesses in the county. Sometimes the county seat is not the largest commercial city in the county. Many smaller communities have significant business operations in town but no counsel. And one benefit of smaller towns is that the townspeople, particularly the business people, will feel strongly about "buying locally." They want the community to shop there rather than to drive to a nearby metropolitan area, and that becomes a way of life for them, too. (And when you are in town, it is a good way of life for you, too. When you need an afternoon soda, walk over to the community grocery store and chat with the owner while you are there. When you need batteries for your radio, stop in the local hardware store. While you may be paying a little more, you are investing in your own future!)

Either way, it's important before you begin to take a day for marketing, making appointments and calling on the major potential clients in the county, introducing yourself to them and telling them about your background, how you are looking forward to opening an office in their county and how you hope they will think of you when they need a lawyer because it is very important to you that this endeavor be a success. Find out what issues are pending in town that you might have an interest in working on in your practice.

Comment to them about issues that you think might not have come up in the town's discussion of those issues and your thoughts about the matter.

Then find a place that fits your budget. Your branch office doesn't need to be fancy. It can be done without even having a full-time staff person in that location. (In fact, unless overhead is not an issue, it's important that you keep expenses down. This office needs to be making a profit the minute you get your first client.) Many communities have phone service that allows you to call-forward your line in the branch office to your regular office when you are home. (If the volume of forwarded calls is heavy, it may benefit you to get an 800 number for forwarding purposes, saving on long distance charges.) Then, on days when the lawyer is "in," you simply answer your own phone. If you are lucky enough to be with a client when a call comes in, you just graciously explain to the caller that you will need to call him or her back later. Most callers understand and are willing to wait.

You will need less equipment than you think. You don't need a postage machine in your branch office—stamps are just fine. A modest desk or table and chairs around it will do for your "office." (Unless you are in a fancy resort community, and particularly if you are in a rural community where the economy is tight, it doesn't make sense to go lavish with your surroundings.) In fact, it's nice to have your desk by the front window, if you have one, so that folks driving or walking by can see the lights on and you inside working to remind them that you are in the office that day. You will be surprised at how many folks walk by and wave at you if you are in a storefront location. And that is good!

You definitely need a computer and printer and basic office supplies. Printers are a dime a dozen. Perhaps it makes sense to use your laptop for this office, taking it home with you between visits. Or perhaps it is better to just leave your outdated computer in this office, since you won't need the newest equipment there when you are only there one day a week. While occasionally you'll need to do some quick and dirty work in a hurry for a client, for the most part it makes sense to not attempt to complete the clients' work while you are there for the day. First, sometimes clients don't understand why fees are so high when you whip out your quitclaim deed form and throw together a deed in five minutes. They can always come back later in the day to pick it up. And if a major project comes in, you probably will need your staff's assistance, and most clients are willing to allow you to use this first visit for "intake," making a subsequent appointment to come back next week to pick up the finished products.

In fact, if you do elder law, you may want to locate near a major retirement home in the area, because you may find yourself making house calls and it's handy to be five minutes away from the nursing home. Further, unless you believe that it is a conflict to notarize documents you have prepared for a client, it's important to have your notary seal so that you can provide this service.

Finding witnesses for wills is a little trickier, since there's no one else in your office to assist with that task. However, there are other small community offices nearby—the local insurance agent and the local grocer we just talked about, plus citizens in a small town are much less likely to be concerned about being pulled in off the street to serve their fellow citizens as witnesses, a function much closer to the old-fashioned idea of witnesses who really knew whether the signers were competent to sign the documents. Sometimes in today's law offices, it is a much greater issue of concern that the staff pulled in to witness a signature has never seen the testator before the signing process begins.

But it is important to have a regular schedule of being present at this office. When you are not there every day, it is critical that residents in the area know when to count on you being there. If you are not there regularly, folks will forget about your presence. When you are there every week on a certain day, the community will plan their visits around your schedule. Consistency is one way you establish dependability and your reputation.

Perhaps you want a conference room. Frankly, a long worktable and some cheaper chairs will do the trick. You won't be taking a lot of depositions in this office, probably. But you definitely need a fax machine. A second telephone line isn't that expensive and it can serve as your dial-up service line, allowing you to talk while on the Internet. (Your staff back home can use the fax or e-mail to send you important messages from your primary office, and e-mail works great for sending you computer files if you've forgotten to bring certain documents that day.) And a copier is pretty important, although you'll have to weigh whether to invest in a fancy one that has lots of features or whether in this office you can live with just a basic tabletop that does limited tricks. When you get a little loose change, pick up a microwave and small refrigerator at a garage sale and you'll have all the luxuries of home.

Getting the word out about your presence is key. While those community visits will get you started, look around you at how people in the community get their information. In smaller towns, the local newspaper is a key source of information. Sometimes Yellow Pages ads are important, but a weekly or biweekly (or maybe even monthly) business-card ad in a community paper will regularly get your name before those in the community and keep your number handy. (Plus, sometimes the editor can send business your way.) Get to know those in the community who have the potential to send you clients. For example, if you do probate work, get chummy with the local funeral director, the public administrator in the county, and the coroner. Don't laugh—each of those persons is the first line of entry for folks who will probably eventually need a probate lawyer. Every practice has those kinds of contacts which can send you business.

Finally a word about fees: After spending 12 years doing exactly what I'm talking about doing, I have concluded that my fees in the branch office can be almost on par with my fees in my metropolitan office. Most of the clients that a profitable practice seeks will be willing to pay for the lawyer's expertise. If they don't hire you, they will hire someone in a nearby metropolitan area who is nearly as high as you are. Indeed, there is some benefit to being a highly priced lawyer if you remind clients that they get what they pay for when they hire a professional.

In time, you'll be driving to your second office one day and suddenly realize how wonderful it is to have a day when you are away from all those phone calls at your primary office. It is incredibly peaceful to spend a day in a community where life moves slower and where you can walk across the street to the courthouse, have lunch with the judge at the local diner, and walk down the street when you need to ask the local banker a question about a client matter.

Plus, you can make money, too!

# §4.6 The Myth and Reality of Volunteerism
## Jeffrey Allen

*Sam, an experienced lawyer with 20 years in practice (spoken sincerely, if a bit patronizingly): "John, you really impressed me in court today. I think you have a bright future as a lawyer. I understand you practice by yourself. Can I give you some advice? If you really want to build your practice, you need to get better known in the community. You should join the Rotary/Elks/Lions/etc. club. By joining, you will find that you have access to a large group of potential clients. . . ."*

It's time to talk about the Big Lie of practice building. You have all heard it, probably many times. The Big Lie says that if you want to build your practice and increase your client base, you should join service clubs and volunteer your time. The Big Lie operates on the theory that the more people who know a lawyer, the greater the number of possible clients or client referrers that lawyer has. That reasoning seems pretty sound, creating the appeal of the Big Lie. Having gone along with the logic to this point, how can one argue with the concept that a lawyer should join available service clubs as each service club brings that many more potential clients and client referrers into the fold?

When I first started practicing, I must have heard the Big Lie at least a hundred times from a variety of people, mostly experienced lawyers who told me that they had received and followed the same advice when they started out in practice. The Big Lie may account, in part, for why lawyers, as a group, make up a very substantial portion of the membership in service organizations and why so many lawyers volunteer their time for community

> The Big Lie: Build your practice efficiently—join a service club!

service activities (and you all thought it resulted from the kind and benevolent nature of lawyers).

Kidding aside, I firmly believe that lawyers, like all other citizens, owe an obligation to give back to the community. I have followed that credo throughout my adult life. As a result, I joined a service club (Rotary International) and volunteered my time for a variety of community service activities and organizations. I have found that participation personally satisfying and emotionally rewarding. I strongly encourage you to make the time to undertake similar activities.

"Now, wait a minute," you say, "I thought we were talking about the Big Lie. First you tell us that joining a service organization to build your practice is the Big Lie; now you tell us to join service organizations. I can't make sense out of this."

While my comments may, on their face, appear at odds with each other, I assure you that they do not conflict. I strongly encourage you to join service organizations and otherwise volunteer your time to community service activities. *But* I want you to volunteer for the right reasons. If you do, I think you will find your participation rewarding. If you join for the wrong reasons, you will probably end up frustrated and unhappy.

Undoubtedly many lawyers have augmented their practices through contacts made in service organizations. Understand, however, that simply joining a service organization does not automatically get you clients. To get clients through service organization membership, a lawyer needs to actively participate in the organization's work. Active participation requires an often substantial time commitment. Time spent working on community service

Membership in a service club can provide a great deal of personal satisfaction.

By all means, join service clubs if you have an interest in their activities. Be sure to join for the right reasons though!

activities has to come from someplace. Generally, it comes from your practice, your family, or your personal time.

If you look at participation in service organizations and volunteerism as a loss leader to get your name out and in front of more people that could bring you legal business, then you should analyze the time and money you will put into your participation as an investment.

You can calculate the cost of membership in the organization as your billable rate times the number of hours you spend on community service activities plus the out-of-pocket expenses you incur (travel costs, membership, etc.). The amount of your time that will go toward the volunteer activities will vary from lawyer to lawyer and depending upon the nature of the volunteer activity you choose. Service clubs generally charge membership fees, and you will incur additional expenses through your participation. Additionally, service clubs generally get involved in fund raising and almost always look to their own members first for contributions. If you rise to a position of leadership in the organization (the product of great involvement and devotion of substantial effort and resources), you will find that leaders need to set an example for the rest of the members by contributing often and much.

In talking about the community service road to practice building, lawyers often neglect to do this investment analysis. If you do not consider the value of any time or money you contribute to the organization and its programs in the equation, anything you get back by way of collections from resulting work looks like a good deal. If you realistically estimate the amount of time and

> If you plan to join a service organization to grow your practice, do the math!

money you will end up devoting to the organization and apply that cost (investment?) against collections from work you get as a collateral result (return?) of your participation in the organization, you will likely find it hard to break even, let alone see any return on your investment.

The return on investment analysis suggests that the theory of volunteering your time as a means of building your practice works poorly and inefficiently at best. That leads logically to ask where the theory breaks down and why it does not work. Several facts jump to the surface in response to such an inquiry. First, we know that lawyers have a high rate of volunteerism. Without regard to whether that results from civic mindedness or more crass motives, it means that you will probably not be the only lawyer in the organization. While the ratio of lawyers to other members of the group will vary from organization to organization, it will probably result in a division of available work among the lawyer members.

If we assume that all lawyers who belong to the organization would happily accept work from members of the organization and that all lawyers who join and actively participate in its programs will get some work from members, the available work gets divided up among those lawyers. It may turn out that some of the lawyer members have different focuses on their practice than others. That may cause some shift in the proportion of the work that each lawyer gets. Recognize that the lawyers best known and most respected in the organization will likely attract the largest share of available work coming out of the organization. Becoming well-known, however, usually means raising the ante in terms

Where does the theory go wrong?

A workload divided may not support all the member lawyers.

of requiring more of your time to participate in activities so that your name gets around and you meet the other members.

As your reputation increases within the organization, you may well get a request from the organization to do some legal work on its behalf—as a volunteer. These requests often come from the president of the organization. If you don't accept, your stock in the organization may suffer. If you do accept, you will spend yet more time on the organization's work, increasing the amount of your investment, making it even harder to get to a positive return.

Dealing with the *quid pro quo*.

If you work hard and become well-known and respected in the organization (traits that will also get you some business), you may ultimately hold leadership positions in the organization. Generally people consider it an honor to hold such positions. If you joined to generate business, you will take the opportunity if it presents itself (you may actively seek it out) to enhance the likelihood that you will get such business. Properly done, these positions require that you devote considerable additional time to the activities of the organization in order to perform your leadership functions. As leadership positions in such organizations generally do not include compensation for your time, holding such a position increases your investment again, thereby making it harder yet to see a positive return on your investment.

The investment analysis makes it appear that I received good advice from one senior lawyer who told me to eschew community service organizations and bar association participation as they did not generate fees and absorbed time like a dry sponge absorbs water.

I have talked to many lawyers who joined community service organizations with the intent of generating business and found the exercise frustrating at best. I have talked to others that told me they joined initially for that reason, but stayed even though it did not generate the kind or amount of business that they hoped. They continued their involvement as they found other satisfaction from their participation in the organization.

Please understand that I am not telling you to not join community service organizations or bar associations. Neither am I suggesting that you do not participate actively in those organizations, giving freely of your time and resources. To the contrary, I strongly encourage you to join them. But if you join, do so for the right reasons. I have actively participated in community service work and in bar association work for many years. I have devoted thousands of hours and considerable financial resources to such activities. It has produced its share of trials (not the court kind) and tribulations. If I had it to do over again, knowing what I know now, I would still have volunteered my time and effort as I did.

*Joining for the right reason.*

Participation in community service organizations can mean many positive things in your life:

- It gives you the opportunity to meet new people, some of whom may become social friends. I have made many close friends over the years through such activities.

*Let's look at some of the benefits. . . .*

- The whole is greater than the sum of its parts. Community service work gives you the opportunity to help others. Doing it through an organization allows you to join your efforts with others in an organized manner that can result in a greater return for your efforts than you could have achieved on your own.

- If you share my belief that each of us has a duty to give back to the community in return for the benefits we received from it, community service offers an excellent opportunity to discharge that duty effectively.
- Many people (myself included) get great personal satisfaction from the community service work that they do.
- Some types of community service work can become something for the family to share.

Participation in bar association or other professional organizational activities can provide all of the benefits of other community service activities, plus the knowledge that your work gives something back to your chosen profession and may result in other changes that positively affect the administration of justice.

In short, as I have said for many years with respect to participation in community service organizations, "the money stinks, but the pay is great!"

Bottom line, if you join community service organizations, do it because

- You believe in the organization's goals.
- You support the organization's activities.
- You want to participate in the organization's programs because you think that they are interesting or will achieve some positive good for society.
- You like the members and want to join for social reasons.

If you approach community service and participation in bar associations from the perspective described above, I believe that you will enjoy your participation much more than if you join in the expectation of increasing your client base. If you join for the right reasons and actively participate, you likely will see some business as a result of that activity. Accept the business as a fringe benefit resulting from your participation rather than as the primary reason for your involvement.

# §4.7 Do You Still Need to Join Kiwanis?

## Lynne J. Stadjuhar

On any given day, most lawyers receive multiple membership opportunities through traditional mail or e-mail. "Don't miss this great opportunity to meet prospective clients and network with other lawyers in your field. Join today for the discount price of . . ." Sound familiar? While membership in these legal organizations is extremely important to the practice of law, the time spent networking and attending these events will not pay the bills. Most of us hardly leave enough time in our day to complete the required amount of CLE credits necessary to maintain our licenses, let alone attend meetings and luncheons, serve on boards, and make appearances at charity events. Today, lawyers are much more focused on billable time—after all, that's how we make money, right? With the time crunch of the modern-day law practice, is it still imperative that we belong to civic and charitable clubs? The answer is a resounding "yes."

Clubs like Kiwanis have their roots in American business society. The Kiwanis club was founded in 1915 in Detroit by a Moose Lodge organizer and a tailor. The club was started as a networking club for local merchants and salesmen to make contacts with prospective clients. The name Kiwanis is derived from a Native American phrase meaning "to trade or advertise." The Kiwanis club contributes $70 million yearly to charitable organizations, and each year its members donate close to seven million hours of their time.

Most of us pass up the opportunity to get involved in organizations such as Kiwanis, not because we believe such involvement isn't worthwhile, but simply because we don't have the time. Perhaps in the name of community service, marketing, and client development, we should make the time.

Although the idea of marketing has been widely accepted by most firms and practitioners, how to market is still a mystery to most. Today there is a great amount of emphasis on the firm résumé, direct mail, newspaper, legal publication, and television advertising. However, most lawyers have realized that these traditional forms of business advertising do not necessarily create a windfall of client work. Because of the lack of success through these traditional channels, many firms

have given up on marketing or have hired professional marketing consultants to do the job. Have
we forgotten that the basis of client development
is creating a relationship?

## Building Trust

Let's start with the basics. How do clients choose
a lawyer? In most cases, when people make the
decision to contact a lawyer, they call their friend
or a friend of a friend who is a lawyer to discuss
their particular legal issue and ask for advice on
whom to hire. People feel more comfortable
sharing this information with someone they trust.
Trust is the basis for creating any type of relationship, and as we propose, the basis for generating business.

Trust cannot be created by simple advertising.
Trust is built over time after a person or company feels comfortable with the character, ability,
strength, and truth of a person or a firm. Think
about it: How do you hire a babysitter, a plumber,
a contractor, or any other service provider? Most
of us ask people we know and trust to recommend someone they know and trust. Although it
is true that some services can develop business
from the traditional forms of advertising, most is
generated on referrals. Membership in an organi-

zation or club creates this type of relationship
and often generates business.

Membership here does not mean attending
an occasional dinner or cocktail hour; it means
attending regular meetings and activities as well
as contributing to the cause, not only financially
but also by donating your expertise. You need to
show the other members that you are not only
trustworthy but that you have an expert knowledge of the law. By participating or perhaps donating your professional time, you will become more
than a name on a roster—you will take on a
persona.

Historically, each town or community had
one general store, one doctor, and one lawyer.
All of the residents of the town knew each other
and knew whom to contact when they needed
these services. Think of these clubs and organizations as communities. If you participate and get
to know the members, they will get to know you.
You will develop a trust relationship with the
members, and when they are faced with a legal
issue or are asked if they know of anyone who
can help, you will be the first friend on the list.

Although this marketing plan is logical and
simple, it may require some time and training for
your partners and associates, as well as some discipline on your part. This type of thing is not

taught in law school. Although there are several opportunities to network with potential employers and gain experience through legal aid clinics, this type of marketing is different. Once young lawyers land their first job, most relax and spend their extra time learning the practice of law. It is important to instill the mindset that law is a business, and although they have landed that coveted first job, their job does not exist without a steady stream of work. All lawyers must market their practice to stay profitable.

## Relationship Marketing in Trade Groups

Most firms and practices already rely on current client referrals for business development. That is a good start. However, there may be an entire world of untapped referrals that you are missing if you fail to practice the oldest form of advertising: good old-fashioned relationship marketing.

By building relationships with people, lawyers create the natural flow of business. Lawyers must rely on referrals to keep their practice up and running, let alone profitable. Referral advertising is the most common way to attract new clients in the field of law. There are so many potential client bases that have remained unexplored by the legal profession. For example, when you are developing your marketing plan, whether it be individual or for a firm, take some time to investigate different trade groups and organizations. Look beyond the traditional membership groups such as bar associations and other law-related organizations. There are vast gold mines of clients lurking in associations and groups that are not even aware of their legal needs. Undoubtedly, your current clients belong to several trade groups, attend trade shows, and keep in contact with people they have met through the years in the industry. Ask your current clients to advise you regarding what groups are reputable and what groups will allow you to get to know the industry in addition to the people in it. Not only will your client realize that you are truly committed to representing their best interests, you will gain their respect as well as the respect of their colleagues.

Again, this marketing technique will not work if you do not take an active role in the group once you become a member. After you join the group, take an educational or consulting role. Perhaps offer your legal services to the group in exchange for a sponsorship position. Make sure your information is accessible to the members of the group so that when they need you they can easily contact you. Be aware and prepared that you may not develop a client relationship overnight, but when these people need help, they will remember the name of the lawyer in their industry group they met at the annual dinner or the lawyer who talked about issues in law that concern the industry.

If you are a small firm or solo practitioner, marketing the name of the firm will not give you the same name recognition as it does for large, well-known firms. Emphasize your name, not the name of the firm. Capitalize on the personal relationship you have created.

One way to make them remember your name is to use your expertise to educate the members about why they need legal assistance. Place yourself in an expert role for all members of the group. Study the industry and the legal needs of its members, then ask the group for time to give a presentation. If the group has a publication, ask for permission to submit an article regarding the legal issues that apply to the industry. Explain when and why legal representation is important to their business. No matter what field of law

you have chosen, offering legal advice will automatically gain respect for you and your firm.

Perhaps the most significant reason to pursue membership in these clubs and organizations is our civic duty as lawyers. The Model Rules of Professional Conduct state, "Lawyers, as guardians of the law, play a vital role in the preservation of society." This is true not only in the courtroom but also in the context of providing legal education to clients and society alike. As lawyers we have special skills that, when used correctly, can benefit society. By offering our time to these clubs and organizations, we can fulfill our civic duty.

The American law system is based on the theory of stare decisis, dictating that we shall rely on precedent when presented with the same set of facts. Membership in civic and trade organizations has been the practice of lawyers since the creation of the American legal system. Who are we to disrupt this tried-and-true method of legal marketing? These groups and organizations are the perfect forum for us, as lawyers, to build our businesses and develop professional relationships with people in our communities.

# 5

# How to Build a Law Firm Brand

*Corinne Cooper*

I've just come home from a bar meeting and, as usual, my briefcase is full of business cards collected from the people I've met. I've never been good with names, so I ask people for cards to help me remember them. But I've realized lately that unless I write something additional on the card, I still won't remember the person. The cards are indistinguishable. Is this the man who wanted a former student's resume? Is that the young woman I shared a cab with to dinner? Is this the lawyer who does only bankruptcy law?

One card stands out. It is pale blue and has a seashell logo. The card belongs to a young lawyer who does environmental and water law. I won't forget what he does, and I won't forget him.

Corinne Cooper, professor emerita of law, spent almost 20 years teaching UCC. She is the author of several books, including *The Portable UCC* (4th ed. ABA 2005) and *The New Article 9* (2nd ed. ABA 2000). She is a member of the editorial board of the *ABA Journal*.

In 1993, Professor Cooper began to focus on the realm of professional communication, culminating in development of her multimedia presentation, Professional Presence®. She has presented to firms, judges, and legal organizations throughout the United States.

In 2000, she left teaching to focus on communication consulting. Her company, Professional Presence®, offers comprehensive communication consulting to lawyers and other professionals, including firm branding.

Professor Cooper was born and raised in Albuquerque, New Mexico. She received her BA and JD degrees from the University of Arizona. She attended the Wharton School, University of Pennsylvania, where she studied finance in the MBA program. She is a member of Phi Beta Kappa, Phi Kappa Phi, and the Order of the Coif.

You can learn more about her, read more of her writing, and find out whether your firm might benefit from her firm's services at www.ProfessionalPresence.com. Contact her at c2@ProfessionalPresence.com.

Law firms and lawyers have been identified for generations solely by name. At a time when most professionals were known in their community, a name was a perfectly suitable form of identification. If you wanted a good lawyer, you asked around and got a name. You joined your mother's law firm, and it became "Jones and Butler-Jones." Every large firm was known by name long after those partners joined the dearly departed.

That was then. The world has changed. Professionals are more anonymous, and law firms seem fungible. It's time to take a more sophisticated approach to identifying your practice. A comprehensive image for your firm is called a brand—or firm—identity.

## What Is a Brand Identity?

A brand identity is a way of communicating about your firm that helps your target audience understand and remember more about your firm. Creating a brand identity requires you to:

- pinpoint the core message that you want to convey about your firm,
- define and deploy an identity that embodies that message, and
- communicate with your audience consistently using the brand identity.

## The Core Message

Think about the one sentence that would encapsulate the goal of your practice. In business, this is known as an elevator pitch. In marketing, it's called a positioning statement. We call it a core message. What kind of firm are you? Think of your core message as a promise you are making to your clients about your firm. Your brand identity should communicate that promise on every level.

More importantly, your *firm* should communicate that goal on every level. The core message shouldn't be an aspiration; it's a description of what the firm can and will deliver. If you aren't prepared, at every level of the firm (from managing partner to receptionist), to deliver on that promise, don't waste your time building a brand identity that is based upon it.

In my firm, we have a very narrow goal. Our core message is:

*We help lawyers and legal organizations change the way they communicate to be more effective with their target audience.*

Although we approach this task in many different ways, this is the promise that we make. Our brand identity builds on that core message.

Identifying and understanding your core message is important. One marketing pundit described a brand identity that ignores this important step as a costume. You can spend a lot of money on it, but ultimately it will just confuse your target audience.

## But Wait, There's More!

When you identify your core message, and develop brand elements that advance it, there are additional benefits. A brand identity will

- professionalize,
- unify, and
- improve the quality of your communication.

By focusing on your audience, and on how to reach them most effectively, your firm's communication will improve. Too many lawyers think about what they want to communicate about themselves and their firms; surprisingly few focus on their audience and what that target audience needs to hear to solve their problems.

A brand identity isn't all form and no substance. It must build upon your firm's strengths and core message. Your brand isn't just your logo and typeface: It's the personality of your firm, from the substantive focus of your practice to the way you treat your existing clients.

**The Core Message**

*Here are some examples of target audiences and appropriate core messages:*

- A law firm aimed exclusively at divorce clients might have a very narrow message:

  "We specialize in collaborative divorce.™"

- For a wider target audience, the message might be broader:

  "Corporate Counsel, LLC, provides your small business with all its legal needs."

- The Real Property Law Group, PLLC, a firm in Seattle that does nothing but real estate law, identifies its target audience right on its web page:

  "Our client base includes both buyers and sellers, borrowers and lenders, developers and contractors, investors and managers, landlords and tenants."

The firm's core message is precisely directed at that target:

  "Our attorneys are experienced in assisting clients with all phases of their commercial or residential real estate project, including development, tax, land use, leasing, lending, joint venture/LLC formation, acquisitions, sales and workouts."

A brand can also unify the firm's thinking about its goals. Firm personnel will understand more clearly what the firm promises, and find it easier to deliver on that promise. Existing clients will understand more clearly how the firm can help them.

## A Brand Identity Has Three Main Goals

1. Your brand will identify your firm as the source of all its communication:

   - It quickly distinguishes your communications from the "clutter."

2. Your brand will increase attention and response to your communication:

   - A brand professionalizes, unifies, and raises the profile of your firm.

3. Your brand will teach your target audience to value your firm:

   - Brand identity builds confidence in and loyalty to your firm.

### Elements of a Brand Identity

**Brand Name**
What is your firm called?

**Logo**
What graphic identifies your firm?

**Fonts**
What fonts will convey your message?

**Tagline**
What additional line of text will convey the brand message?

**Color Palette**
What colors are right for your firm and audience?

**Design Elements**
What design elements will be used to reinforce the brand and assure identification of the product with your firm?

## Elements of a Brand Identity

Once you identify the core message, you can begin to build a brand that carries that message. The key elements of a brand identity are:

### 1. Brand Name

Law firms are gradually moving away from the practice of naming the firm for its members. There are good reasons to avoid this anachronistic system: You will not have to rename the firm when people join or leave, and your brand will not be tied to partners deceased or disowned. (Note how fast Andersen partners ran from that name after Enron.)

Small or boutique firms are particularly suited to trade-name branding. Large firms with diverse practices may have difficulty identifying a trade name that describes their substantive strength or geographic location (although it's only a matter of time before major law firms start grabbing brand names like "Global Legal" or "All Law"). But a firm doing nothing but adoptions and custody cases may find it easier to do business as "Kidlaw" than as "Smith & Smith & Smith."

Many law firms practicing domestic relations law operate under trade names that include the word "family." Several firms now use trade names that include the words "bankruptcy," "patent," or "intellectual property."

TWO WARNINGS

1. Be sure that the trade name you select isn't intellectual property belonging to another firm, that you protect your exclusive right to use it, and that the URLs that incorporate the trade name are available.
2. Check your state bar rules before opening a firm under a trade name. Although the restrictions may not be enforceable, many state bars still prohibit law firms from operating under trade names (see "The Ethics of Branding" sidebar).

For many firms, trade names are not an option. If you have a multiple name firm, consider shortening your firm name, as most national firms have done. "Cooper, Smith, Jones, Davis & Black" should be "Cooper Smith."

## The Ethics of Branding

**Warning:** This is not the chapter on ethics! See *How to Capture and Keep Clients: Marketing Strategies for Lawyers,* ABA Publishing, May 2005.

**Beware:** There are lots of ethical landmines in the branding field. Check with your state bar before you print if you have any questions. Here are some guidelines and some resources:

| You should be okay if you: | But beware: |
| --- | --- |
| Use your name or your firm name. | ■ You cannot use a fictional name, or the name of a dead lawyer who was never in your firm! <br> ■ Nevada recently challenged an out-of-state firm because the firm name did not contain a Nevada lawyer. The bar settled with the firm, and it's questionable whether its position is enforceable. |
| Use a trade name that accurately describes your practice. | ■ The ABA Model Rules permit this so long as the trade name is not misleading. <br> ■ You may not use a trade name that makes you seem like a government agency, or legal aid, such as "clinic." <br> ■ Some states have not adopted the Model Rules, and some have not adopted this rule. Your state bar may challenge you if you use a trade name (but you should win). |
| State that you practice exclusively in one area, or that your practice is limited to one or more areas of law. | ■ Many states will not let you use the word "specialize" unless you have been certified as a specialist. Others require disclaimers. <br> ■ Some states are trying to crack down on the "practice limited to" description. <br> ■ You must actually practice in the area! |
| State that you practice a specific kind or substantive area of law. | ■ Be sure you actually practice in the areas described and do not mislead. |
| Use a tagline that describes your firm or your work. | ■ Again, the description cannot be misleading. Statements that compare you to other lawyers or law firms, or that are self-laudatory, have to be verifiable. |
| Use a tagline describing your clients or target audience. | ■ You may not state or imply that any client or group endorses you. |

| *You should be okay if you:* | *But beware:* |
| --- | --- |
| Use a logo that conveys an idea or message. | ▌ You may not use a logo that is misleading.<br>▌ Your logo may not give the impression that you are affiliated with any other firm or organization when you are not.<br>▌ Your logo must be either your intellectual property or in the public domain. |
| Use your degrees as a part of your firm or brand identification. | ▌ You cannot call yourself "Doctor" with just a J.D. degree.<br>▌ You can display other degrees that you have earned. |
| Call yourself a lawyer, attorney, or counselor. | ▌ In some states, there are limits on what you can call yourself if you are not a member of that state's bar. |
| Call yourself something else, such as "business advisor," "arbitrator and mediator," "communication consultant," or "marriage counselor and advocate." | ▌ Be prepared to defend this description as "not misleading" if you are actually practicing law.<br>▌ If the professional description requires licensure in your state, you must have the requisite license. |
| Use the same brand identity on paper and on the Internet. | ▌ The general rule is that you can use the same branding and marketing on the Internet that you can use in any other medium.<br>▌ In some cases there are fewer restrictions for websites than for print! One state said it did not require the same disclaimers on the web that it requires in print newsletters. |
| Use a URL for your website that is not your firm name. | ▌ You can use a URL if it is not misleading. See Arizona Ethics Opinion 2001-05. |

Resources: *Your state bar ethics opinions; ABA Model Rules; ABA/BNA Lawyer's Manual on Professional Conduct.*

To be memorable, your firm name should not contain more than two names. Pride may get in the way of this process (see "Trade Names" sidebar) but if you are serious about branding, you must consider this option. "Skadden, Arps, Slate, Meagher & Flom" became "Skadden Arps" and is now just "Skadden."

On the other hand, if your firm name does not clearly identify you as a law firm, take steps in your brand to make that point clear. A surprising number of firms assume that people will understand that their business is law, but the market may not be able to distinguish a law firm from an accounting firm when the brand is just a series of names. Recent research showed that participants could not identify the business of a law firm sponsoring a prominent charitable event. This qualifies as good works, but it's poor branding.

## 2. Logo as an Element of Brand Identity

A logo is a graphic that is associated with a company or product. More than any other element, your logo creates a brand identity and helps your audience identify your communications. A good logo is always identified with the firm.

Most law firms have no real logo. Instead, they use a common typeface to identify the firm on their letterhead and business cards. This is a fairly antiquated approach. It conveys the impression that the firm is new, or old-fashioned, or has not focused attention on its professional image. It fails completely to differentiate one firm from another, or to tell the audience anything about the firm's practice.

### Trade Names

**REAL PROPERTY LAW GROUP** PLLC

In Seattle, the Real Property Law Group was interested in identifying its area of practice clearly to potential clients. As partner Vincent DePillis put it, the name choice "was simply a reaction—a reaction against the cult of personality that is fostered in traditional law firms. I wanted the ability to let people come and go without always changing the name. The name 'Real Property Law Group' affirmed pride in my practice area. Finally, there was a practical component to the choice. When we were setting up, we did not know who would be joining the firm."

Legal Venture Counsel, Inc., describes itself as a firm meeting the legal needs of growing businesses without an in-house general counsel. Founder Jean Batman explained, "The factors that influenced my selection of the firm name were all about marketing and branding. I wanted the name to indicate the firm's specialty to clients looking for help in that area. I also wanted a name equally appropriate for a firm with one lawyer or a firm with 10, 20, or more. Finally, the firm name was selected simultaneously with our domain name, which had to be similar to the firm name, easy to remember, and easy to spell: www.legalVC.com"

HERE'S THE LECTURE IN TWO LESSONS:

1. **Hire a professional.** Lawyers developing logos are like graphic designers doing divorces. If you are doing your own brand identity, you are almost certainly wasting valuable professional time that could be spent more productively elsewhere. And you are likely to wind up with art that is worse than no logo at all. A large legal organization recently put together a committee of lawyers to pick a new logo. Their selection was so generic that it was a less effective identity than the one it replaced.

2. **You cannot design by committee.** I'm *not* suggesting that you shouldn't have a brand committee. A committee will be key to developing the core message, and the members of your firm must buy into the brand or it won't be used. But don't get a group together to design a logo or tagline. Hire a professional whose work you admire. Let the professional create two or three logo designs, and explain the options. Then ask the committee to select the one that best delivers your core message to your target audience.

**Law Firm Logos**

Quarles and Brady was one of the first firms to develop a brand identity that incorporates color. This logo, with a red slash behind a reversed ampersand, was adopted in 1985 and won several national awards. A Quarles attorney notes, "For several years, there were partners who would only use the old black and white letterhead—until their clients started asking why they weren't getting the better stationery!"

## 3. Font Selection

If you only do one thing to unify your brand, pick one font and stick to it. Use it for all your firm communications: business cards, letters, brochures, website, and documents. It's amazing how many firms let each staff member decide what font to use, with no uniformity or regard for impact.

Font selection is important for several reasons beyond brand identity (forgive me if these seem obvious, but sometimes we overlook the obvious):

- The font affects the readability of your documents.
- The font affects the size of your documents.
- Fonts take up the majority of the visual field law firm documents.

As a result, you and your clients (and opposing counsel and judges) will spend a lot of time staring at the font you choose. You want to pick a good one.

WHEN SELECTING A FONT, ASK THREE QUESTIONS:

1. What font(s) will help your communications stand out?
2. Which font(s) will appeal to your target audience?
3. How will the font(s) selected enhance readability?

Professional Presence

### Font Selection

**Warning!**

**Please,** don't **PICK** a **CRAZY font** *for* **LEGAL BRANDING**.

When word processing programs first offered a variety of fonts, the world became drunk with the choices, and suffered from font madness. Everyone started using truly terrible fonts just to be different. The result was generally unreadable, ranging from "cluttered and awkward" to "ransom note." Now, an inappropriate font screams "amateur" not "cutting-edge professional."

My advice is to consult a professional. I hired a professional designer to select the fonts used in our firm logo. As noted in the text, if you insist on developing your own brand, you are like a graphic designer practicing tax law: wasting valuable time and probably in over your head.

Still, if you insist on a do-it-yourself approach (or even a "don't bother branding" approach), settle on a single font for all your documents and use it uniformly. Without getting technical, you can pick a font most easily by typing a typical page, copying it, and printing it out using several different fonts. In a page-length document, you will easily be able to tell a great deal about readability, size, and impact of the font. Have several people of different ages look at it. Make sure there is a comparable web-safe font available (and see the "Beware Font Substitution" sidebar). When you have settled on one font, try it out in several different types of documents to be sure that it is sufficiently versatile to meet all your font needs.

If you want to get technical, and discuss kerning and leading, serifs and sans, and the mysterious x-height—all important typographic issues—hire a professional. That discussion is beyond the scope of a sidebar!

## Beware Font Substitutions

You develop a beautiful brand identity, using unusual and visually appealing fonts. You create documents, e-mail signatures, a .pdf brochure, and a website using your signature fonts. Brand in place? Not quite. When you transmit a document electronically, there is a chance that fonts will be substituted when they arrive on the recipient's computer. The more unusual the font, the more likely it is that the recipient will not have it. Of the items listed above, only the .pdf file will arrive looking like it does on your computer.

In preparing this chapter, I asked to use a logo that I've admired. My colleague sent the logo—a word mark—as text via e-mail. I didn't have one of the fonts on my computer, so my browser promptly substituted Helvetica (my default font) for the specified font.

The firm logo: **Firm Name**

My browser changed it to: Firm Name

When I opened it in Word, my default font substituted for the missing font again. By leaving any part of your brand as a text element, you risk change by the recipient's computer. What to do?

| You should be okay if you: | But beware: | You should be okay if you: | But beware: |
|---|---|---|---|
| *Send everything out as a .pdf.*<br>■ This will accurately display brand fonts whether your recipient has them or not.<br>■ Many print programs (including current versions of Word and WordPerfect) allow you to "print" as a .pdf without additional software.<br>■ Sending documents as .pdfs can be an advantage, as .pdf also hides metadata in a Word document. | ■ The recipient will not be able to edit the document without the full version of Adobe Acrobat.<br>■ In some systems, you may have to check "include fonts."<br>■ Including fonts may exceed your license if you have purchased fonts. | *Use graphics in document files.*<br>■ In a Word document, go to "Insert" and select "Picture from File" to place a brand element created as a graphic into your document. The process is similar for WordPerfect.<br>■ In Word, you can embed fonts into the document, and they open when you send it. | ■ Word documents with incorporated graphics or fonts are much bigger, which slows sending and printing speeds.<br>■ Word won't display some graphic formats. Use a high-quality .jpg unless print quality isn't an issue, because small .jpg files print poorly.<br>■ Embedding fonts works in Windows only; this is not supported in Word for Mac OS X. |
| *In e-mail, send brand elements in a graphic format.*<br>■ Insert your brand graphics into your automatic signature using a widely accepted graphic format, such as .jpg, .bmp, .gif, or .tif. | ■ Some e-mail systems turn graphic elements into attachments. Others reject e-mail that includes graphic elements, fearing viruses. These limitations make it more difficult to brand e-mail uniformly. | *Choose widely available fonts.*<br>■ Pick fonts that, while combined creatively, are widely available. If it comes with Word, your recipient is likely to have it.<br>■ Use web-safe fonts in your web pages and HTML documents. Insert other fonts in web pages as graphic elements. | ■ Not all fonts look alike. Versions of the same font are different in different operating systems.<br>■ Even web-safe fonts will be substituted if the recipient has specified a different font in the browser preferences. |

As long as you know the benefits and risks of each choice, the brand's consistency is in your hands.

*Thanks for help with this sidebar to Jerry Haley, Bruce Bohannan, Vicki Kalcic, and Maureen Lawlor.*

Most documents use two typefaces: one for headings and one for body text. The heading face may be the same font in a larger point size, or bold. Some designers prefer two complementary fonts, often one serif and one sans serif font. (Serifs—French for "tails"—are tiny decorative cross-strokes in a letter. Compare a capital T, H, or A in the main text of this chapter, which is set in a serif type, with the same letter in one of the sidebars, which are set in a sans serif.)

But you don't need two fonts. You can create a brand identity with a font in the simplest possible way. The editor of this book, jennifer rose, created a brand identity years ago using lowercase letters for her name on her business cards, letterhead, and in all her professional work. She is known and remembered for this simple homage to e. e. cummings. It's clever, and it doesn't hurt that the subtle message of all lowercase is "the opposite of ALL CAPS NAMES."

## 4. Taglines

A tagline is a short, memorable phrase that conveys your core message and distinguishes your law firm from the competition. For years, the law firm tagline of choice has been "Attorneys at Law."

How can I put this delicately? Most law firm taglines are a disaster. A survey of 100 was collected a few years ago (part of the list appears in the "Law Firm Tagline Game" sidebar). Of 100, 16 use the word "global," "world," or "international." Fifteen emphasize tradition or length of existence, and 18 emphasize "future," "innovation," or "change" (and some mention both). Many talk about value, excellence, business, technology. Obviously, these taglines cannot differentiate one firm from its competitors.

Very few say anything memorable—much less capture the firm's core message. Some are exaggerated or represent more of an aspiration than reality. One pundit described most firm taglines as reverse disclaimers in their attempt to include all possible potential clients. I recently suggested to a firm that they would be better off with the tagline, "Longer hours, shorter bills" than their actual firm tagline, which was pablum.

Small and boutique firms again have an advantage in developing taglines. Because you do not purport to do everything, you can identify a core message and find a tagline that captures it more easily than large law firms can.

Not every firm needs a tagline. If you cannot find a short, memorable phrase that specifically identifies and distinguishes your firm, forget it.

## Law Firm Tagline Game

Can you identify any of these taglines with the law firms that use them? No? Didn't think so.

*The two-period approach:*
- Practical Professionals. Practical Solutions.
- Practical Advice. Sound Solutions.
- Legal Insight. Business Instinct.
- Uncommon Wisdom. Common Sense.
- Legal Minds. Global Intelligence.
- Clients First. Excellence Always.

*The three-period approach:*
- Leadership. Teamwork. Solutions.
- Service. Strategy. Success.
- Trust. Commitment. Integrity.
- Experience. Expertise. Excellence.
- One World. One Firm. Connected.
- Legal Excellence. Practical Solutions. Worldwide.
- Integrity. Excellence. Dedication.

*The rare four-period:*
- Global. Connected. Collaborative. Client-Focused.

*Trite, even if true:*
- Lawyers for the global economy
- A law firm serving global clients
- A global law firm for the 21st century
- A tradition of innovation
- A tradition of excellence
- Serving the World's Leading Innovators
- Strategic legal counsel
- Legal Innovators

*Are you kidding?*
- A source of strength
- Out in Front
- Staying Ahead of Change
- Ahead of the curve
- Take the Lead
- Vision in Practice
- Seeing things differently
- When it counts
- When your future is at stake
- Your guide to the top
- Challenge us
- Not if, but how
- Attorneys who make things happen
- It's not just business. It's personal.
- Leaders in the law of ideas
- Where leaders go
- A history to leverage
- Think/Results
- Thinking Ahead
- A Better Legal System
- Exceeding expectations

*And the longest:*
- A tradition of quality services, hard work and innovation has established X as one of the Nation's leading law firms

**Source:** http://www.lawmarketing.com/pages/articles.asp?Action=Article&ArticleCategoryID=6&ArticleID=173

## Two Good Taglines

In reviewing over 100 taglines for this chapter, I found very few that do a good job of identifying the firm mission and differentiating themselves from the pack. Here are my selections:

### Osler Hoskins & Harcourt

Class Action Defense in Canada

*This firm clearly understands its mission.*

### Jackson Lewis

All we do is Work

*This is a labor law firm, and I love the sense of self-deprecation, which makes it stand out against the self-importance of other law firm taglines.*

### Runner-up: Baker & Daniels

Est. 1863. We Know the Territory.®

*While it says little about goals, at least this tagline clearly differentiates the firm from its competitors!*

## 5. The Use of Color

Color can be an important element of brand identity. Colors and color combinations, used consistently, can powerfully reinforce the identity and remind the audience, even in the absence of text, of the source of the information. Think about:

- McDonald's Golden Arches
- The red frame cover of *Time*
- IBM's signature blue

While we are accustomed to color in commercial brands, we don't think of it much in law firms. But a study of law firm letterheads and logos showed that 25 of the nation's 100 largest law firms had added color by 2000, up from 18 in 1997.

The fields of psychology, graphic design, and industrial design have all added to our understanding of the impact of color. Individual colors, and color combinations, may have connotations within the target audience that make them particularly effective—or unsuitable:

- Red, white, and blue connote patriotism.
- Primary colors may evoke childhood or basics.
- Pastels may be perceived as feminine, subtle, or comfortable.
- Black and white can be clean, even stark, or may evoke a lack of nuance.
- Silver, purple, and other unusual shades are associated with modernity, and with change.
- Some colors are too trendy to use in a brand identity. What works for this year's fashion probably won't work for your letterhead.

### Color

One law firm has taken a bold and innovative approach to the use of color. Sonnenschein (formally Sonnenschein, Nath & Rosenthal) launched a firm identity that played off this name, which means "sunshine." To reinforce this point, and make a difficult name more memorable, the firm brand uses tones of yellow and gold, the purple of sunset, and a charming little golden ring in the middle of its name. The firm website and brochures reinforce the message with pictures of skies, sunsets, and clouds, as does the firm tagline, "See the light."

There are only two reasons to use color, and they reinforce each other:

1. To make your brand more memorable.
2. To reinforce your core message.

To accomplish these goals requires you to use color thoughtfully. Consider how the color works in all brand contexts (including the web), how it will affect readability, and what connotations might be associated with the color within your key audience. Should a bankruptcy firm use red, or green, both of which are associated with finance and money?

## 6. Design Elements

A brand identity is not just an explicit message. All the elements of the brand should work together. Every aspect of the brand should reinforce your core message.

Some lawyers think that design is beneath them, that it detracts from their substance.

That's a lot of high-minded hooey. Greenfield/Belser, a national marketing design firm, puts it beautifully:

*Design gives form substance.*

You are designing already—by putting print on paper, by putting color on a website. If you don't have a brand identity, you may be making one randomly, without advancing your firm's core message.

Design elements are merely templates, patterns, and graphics that are used consistently to unify your communications and to reinforce your core message visually. They tell the reader in nonverbal ways that this communication comes from your firm. The use of a design template, with consistent elements across various delivery platforms, will strengthen your brand identity. Combining your color palette with consistent use of design elements will evoke a stronger brand identity.

Design elements like typefaces, borders, and templates work with logos and taglines to create and reinforce the message. Coca-Cola and *Time* magazine use not only recognizable colors but also design elements (a wave logo and bottle shape for Coke, and a masthead typeface and cover frame for *Time*) that reinforce the brand through repetition.

You may think it boring to repeat your design elements. But you have limited opportunities to get the attention of your target audience, and brand must be repeated to have any impact. Any message that is delivered without your firm brand is an opportunity wasted.

Creating a brand identity through visual cues is as much a process of subtraction as addition. The busier the designs, the more difficult it is to identify the consistent elements that make up the brand identity. With visually strong design elements and a powerful color palette, the overall design must be spare to remain recognizable.

Consistent use of color and design templates does not mean that the brand identity has to be repetitive or boring. Simple design can be both creative and powerful. Even within templates, there is ample opportunity for creativity without undermining the elements that reinforce brand identity.

**Visual Cues**

In our firm logo, dots help to identify all messages as coming from the firm:

The visual element reinforces the message of change, as the dots change from circles to squares. We repeat this design element, sometimes straightening the curve, to increase its impact. Even our outgoing mailing labels incorporate our signature dots.

The Nike "Swoosh" is an extreme example of spare design that has become an instantly recognizable and powerful brand identity. In fact, the Swoosh logo is so powerful that Nike regularly uses it without any brand name.

## A Case Study

When the client came to us, they were using the name "Knowledge Connections, Inc." and had no formal brand.

In discussion with the clients a core message emerged:

*KCI brings knowledge management to corporate law departments, to help identify organizational knowledge and connect those who need it to those who have it.*

We worked with the client to develop a brand identity to convey this message to target audiences.

**Brand Name:** We recommended that the firm change its name to KCI, for KnowConnect, Inc. This name is simpler, more memorable, and conveys the cutting-edge nature of the work. We suggested that they reserve the URL, www.knowconnect.com because it was easier to remember than their former URL.

**Tagline:** The tagline "know. connect." conveys clearly and concisely what knowledge management does for law departments.

**Logo:** The bridge emerging from the fog became KCI's logo because it is the perfect metaphor for the firm's message: In most law departments there is too much information (the fog); when you identify key information (emerge from the fog) and make it easier for people to connect to information and to one another (the bridge), you create efficiency (you get there from here).

In the logo, the letters "KCI" emerge from the fog, leading to clarity. On the firm business cards, the partner's first name similarly emerges from the rectangle, also creating a subtle frame for each partner's nickname:

**Fonts:** Hei, an unusual sans serif font, gives the brand identity its modern, clean lines. Formatting the logo without caps emphasizes simplicity. Periods in the phone number echo those in the tagline, eliminating additional characters.

**Color Palette:** Black and white, with elements of cool grey, provide the right palette for the client's message of simplification.

**Design Elements:** A simple thick horizontal rule completes the design elements:

———————————————— know. connect.

The rule leads sometimes to the firm name, sometimes to the tagline. Like a bridge or a road, it arrives at a destination.

Subtle variations of the font, logo, tagline, and rule combine to create all the firm's communications: letterhead, business cards, website, and PowerPoint template.

The result is a clear, unified brand that

▌ reinforces the firm's core message,
▌ clearly identifies the firm as the source of its communications, and
▌ builds confidence in and loyalty to the firm's communications.

## Where to Brand

Once you develop a brand, the next question is where to use it. The simple answer is, everywhere. Everywhere that your firm name appears, your firm brand should be used. Okay, you may not be able to brand in the state bar directory listing, but wherever you have control over the output, your brand should be used.

It's amazing, when you stop to evaluate it, how much comes out of your firm and how little of it is currently branded. So when you are developing your brand, do this kind of inventory, and create a list of places (called "platforms") where your brand should be implemented. At a minimum, this list should include:

- Business cards
- Rate or service information cards
- Letterhead
- Invoices and statements
- Note cards
- Packaging, including envelopes, mailing labels, and even stamps
- Website, including the URL
- Signage, including building lobby and office reception signage
- PowerPoint presentations
- Deliverables, including firm brochures and client information sheets
- Corporate gifts
- Advertising, including Yellow Pages ads

### Heller Ehrman Brands Right Down to Its E-mail

At Heller Ehrman, the brand goes all the way to its e-mail auto-signature.

The firm stylebook explains how the auto-signature works:

**AutoSignature Format**

- The HEWM standard AutoSignature is as follows:

**AutoSignature for Heller Ehrman:**

| Arial 10 Bold | | Arial 10 | | Garamond 12 Bold |

**Barry S. Levin** | [Title] | **HellerEhrman** | 333 Bush Street | San Francisco, CA 94104
tel: 415.772.6646 | fax: 415.772.6268 | email: blevin@hewm.com | web: www.hewm.com
Heller Ehrman White & McAuliffe LLP

Use non-breaking spaces (Ctrl, shift space) between the special character | before each word and between the sections for names, titles, VLG, street address, city, etc.

The firm explains the decision to extend its brand in this format:

"Because e-mail is becoming the predominant form of communication (almost more than the use of business cards, stationery, and other printed materials), our electronic closing must be the same across the firm. One of the hallmarks of a strong brand is the consistent, professional presentation of its identity."

*Thanks to John Buchanan of Heller Ehrman for the information in this sidebar.*

## Launching a Brand

Your brand is ready to deploy. What do you do next?

1. Have all your printed material done at once. There's no sense spending the time and money developing a brand and then rolling it out piecemeal. Printing costs are often cheaper if you do it all at once.
2. Have everything (letterhead, envelopes, labels, business cards, coffee mugs) delivered and staged in a holding area. Release everything to your staff at one time. Make it a party!
3. Produce a firm stylebook. The book will give everyone an overview of what you are doing and why. Include samples of the new letterhead, labels, note cards, envelopes, as well as guidelines for using the new brand.
4. Use Word, WordPerfect, or Adobe Acrobat Professional to design new templates for your computer-generated forms, letterhead, memos, and fax cover sheets. Create a file on the server with the elements of the brand and the templates. When users log into the system after the rollout, the new firm identity should load onto everyone's computer.
5. Write an "open letter" to the firm on the new letterhead. Every employee should receive a corporate identity launch set that includes your note, a branded coffee mug, the stylebook, new stationery, and business cards.
6. Remove all old materials from desks, the supply room, and printers, and restock them with the new materials.
7. Replace all of the graphics and logos on your website.
8. Create a gift box for your best clients with a note, a coffee mug, and your firm brochures and business cards with the new brand.
9. Ask your staff to let you know how else they think the new firm identity should be used, and have a cake with the brand in the icing to celebrate after your first week, when the change is completed.
10. Purchase a branded item every few months to keep the momentum going. Add self-stick notepads, pens, or luggage tags—whatever your staff and clients would find useful and keep handy. Make sure your law firm holiday card is branded.

*Thanks for permission to use this list to Steven R. Boutwell, Director of Client Services, Kean, Miller, Hawthorne, D'Armond, McCowan & Jarman, LLP, Baton Rouge, Louisiana 70821-3513; steve.boutwell@keanmiller.com*

## Conclusion

- Branding starts with the identification of your firm's core message.
- A brand should reinforce your firm's core message, verbally and visually.
- In a competitive environment, it is essential to deliver a brand identity to support and reinforce your firm's core message.
- A brand should differentiate you from your competitors.
- A brand identity can dramatically improve audience attention to your communication.
- A good brand clearly identifies your firm as the source of information.
- A strong brand identity will convey the message that you are a sophisticated and polished professional.
- A strong brand helps you communicate clearly and effectively, a key to convincing clients of the value of your services.
- A clear message will help potential clients, and referring lawyers, understand and remember your firm's unique qualities.
- Your firm communications are a key piece of your deliverables. They should be as professional and polished as the substance you deliver.

## *Branding Bibliography*

### Branding Books

Beckwith, Harry. *Selling the Invisible: A Field Guide to Modern Marketing.* Warner Business, 1997.

Belser, Berkey, and Donna Greenfield. *25 Years of Legal Branding.* Sunnyside Press, 2004.

Gobe, Marc. *Emotional Branding: The New Paradigm for Connecting Brands to People.* Watson-Guptill, 2001.

Mark, Margaret, and Carol S. Pearson. *The Hero and the Outlaw: Harnessing the Power of Archetypes to Create a Winning Brand.* McGraw-Hill, 2002.

Morgan, Adam. *Eating the Big Fish: How Challenger Brands Can Compete Against Brand Leaders.* Wiley, 1999.

Ries, Al, and Laura Ries. *The 22 Immutable Laws of Branding.* HarperBusiness, 2002.

————. *The 11 Immutable Laws of Internet Branding.* HarperCollins, 2000.

————. *The Origin of Brands: Discover the Natural Laws of Product Innovation and Business Survival.* HarperCollins, 2004.

Ries, Al, and Jack Trout. *Positioning: The Battle for Your Mind.* McGraw-Hill, 2000.

Schmitt, Bernd H. *Marketing Aesthetics: The Strategic Management of Brands, Identity and Image.* Free Press, 1997.

Trout, Jack. *Differentiate or Die: Survival in Our Era of Killer Competition.* Wiley, 2000.

————. *The New Positioning: The Latest on the World's #1 Business Strategy.* McGraw-Hill, 1997.

Wheeler, Alina. *Designing Brand Identity: A Complete Guide to Creating, Building, and Maintaining Strong Brands.* Wiley, 2003.

### Communication Books

Johnson, Sammye, and Patricia Prijatel. *The Magazine from Cover to Cover: Inside a Dynamic Industry.* McGraw-Hill, 1999.

King, Stacey. *Magazine Design That Works.* Rockport, 2001.

Lancaster, Lynne C., and David Stillman. *When Generations Collide: Who They Are. Why They Clash. How to Solve the Generational Puzzle at Work.* HarperBusiness, 2003.

Marton, Jill. *Color Voodoo #1: A Guide to Color Symbolism.* ColorCom, 2001.
and the other CDs in the Color Voodoo series.

Rostelnick, Charles, and David D. Roberts, *Designing Visual Language: Strategies for Professional Communicators.* Longman, 1977.

Tufte, Edward. *The Cognitive Style of PowerPoint.* Graphics Press, 2003.

————. *Envisioning Information.* Graphics Press, 1990.

————. *Visual Explanations: Images and Quantities, Evidence and Narrative.* Graphics Press, 1997.

Wurman, Richard Saul. *Information Anxiety 2.*
Pearson Education, 2000.
———— . *Understanding.* Ted Conferences, 1999.
and other *Understanding* books.

## Online Resources
### Branding
Bodine, Larry. "Regis McKenna Dumps on
Branding."
http://www.lawcommerce.com/clientdev/
art_bodine_marketingrelations.asp
Buchdahl, Micah. "Establishing Your 'Brand'
in the Law Firm Marketplace."
http://marketing.lp.findlaw.com/articles/
buchdahl01.html
Greenfield/Belser, Ltd., http://www.gbltd.com
The best legal branding site on the Internet;
their 1999 study on law firm branding is the
original authority on the topic. Lots of valuable
information that you can download for free to
see how the big firms do it.
Lawson, Jerry, Brenda Howard, and Dennis
Kennedy, ABA Law Practice Management
Section, "The Internet Roundtable #34:
A Continuing Discussion of Law Firm
Marketing on the Internet."
http://www.abanet.org/lpm/lpt/articles/
mtk0214033.html

The Law Marketing Portal,
http://www.lawmarketing.com
Search for "branding."
Legal Management Resource Center,
http://thesource.alanet.org
Lots of valuable information; search for
"branding."
TheManager.org, http://themanager.org
Search for "branding" at this management
portal.
Semmes, Elonide C. "Why a Down Market is the
Right Time to Brand."
http://marketing.lp.findlaw.com/articles/
semmes01.html

### Color
Color Matters, http://www.colormatters.com

Resources on Color:
http://www.colormatters.com/link.html
Lee, Na Ree. "Colour as a Tool for e-Branding."
http://www.colormatters.com/research/
nrl_ebrand.pdf

### Design
Timoshenko, Walter. "Own Thy Own Logo."
http://www.lawmarketing.com/pages/articles.asp
?Action=Article&ArticleCategoryID=7&ArticleID
=102

**Fonts**

Bernard, Michael, Melissa Mills, Michelle Peterson, & Kelsey Storrer. "A Comparison of Popular Online Fonts: Which is Best and When?" http://psychology.wichita.edu/surl/usabilitynews/ 3S/font.htm

Resources on Fonts: http://desktoppub.about.com/od/typelegibility/ or search "font readability"

Sanchez, Mario. "Web-Safe Fonts for Your Site." http://www.accordmarketing.com/tid/archive/ websafefonts.html or search "web-safe fonts"

Website Readability: http://www.leafdigital.com/class/lessons/ graphicdesign1/3.html

Wilson, Ralph F. HTML E-Mail: Text Font Readability Study http://www.wilsonweb.com/wmt6/ html-email-fonts.htm

**Naming**

Javed, Naseem. "Three Golden Rules of Naming." http://www.abcnamebank.com/GoldenRules .html

Meyerowitz, Steven A. "Law Firms Gain Notice by Adopting Shorter Names." http://www.lawmarketing.com/pages/articles.asp ?Action=Article&ArticleCategoryID=7&ArticleID =308

# 6

# Making Rainmaking Part of Your Daily Practice

# §6.1 Five Easy Ways to Use Daily Activities as Marketing Tools

*David J. Abeshouse*

Those solo and small firm practitioners who neither were born with nor inherited a built-in client base must develop a solid client foundation and steady stream of new clients the old fashioned way: They must earn it. Various ways to do this have been well documented. Now we will focus on everyday things you can do that might come to you naturally—those that therefore are, relatively speaking, easy, at least in terms of overcoming the motivational barriers to starting and following through, and also are low-cost and low-tech. Drawing an analogy to diets and exercise, these marketing techniques also can become valued components of daily life, once the initial mind-set barriers have been surmounted. In addition to basic considerations such as the nature of your practice and the amount of time you can make available for this purpose, selecting the particular techniques with which you'll start should be predicated upon which appear most attractive to you, as those are the ones that you'll likely pursue with the most ardor. The best strategies for law marketing often tend to focus on what comes naturally. Perhaps some of the handful of ideas that follow will appeal to you, or at least spark other ideas consonant with your personality. A measure of inspiration is beneficial, if not essential, in the quest for networking success.

## #1: Send a Useful and Personal Message

Many of us are voracious readers, "information hounds" who sniff out a wealth of useful knowledge on a wide variety of subjects across many different contexts: business, professional, personal, and even trivial. We seek knowledge that is both broad and deep.

Others of us are not, perhaps because we lack the time, interest, initiative, or other characteristics necessary to such an undertaking.

Those of us who are information hounds can help those of us who are not, and if it is done thoughtfully, the "nots" often will appreciate this assistance from the "ares." Here's one simple way you can make it happen.

For many years, even long before I ever thought about business or professional networking (which, I confess, I think about a lot these days), I regularly felt the urge (and acted upon it) to share my informational discoveries with those who I thought might benefit from them. This was altruism for the sake of helping colleagues and acquaintances. As many networkers have come to realize over the years, a good measure of altruism—in its various forms—ironically is perhaps the best basis for building one's business or professional practice. That the intent to help others now may be accompanied by the realization that they later may in turn reciprocate does not detract from the value of the assistance provided; instead, it reflects the development of a relationship and a stronger basis for working together in the future.

Back to our simple way: A couple of years ago, I asked my business printers to create for me a mini-letterhead card about four by six inches containing my name and contact information at the top, just beneath a horizontal fold line about an inch from the top of the page. Whenever I come across a Web or print article or other item likely to be of interest to someone on my list, I copy it, and chicken-scratch a short and simple handwritten note (e.g., "Dear Mary: I thought this article might be of interest to you. I hope it's useful, and look forward to speaking with you soon. Best regards, David"). I fold on the line and staple the mini-letterhead to the article, pop it into a stamped envelope, and hand it over to the U.S. Postal Service. There's no magic here, but there may be a bit of elegance in the simplicity of the straightforward technique.

I often do a variant of this by e-mail or occasionally by fax, but I think these are not quite as effective as the personally handwritten and mailed missive, unless time is of the essence or I know

## More Ways to Use the Five Easy Ways

To overcome motivational barriers, use marketing techniques based on everyday tasks that come naturally to you.

### #1: Useful and Personal Message
Altruistic helping of others is one of the best bases for building your professional practice; sending useful information is an excellent way to convey your helpful nature.

### #2: Business Networking Group
Taking an active leadership role is the key to success in a business or professional networking group; passive members enjoy far fewer opportunities.

### #3: Outside Board of Directors
An outside board can provide the solo with a wealth of viewpoints based on the different experiences of its members, to address a variety of practice management issues better than the solo can alone.

### #4: Volunteering
By volunteering in the community, you place yourself in a position of authority and work toward a common goal with others who will see firsthand who you are and how you operate.

### #5: Mutual Assistance
Many of those close to you may understand far less about what you do than you might think; here is a structured way to let them know how to help refer appropriate work to you, and for you to offer to reciprocate.

### Bonus Way: Advising Others
Help others, and they may help—or hire—you.

the recipient has permanently forsworn opening any nonelectronic correspondence.

Following up with a phone call or e-mail a week or two later provides the icing on the cake. Often, I don't need to take that additional step, because the recipient (the ubiquitous Mary) already has called or e-mailed to thank me and, on occasion, to refer me to a lead generated out of appreciation.

This simple act of information-sharing sends the right message by conveying that you were thinking about the recipient and cared enough to communicate personally. In this highly electronic age, it doesn't hurt to show that you still remember how to use handwritten "snail mail," which is undeniably more personal than e-mail. It also puts your name in front of those who you would like to have thinking about you.

## #2: Join—and Actively Participate in—a Business Networking Group (or Two or Three)

Whether it is a "mandatory bring a lead get a lead" networking group (which may raise some ethical considerations depending on your state's governing laws and regulations), an independent noncompetitive group, a national or local bar association committee, or a new so-called "urban tribe" group (young, single, educated city-dwellers who connect to find romance, friendship, shelter, and work), membership in one or two quality business networking groups can yield significant professional rewards. Membership alone, however, rarely garners satisfactory results. Instead, a demonstrated commitment to active leadership such as service on the executive committee or board of the group, or as its de facto legal counsel, ensures that you are well positioned to reap whatever opportunities might exist within the group.

Experience demonstrates that those who appear most dissatisfied with a particular networking group (or even with the concept of networking) usually are those who invest the least effort in it. This is not a mere tautology. When fellow group members see that you are someone who engages, commits, acts, and achieves results, they are more likely to want to do business with you and to refer to you those in their spheres of influence. In essence, it is the ultimate job interview or sales meeting; but it is better than that because it is in a real setting and takes place over time, allowing you to demonstrate continuity. This falls squarely into the category of actions speaking louder than words. Caution: Not all networking groups are created equal, and many may not serve your particular interests or goals. If you are investing appropriate effort and nevertheless remain dissatisfied, consider finding a different group better suited to your personality and practice.

A colleague (let's call him Larry the Lawyer) asked me not long ago to give him an informal crash course on business networking for lawyers. Larry is a smart, experienced, congenial, able lawyer who throughout his career has not managed to originate sufficient new business to make him as valuable to his firm as he would like. Over lunch, we discussed the sorts of things he likes to do and those that he prefers to avoid. He concluded that he was not well suited for business networking because he saw no networking possibilities in the things he likes to do (perform in local theater, cook, and attend sporting events). I pointed out a few examples of the many opportunities those activities provide (serve on the managing board or as general counsel to a local theater group, join a cooking class geared to business professionals, join a networking group that holds meetings or special events at sporting venues), and encouraged Larry to dip his toe into the waters of business networking through activities in which he demonstrates interest, experience, expertise, and enjoyment. I am hopeful that he will be able to fulfill his wishes while enjoying himself in their pursuit.

## #3: Join—or Form—an Outside Board of Directors Group

Many small-business proprietors complain about the isolation they experience when trying to manage and guide their companies, both on day-to-day matters as well as broader planning and policy issues. It is no different for solo and small law firm owners. General Motors can afford a bevy of well-compensated outside directors; solos cannot. Legal mega firms have a diverse wealth of in-house talent supplemented by outside consultants; solos do not. The solution for small firm practitioners is either to join an established outside board of directors group—there are several national organizations such as The Alternative Board (TAB) and The Executive Committee (TEC)—or form an informal local board of your own: Start with a couple of law and/or business colleagues whom you respect and trust, and ask them to invite others of similar caliber. The legal and business marketing gems offered by group members often will apply to your practice as well. And the group need not limit its focus to marketing alone; it can discuss and analyze various business problems and issues, and even serve as a quasi-networking group, generating leads and referrals as well as answers.

An interdisciplinary group (several different types of law practitioners and even other types of small businesses) likely will yield the richest benefits because this sort of group will have the most diverse experience. You can glean much from the knowledge of those in other disciplines and modify it for application to your practice. If all "board" members are similarly motivated, trustworthy, expert, committed, and ethical, the results can be astounding. Be sure to plan in advance such aspects as frequency and locations of meetings, confidentiality, single or shared leadership, meeting format and agenda, cost of membership, whether competitors will be permitted in the group, and other requisites. The efforts expended in organizing and maintaining the groups simply constitute the price you pay for the rewards, and experience teaches that it can be well worth it.

## #4: Volunteer in Preferred Arenas Using Unique Skills

By their very nature, small businesses and law firms depend more on their local communities than do large corporations and firms. You don't succeed in a community without getting involved. It's good for business, for the community, and ultimately for you. To enhance your work satisfaction and enjoyment of your local community, you and your law firm should become good corporate citizens.

The range of rewards for good corporate citizenship is broad:

- It brings personal satisfaction, because you can choose the public service arenas in which you and your firm will become active.
- You'll meet other legal and business leaders and get to know them face to face, often outside their normal "business personalities." This interaction can be personally rewarding—and it expands your network of legal and business contacts.
- You'll keep from being too one-dimensional through your work. If you don't have time for community involvement, you probably should make time for it.
- If you're running your own practice, you may have been luckier than many. Making your firm a good corporate citizen is a way to give something back.
- When businesspeople go out of their way to make an impact on the community, that's news. You may garner positive press coverage for your efforts.

- You can increase the quality of the employees you draw to your firm. Your community commitment will attract other hard-working, like-spirited people.

In the context of the small firm, your community activities will typically have a greater impact on how your firm is viewed than the activities of a single partner at a larger firm will have on the community's view of that firm. Thus, your community efforts are arguably even more meaningful for rainmaking than those of the Big Firm lawyers. Take advantage of this and you have the proverbial win-win situation.

So what can you as a solo or small firm lawyer do in your community as a volunteer that also will enhance your reputation and help position you for bringing in new business? That depends on the nature of your community (what is available) and the nature of your practice and personality (your unique skills and interests). As a general rule, managing or administering or advising or consulting are roles often undertaken by lawyers volunteering in the community, beyond pro bono lawyering. Find something that will expose you directly or indirectly to your target audience and is either related to your principal practice areas or to your outside interests and hobbies; or find something new that appears

attractive even if unrelated to your past experience. Join the board of directors of a not-for-profit corporation or serve as its general counsel. Experience demonstrates that placing oneself in a position of some authority while volunteering toward a goal with others who are similarly inclined is a strategy designed to be fulfilling in more than one respect.

## #5: Send a "Mutual Assistance" Message to Those with Whom You Are Close

Following this suggestion takes some careful thought and preparation, and should be implemented on a slow, selective basis. Again, the potential rewards are considerable. This technique is founded upon two basic circumstances:

### Circumstance #1

Many lawyers simply assume that those close to them (friends, relatives, cocounsel, long-time clients) know what the lawyer's areas of practice, experience, and abilities are. This often is a mistaken assumption. Others' understandings of what a lawyer does frequently are at considerable variance with reality, even if the others are regularly in contact with the lawyer.

## Circumstance #2

Those who are close to you care about how you are doing. They want you to do well. This sentiment is heightened when you demonstrate the reciprocal sentiment to them. When someone expresses an interest in helping you, you in turn are more likely to want to help him or her. What goes around, comes around.

So what is the "mutual assistance" message concept predicated upon these two circumstances? Simply put, it is a document, carefully crafted by you and sent by e-mail or regular snail mail (preferably to one or two test recipients initially, and never more than a few at one time) that tells others concretely what you do, whom you tend to represent, and what you seek; it also asks them to provide their own information so that you can reciprocate. The personal nature of this communication militates against a mass mailing, and is best undertaken on an individual basis.

This technique has been quite successful when prepared and presented carefully, used sparingly (in a targeted fashion, directed toward the right people), and offered in the true spirit of reciprocity.

## Bonus Way: Give Nuggets of Advice in Your Areas of Expertise

Welcome phone calls from colleagues and networking acquaintances seeking limited legal or similar advice. Help them write a basic letter that may secure or bolster their legal position in an area of concern to them, if you are familiar with the area. Some may deem this a bit controversial because it can be misunderstood

### "Mutual Assistance" Document Outline

Dear Friend/Colleague:

Here are several **key characteristics of prospective clients** that would be good leads for me:

_____

**Types of client entities** I represent include:

_____

**Key contacts** at client companies usually are:

_____

Some **representative clients** include:

_____

Sample **categories of cases** include:

_____

Illustrative **examples of several specific matters** include:

_____

My firm is **dedicated** to _____
An important focus of the practice is
_____

I also undertake _____

Several ways in which I believe I **distinguish** myself from other able lawyers who serve a similar clientele include: _____

My **top wish** at the moment:
_____

So—what's your info?
And what can I do to try to help you?
Best regards,

David Abeshouse
davidlaw@optonline.net

as "free legal advice" that may create the same sorts of lawyer responsibilities as a regular attorney-client relationship without the attendant client responsibilities. However, a straightforward approach can communicate to the beneficiary of your legal largesse that this simply is a favor that does not create a formal relationship. That discussion can lead, however, to the explanation that if the matter proceeds further, your acquaintances may wish to formalize the relationship so that you can represent them in connection with the matter.

## Conclusion

No universal marketing panacea or rainmaking magic bullet exists. Rather, successful practice building generally requires strategic planning and consistent, regular implementation over time. Small firm and solo lawyers who wear many hats enhance their likelihood of success by designing a set of procedures that incorporates activities that are personally palatable because they will be better motivated to adhere to the program. In sports, it is not enough to hit or throw the ball hard; follow-through is essential to ensure directional accuracy. So it is with legal marketing, and if you enjoy implementing the elements of your marketing plan, you likely will do so with sufficient continuity to achieve success.

# §6.2 Effortless Marketing: Putting Your Unique Qualities to Work

## Melanie D. Bragg

If all lawyers were as naturally skilled in the courtroom as Perry Mason, we would live in a perfect world and rainmaking would not be an important topic. Lawyers are a diverse group of people with a variety of interests and abilities. For most of us, our professional skills are learned and honed until they become as ingrained as brushing our teeth.

There are many reasons you became a lawyer, but in today's highly competitive, increasingly technological work world, one thing is certain— cultivating the art of rainmaking is a vital necessity. Whether you are a member of a firm, on staff at a corporation, or on your own, you must develop and maintain a marketing "edge" in order to survive and thrive.

Let me demonstrate how easy it is to ADD to your law practice by following a simple formula: (1) *Assess yourself*; (2) *Decide what works for you*, and (3) *Do it!* By going through the three steps, you will determine your strengths and weaknesses, match them to your marketing activities, then develop a natural strategy to make the most out of your chosen profession. The goal is for you to enjoy yourself as you build and create the law practice of your dreams.

## A: Assess Yourself

You can't sell something you don't believe in. And you can't flourish in an environment that is not in harmony with who you are. When it comes to effortless marketing, the old saying you can't fit a square peg into a round hole applies. No matter where and how you started or where you are now, the path to effortless marketing is to know yourself, determine your assets and deficits, and identify what you really want out of the practice of law.

Sit down with a pen and paper. Pick a time when you can spend a couple of hours. Turn off the cell phone, close the office door, and then take a couple of deep breaths. With a pen and legal pad, draw a line through the middle of the page and begin your assessment. On one side, list your strengths; on the other, list your weaknesses.

Just thinking about these things isn't enough. When you write and see them on the page, you gain a better understanding of yourself. As you go through this process, think about where you are now and how you got there.

Start with your strengths. Make a list of what, so far in your practice, you like and what you are good at. What aspect of your workday gives you the greatest pleasure? Do you shine in the courtroom? Are you happiest in the library researching a legal concept? Or do you prefer to draft documents and conduct discovery? Are you best one-on-one, or do you love crowds? Does client interaction come easily? Do you like administrative tasks?

Elisa Southard teaches us how to take and utilize a personal inventory in her book, *Break Through the Noise: 9 Tools to Propel Your Marketing Message*. Don't rush. Take your time and just do some free association.

Then, in the other column, write down the daily activities you don't like. Think about what makes you procrastinate and what makes you pull your hair out. This list will give you insight into how, daily, you may go against your natural grain. Rainmaking will become effortless only when you excel at what you like.

Next, turn the page and start another list by detailing how you spend each day. What percen-tage of your time do you devote to work, to family, to exercise, to your spiritual development, to leisure, to friends, and to your community? Are chunks of time allotted to nonproductive activities that neither nourish nor develop your life? What tasks could be delegated to increase your productivity?

Take it a step further and really get in touch with where you are now. Think back to your roots. What were your happiest moments in college, law school, and the early years of your law career?

If you are on a roll, take it a step further— go back into your earlier years. What were you good at in school? What teachers did you like? Did sports or extracurricular activities occupy your extra time?

When I did this exercise, I remembered how in third grade, I was fascinated by a little collection of books in our school library about first ladies like Martha Washington, Dolly Madison, and Abigail Adams. From an early age, I read anything I could get my hands on. I worked in the school and law library. And I served as a research assistant in college and law school. I've been an adjunct professor and plan to return again in the future. It is no surprise that I derive the most joy and pleasure in my profession in these areas.

Look at where are you in your practice. Are you satisfied with what you have? If so, maybe you just want to take on a few new clients, or start up a new area of practice. Or maybe you want to switch gears. Would you admit it to yourself if you are sticking with a job or practice area you don't truly enjoy because of security or the fear of starting something new? If you are opting for security, is it an illusion, or is it real? Be honest with yourself.

In your self-assessment, whose voice are you listening to? Be sure it's your own. I know people who are miserable because they are living out someone else's plan for their life, rather than their own dream.

Think about how you take in and give information. Are you visual, auditory, or kinetic? Awareness in this area will help you figure out which marketing activities will work best for you.

As you take inventory, some new ideas may just jump out at you. You may recognize a pattern you didn't see before and learn why rainmaking may be a challenge.

And be realistic about your abilities. Some people are meant to be Olympic skiers and some are meant to sell skis. Your goals and dreams should line up with your skills and strengths. After serving as a briefing lawyer for an appellate court, I started my own practice. Business came easily, but I didn't have a plan. Years later, I ended up with a staff of five and a heavy caseload.

For me, the lightbulb came on late one Friday night. I sat in my big, expensive office and realized I was burned out. I had become an administrator. My days were spent answering questions about whether to use Ozarka Spring water or Mountain Valley, Folgers or Starbucks. I spent more time delegating and checking on delegation than doing legal work. The accumulation of stress was reflected in my health.

That night was a turning point. I made the list I recommend today and realized that I was not doing what best suited my nature. Administration was not my forte and I realized I didn't want to build a big law office. I'm more inclined toward the creative aspects of the law than the details. As a result of my analysis, I scaled down my caseload and reduced my expenses. (Like Tom Cruise in *Jerry McGuire* said, "Fewer clients, less money.") As I worked toward the transformation of my practice, my health improved and I began to have more fun. I've spent the last ten years building a business that suits my interests and needs, and allows me to still be truly excited about the practice of law.

Keep in mind that there isn't one formula for all. Some lawyers, like Jane Barrett, the first woman chair of the American Bar Association Young Lawyers Division, have a natural affinity for law practice management. At the ripe old age of 36, Jane was the youngest managing partner in a major California firm at the same time she was serving as the first woman on the ABA Board of Governors. The key is understanding yourself, knowing where you want to go, and where you need to be.

## B: Decide What Works for You

Armed with your self-assessment, now begin step two of the effortless marketing plan by looking at different rainmaking activities and decide which of them will work best for you. Pinpoint rainmaking activities that will complement your skills and unique personality traits and that will blend naturally into your daily routine.

As I began to write this section, I realized some people might think they don't have the right personality to market effectively and that rainmaking only comes easy to extraverted people. In her book, *What's Holding You Back? Thirty Days to Having the Courage and Confidence to Do What You Want, Meet Whom You Want and Go Where You Want,* author Sam Horn devotes several chapters to this subject. She says, "The good news is that you can nurture a shy nature if you so choose. Even if you are predisposed to being a 'social coward,' as one of my students put it, you can acquire the ability to be more socially confident. That's what being a grown-up is all about—evaluating your behavior to see if it's helping or hindering you. If your current interpersonal skills are contributing to your confidence, great. If they're compromising it, you have the power to change." I agree with her assessment. No one is exempt from the need to cultivate the skill of rainmaking.

Do you currently incorporate rainmaking into your day-to-day life? There are a variety of different ways to market. You can join legal or community organizations, speak at CLE events, publish papers, or coach a little league team. The list is endless. Make a list of possible activities and then figure out which of them fit into your daily life. Commit to do at least one marketing activity each day.

In my case, I am often at the courthouse and carry a file of resumes in my briefcase. Sometimes I get lucky and have the opportunity to walk from the parking garage to the courthouse with a judge or a lawyer I would like to work with.

I simply pull out a resume and hand it to them, along with a card. Earlier this year, I landed a plum guardian ad litem appointment just by slowing down long enough to remind a judge that I needed work. Much to my surprise, his court coordinator called the next morning with a new case. It confirmed my belief that we must always be ready to seize opportunities to develop our business, even when we are not "in the mood," or when we cannot immediately see the outcome.

STRETCH YOURSELF. Sometimes you just have to force yourself to venture into a new area. It's ok to "shake things up." Just for fun, personal growth, and to expand your rainmaking skills, go to a professional group you've never found time to attend; say yes instead of no when the next invitation comes in to go to a social event that doesn't normally interest you; expand your boundaries; and test yourself. You will be surprised at the results.

## C: Do It!

The last step of the ADD formula is *do it!* Don't let the title of this section fool you into thinking you can "do nothing" in order to master the art of rainmaking. The reality is that you often must do things that go against the natural grain of your personality. If you have to, do it afraid!

My friend Rosemary Sullivan, an insurance defense lawyer, told me her first boss, W. Garney Griggs, said that walking into a room to do client development can be like being "whipped with a wet towel, but you just have to get in there and do it."

We may think we aren't good at something because we did it as a child and didn't succeed, or because someone told us we couldn't do it and we never tried.

Along those lines, I try to always remember what Theodore Roosevelt said: "Far better it is to dare mighty things, to win glorious triumphs, even though checkered by failure, than to take rank with those poor spirits who neither enjoy much nor suffer much, because they live in the gray twilight that knows not victory nor defeat." Or, what a well-known trial lawyer once said, "If you don't try 'em, you don't win 'em."

We have to face the fact that failing is a big part of law practice and a big part of life. Step out there and do something different. There is nothing to lose and everything to gain. If it doesn't work out, then you won't be any further behind than you were when you started and there's a good chance you will come out ahead.

Expand on what you are already doing. The better you get at it, the less effort it will take to excel and the more time you will have to devote to other facets of your life.

In his best-selling book *The Power of Focus,* Jack Canfield devotes a great deal of time to the subject of developing good habits. He says that successful people have successful habits and that your habits will determine your future, your quality of life. He says quality is not an act, it's a habit.

Effortless marketing requires momentum. The more momentum you have, the easier it gets. When you are walking at a natural pace and rhythm, there is balance and order to your life; things just seem to fall into place. That's when you are in what the late Joseph Campbell, author of *Myths to Live By,* calls your "bliss spot." When you do what comes naturally and you enjoy it, your business will flourish.

Sometimes finding your bliss spot is not a straight line. You just have to know where you want to go and follow the twists and turns on the way. In the long run, if you do what you love, what comes naturally, the practice of law will become the rewarding career you dreamed of when you sent in your application and sat for the LSAT.

**For Extra Reading**

Campbell, Joseph. *Myths to Live By.* New York: Penguin Books (reprint), 1993.

Canfield, Jack, Mark Victor Hansen, and Les Hewitt. *The Power of Focus: How to Hit Your Business, Personal, and Financial Targets With Absolute Certainty.* Deerfield Beach, FL: HCI, 2000.

Horn, Sam. *What's Holding You Back? Thirty Days to Having the Courage and Confidence to Do What You Want, Meet Whom You Want, and Go Where You Want.* New York: St. Martins, 1997. (See also Tongue Fu and ConZentrate.)

Southard, Elisa. *Break Through the Noise: 9 Tools to Propel Your Marketing Message.* Walnut Creek, CA: MarketSkills Publications, 2004.

***Other Recommended Books of Interest***

Canfield, Jack, and Mark Victor Hansen. *The Aladdin Factor.* New York: Berkley, 1995.

Ramsland, Katherine. *Bliss: Writing to Find Your True Self.* Cincinnati: Walking Stick Press, 2000.

# §6.3 Rainmaking Tips from Solosez
### *Carolyn J. Stevens*

At one time or another, most of us have been responsible for rain-making, even if it was not an official part of our job. Naturally, if you start your career as a solo practitioner, you're also a solo rainmaker, responsible for seeding the clouds and maintaining the business. If you start out in a large law firm, other people or an entire department might research and implement the effective marketing techniques, which is great—but when you leave the firm, you leave their expertise behind.

What makes us memorable? We might advertise, volunteer, network at professional functions, and step by step build our reputations as good lawyers. But, inevitably, we often end up praying for rain. Where do you start? What works?

Rainmaking tips and comments for this discussion come from members of Solosez, the listserve sponsored by the American Bar Association General Practice, Solo and Small Firm Section. For more information about Solosez, go to http://www.abanet.org/soloseznet/.

**Caution:** Don't Try These at the Office without an Umbrella Handy

## Marketing, Branding, Advertising

Jay Foonberg (Santa Monica, California) reminds us that the three P's of marketing are Persistence, Persistence, Persistence. In marketing you don't "make mistakes"; you "learn lessons." Carolyn Elefant (Washington, D.C.) learned lessons early on.

Writing to large law firms for contract work wasn't successful, and neither was hosting an open house. Asking lawyers to lunch to learn about their practices resulted in "Come to my next seminar." But some "mistakes" lead to other things—such as the lawyer who notified her when prime space opened in his office. Randy Birch (Heber City, Utah) hosted a cocktail party and distributed five-by-eight-inch binders imprinted with his contact information. Alan C. Bail (Playa del Rey, California) garnered large-firm business through his legal and social contacts. He developed good professional relationships while working in a large firm and, after he went solo, the firm lawyers sent clients to him. He also had social relationships with decision makers in companies. At a volunteer organization's meeting, Bail talked casually about food, cooking, and Kauai with the chair's husband, who turned out to be president of a company. They met socially several more times and, after Bail visited the husband's headquarters, the company retained his services.

Brendon Carr (Seoul, Korea) created his firm's original website (http://www.auroralaw.co.kr) on a shoestring budget by using off-the-shelf programs. He used a cult program for the graphics, edited photos with a shareware program, and made the portraits with his digital camera. The page layout was courtesy of NetObjects Fusion MX and a few JavaScript components from Coolmaps Components Club. Carr even did the Flash animation. The early returns made him believe that a good Web site should be included in any solo's marketing plan.

Austin, Texas, lawyer Rob Robertson cannot imagine a law firm's URL becoming a household word like Yahoo; he considers his Web site's metatags, which garner hits during a search, more important than the URL. Chris Barber of Houston uses descriptive URLs and descriptive e-mail addresses. Not only are descriptive addresses easier for people to remember, they also allow Barber to filter both incoming and outgoing e-mail, according to whether the sender used Cbarber@TexasAttorney.net, Wills@TA.net, or Trusts@TA.net. Bruce Dorner (Londonderry, New Hampshire) starts with the premise that people are under a lot of stress when they look for a lawyer and often miss details. Instead of having inquiries answered by a "disembodied" e-mail presence, Dorner sends a note saying the caller might have a valid legal point and inviting the person to set up an appointment so they can explore the problem in greater detail. This method also helps to weed out casual shoppers.

## Writing and Speaking Engagements

Alan Clark (Freemans Bay, Auckland) wrote a short article for his local community monthly newsletter and at the same time purchased a small "professional card" ad that appeared on the facing page. Christian Vinaa (Gentofte, Denmark) advises that writing in a journalistic style, not a legal style, will attract many new clients.

Domenic A. Bellisario (Pittsburgh) is a presenter at National Business Institute (NBI) seminars. NBI sends about 10,000 mailings to lawyers and businesses around Pittsburgh and provides extra brochures for him to send clients and other contacts. The brochures include his bio, which increases his exposure. Bruce Dorner is a well-known presenter at CLE programs, where he makes sure to have fun, meet interesting people, and learn something new to take back to his own practice. Presenting is also a great way to become known as an authority in a field. Jimmy L. Verner's work as a presenter in Dallas keeps him current, provides a lot of CLE credit, and affords him many contacts. It's also fun. He suggests you are more likely to get referrals by speaking to groups of lawyers who don't practice in your field; they feel comfortable referring to you because they've heard you speak and you're not competing with them.

Chicago-area lawyer Shell J. Bleiweiss receives high evaluations when he speaks, but positive exposure doesn't often directly result in work. Nevertheless, he doesn't regret his efforts; speaking helps establish name recognition and a reputation as an expert in a field, which can lead to business. A supervisor chose Jay S. Goldenberg (Chicago) to present the IRS training course because he thought Jay would learn more than anyone from doing it. "He was right! You clarify your thinking and knowledge by explaining and you'll research and write many points, and you'll know the stuff." The business Rebecca Weiss gets from being a CLE presenter comes from two groups. First, she handles specialized litigation within her main real estate practice, and she makes sure that real estate lawyers know this. Her CLE presentations spread the word and bring in specific referrals from other lawyers. Second, nonlawyer professionals (real estate agents) who attend CLE classes refer their clients to Weiss when they need lawyers. Adam Shapiro (Philadelphia) appeared on a television call-in show mainly to make the public aware of his practice area, not thinking the callers would become clients. After the show, the other panelist said he was getting away from landlord-tenant work and, because Shapiro demonstrated knowledge on the topic, would refer cases to him. Sharon Campbell (Dallas) employs what she characterizes as an obvious marketing step—she asks for referrals at the end of her CLE presentations.

## Networking

Becki Fahle (San Antonio) recommends cold-calling referral sources and inviting them to lunch, morning coffee, or afternoon tea. Even doing this just once a week, she estimates, provides four or five new referral sources a month. E. Alexandra (Sasha) Golden's practice in Needham, Massachusetts, includes guardianship actions for nursing home residents. Nursing homes need lawyers, and families need information concerning Medicaid and related legal matters, so she cultivates relationships with nursing home social workers. During her first call from one facility's social worker, Golden mentioned she would have to visit the nursing home, read the record, talk with the social worker, and meet the resident before accepting the case. After the preliminary work, Golden invited the social worker for coffee, where she learned that the home's former lawyer considered site visits

a bother and did not do them. By "bothering" with a site visit and networking with the social worker, Golden learned that the employer owned ten nursing homes in the area. She gained a new friend and a lot of potential work.

## Business Cards

Randy Birch found a unique way to hand out cards. An old high school buddy who tended bar at Randy's favorite watering hole asked for a supply of Birch's cards, which he passed out to customers who complained about legal problems. This gambit brought a surprising amount of decent business, and Birch swears he hasn't been tarnished with the "Paul Newman in *The Verdict*" image of the barfly lawyer. (Although he hasn't yet cultivated all the local bartenders, he says there's still time.) A lawyer once told Becki Fahle that she would have a profitable practice by the time she gave away 2,000 business cards. Her closing letters contain two business cards and a request that the client retain one for future reference and give the other to someone in need of legal services. She suggests going one step further by affixing a mailing label "coupon" good for a free office visit to discuss new matters.

## Referrals

Referral services work for some people. Joseph Hughes (Berrien Springs, Michigan) recommends the state bar referral service and prepaid legal services networks. Marion Chase Pacheco (Syracuse, New York) got started by signing up with the local lawyer referral service. After a few months, she had so many cases she had to withdraw her listing. Rob Robertson had a similar experience but cautions that effectiveness varies from program to program. Fortunately, his local lawyer referral service leads to profitable work even if most callers do not engage him. On the other hand, his experience with legal insurance plans is that the clients generally pay small premiums and participating lawyers discount their fees, but clients expect "white-shoe law firm" representation. Sterling DeRamus (Birmingham, Alabama) pays $100 a year to be on a referral service list and considers the five or six hits per month it generates definitely worthwhile.

Volunteer and pro bono work led to business for Joseph Hughes. By connecting with Legal Services offices and volunteering his time, he also receives the bonus of free training. Pro bono legal work for a battered women's shelter, for example, helped him with his grasp of family and immigration law.

But client recommendations seem to be the best marketing tool. Joseph Hughes calls it "priceless"; John D. Kitch (Nashville) agrees. When he completes a piece of work for a client, he reminds the client of additional practice areas and other services he provides—wills, personal injury matters, contract review. Randy Birch keeps in touch with one repeat client, a sand and gravel company, by visiting its office once a month to have lunch, review files, and pick up new cases. "Sometimes I think it works too well," he reports.

## Keeping Clients Happy

Marion Browning-Baker (Stuttgart, Germany) tries to help every caller, even if she simply finds another lawyer who can help. "Do unto others," agrees Rod Klafehn (Laurens, New York); "give the kind of service you'd want from your own lawyer." In Nerino J. Petro's Loves Park, Illinois, area, preparing a client closing book is standard practice in commercial real estate deals, but it's not common in residential real estate. He prepares a closing book for all residential real estate clients and finds that the extra step does lead to referrals. New Zealand lawyer Alan Clark delivers Rolls Royce service from the first call until the case is completed. In Jacksonville Beach, Florida, Wendell Finner cuts to the core: "Diligently and efficiently do the work in front of you." And Shell Bleiweiss keeps it simple: "Answer the phone when it rings."

## Keeping in Touch

When you say goodbye to happy clients, you want them to remember you when they need legal help in the future. Some lawyers use personal cards to keep in touch. Charles Abut (Fort Lee, New Jersey) always sends a personal thank you for a client's or colleague's referral, even if he doesn't take the case. Vicki Levy (Lake Mary, Florida) writes notes for everything from thank you to condolences—and also brings along homemade cookies to the three main courthouses almost every time she's there.

Some lawyers use seasonal reminders. Becki Fahle's Thanksgiving cards are usually the first cards of the holiday season. Karen Robbins (Olney, Maryland) never deletes a name from her holiday card list (unless, of course, the person dies). People who haven't been clients for years still send other clients to her. "They all say they're tickled to know I still care about them even though they're no longer clients."

Each November Andrew Simpson (Christiansted, Virgin Islands), Patricia Joyce (East Greenwich, Rhode Island), and Rob Robertson send calendars. Simpson's calendar features local artists' work printed on high-quality paper ("suitable for framing"). Simpson affixes a clear label with a greeting and his contact information and includes a note with information about the artwork. Client comments throughout the year confirm that they remember the calendars came from him. Joyce's mailing is a tri-fold calendar card with "Best wishes for a healthy and prosperous 200X" and her contact information. The tri-fold doesn't get lost in the shuffle of holiday cards, and clients keep them all year. Robertson's is a 12-month ten-by-four-inch calendar with holiday dates—and the following year printed on the reverse. In early fall, clients and courthouse personnel begin asking Rob about the upcoming calendar; court coordinators hang it next to their seats in court, and judges routinely thank him. The calendars remind some clients to pay him and occasionally, years later, someone comes across an old calendar and calls him for services. He gives remaining calendars to new clients at the first conference.

Some lawyers use newsletters to keep in touch. Alan Clark sends a newsletter every three months to former clients so they will continue to think of him as their lawyer. Nicholas H. Cobbs (Washington, D.C.) sends a two-page office newsletter to clients, prospective clients, and other potential sources of business. The articles feature general legal matters: how to execute a judgment or take a deposition, the theory of negligence, and such. However, family law practitioner Jimmy Verner keeps in mind that family law clients usually aren't repeat customers and that sending materials might even be offensive to remarried clients. Instead, Verner sends a newsletter alert of legal developments to lawyers who don't practice family law and to family law lawyers who might want some help with a big family case.

Successful rainmaking comes from persistence, creativity, and variety. If one technique doesn't make rain today, it might work tomorrow. If a technique produces only a mild shower, thinking about it in a different way might produce a better result. To continue to explore new rainmaking ideas, simply connect with your GPSolo colleagues for new ideas.

# 7

# The Ten Most Common Ethical Rainmaking Mistakes Lawyers Make

*Barbara Glesner Fines*

## Mistake #1: Not Researching the Issues

You would not represent a client without adequate legal research and analysis of their case. You should always be as careful and competent in analyzing your client development activities. That the United States Supreme Court's holding that lawyer communication with potential clients is constitutionally protected speech does not mean it is unregulated speech. *Bates v. State Bar of Arizona*, 433 U.S. 350, 365, 374-75 (1977) (lawyer advertisement of routine legal services constitutes commercial speech, subject to intermediate level of scrutiny, and may not be subject to blanket ban).

**Even if the Marketing Experts Tell You. . .**

Lawyers are increasingly attending seminars or employing marketing experts to develop new and better techniques for rainmaking. Beware taking the advice of these experts without doing your own research on the ethical and regulatory issues. Even advice taken from a CLE program needs to be double-checked against your own state's rules. Learn from the tale of the Oklahoma lawyer who learned about a creative billing method in his family law practice and later received a public reprimand for charging prohibited contingent fees. His defense was that he had learned about the billing method at a state-bar-sponsored CLE program. One judge, writing in a separate opinion, commented, "It is troubling that although the rule is clear to the Court, at seminars conducted by the official arm of the Court, lawyers have been advised to engage in a billing practice which is contrary to the plain intent of the rule" but nonetheless concurred in the result. *State ex rel. Oklahoma Bar Ass'n v. Fagin*, 848 P.2d 11 (Okla. 1992).

On the contrary, lawyer advertising and solicitation are subject to detailed and aggressively policed regulation, regulation that varies considerably from state to state and changes over time. For example, do you know what your state's rules are regarding firm letterhead; e.g., can you include the name of a lawyer who is only "of counsel"? Do you need different letterhead for branch offices in a different state? What is your state's position on the use of trade names?

Have a copy of your state's rules of professional conduct at hand. Keep current on changes in the rules. Know how to locate any ethics opinions issued by your state's professional regulatory body (while rarely binding, they often provide the only answer for very specific situations).

Don't rely on gossip, assumptions, or the seat of your pants. If your instincts are that an idea sounds improper, it probably is. But even if your instincts tell you "there can't be anything wrong with that," do your research!

## Mistake #2: Not Cultivating Current Clients

Obviously, we represent our clients competently and professionally because our ethical duty demands nothing less. But in the rush to find the newest approach to rainmaking, we may forget that this competent and professional representation of our current clients is the best advertisement available. Even today, in our competitive and diverse legal market, most clients still prefer to find a lawyer by personal referral. You want your name to be

### Do Your Billing Practices Sell Your Practice?

Once you are representing a client, you should continue to "sell" your services. One of the best opportunities to be sure your client knows what good work you are doing is to let your regular billing statements reflect that work. Compare the marketing of a billing statement that reads "For professional services: $300" and one that reads: Professional services completed:

| | |
|---|---|
| 1.5 hours Legal research | $150 |
| 1.5 hours Investigation (witness interviews) | $150 |
| .25 hours Client phone consultations | no charge |

Obviously a billing statement will be effective in continuing to keep your clients informed only if the clients understand from the beginning what they are likely to be seeing in billing records.

the answer that is given when someone asks, "Do you know a good lawyer?"

It pays, then, to spend extra effort ensuring that your current clients are satisfied with your representation. The most common complaints clients have about their lawyers are also the most easily remedied.

## Expectations management

From the initial contact with your clients, learn what they expect from your representation. Make clear what you can and cannot do, how long it is likely to take, and how much it is likely to cost. Don't promise more than you can deliver.

## Communications systems

The most common complaint to lawyer disciplinary systems is that lawyers won't return phone calls. Set up a system for regular and prompt communication with your clients. Make sure they understand what they can expect from you by way of communication. Don't let your billing statements be your client's only window on your hard work. Ask your clients if they are satisfied and remedy their complaints if possible.

## Understandable fees

Never give a client "sticker shock" with your bill. Clients should know how much you charge and why. If you use a billable hour method, make sure your base rate is sufficient that you need not nickel-and-dime the client by charging for such things as "photocopy surcharges" and the one-minute phone call that is charged at a quarter-hour rate. Not only do these billing practices walk an ethical tightrope that regulators (and consumers) are increasingly unwilling to tolerate, they create the kind of relationship with your client that makes them reluctant to sing your praises to others.

## Mistake #3: Putting Yourself on the Hook through Cross Selling

Even after they have completed their representation, savvy lawyers recognize that continuing a relationship with former clients can pay off in referrals and return business. Some lawyers use their termination letters to remind the client of additional practice areas and other services available from the firm. Some lawyers keep in touch with former clients by providing them legal updates newsletters, arranging personal meetings, or sending holiday greetings.

There is nothing wrong with these efforts to keep your name on the radar screen of former clients. There is little risk of violating advertising and solicitation rules in these contacts. The rules of professional conduct even permit in-person solicitation of former clients (unless they have told you otherwise). Rather, the risk is that you will "sell too well"—that is, your contacts with a client after the close of representation may create the impression that you are continuing to represent the client. This can make the client a "current client" for purposes of malpractice liability or disqualification for conflict of interest.

To avoid this result, be sure to send each client a termination letter with clear language of termination, such as "our representation is now completed . . . the attorney-client relationship between us has ceased and we will have no further obligation to advise you in connection with this matter." If you want to include in this letter some cross-selling information, keep that information separate. Be sure your language describes any future representation as a possibility, not a guarantee (e.g., "if you find you have need of our services in the future, we would be pleased to consider possible representation at that time.").

If you intend to contact the client with newsletters or other future contacts, give notice in your termination letter of your intent to do so, make it clear that this is simply a general service you provide to former clients and others, and give the client an

## An Engaging Disengagement Letter

Dear [former client]:

With [result or event that ends case], our representation of you in the matter is now completed and our attorney-client relationship has ended.

It has been our pleasure working with you. If you should find you need our services in the future, we would be happy to consider representing you again at that time. In addition to [type of matter handled for client] matters, we also provide client assistance in [other areas of practice]. As a general service to all our former clients, we do occasionally send newsletters with general developments in these areas of practice. Unless we hear otherwise from you, we would be pleased to send you these bulletins.

Sincerely,
Lawyer

opportunity to opt out ("unless we hear otherwise" would be sufficient). For more suggestions, see the ABA Section of Business Law publication "Documenting the Attorney-Client Relationship" (ABA 1999).

## Mistake #4: Misusing Referrals

Referrals are indeed a powerful method of bringing clients to your door. How to generate those referrals ethically is another matter. Lawyers may ethically participate in lawyer referral services. The general rule in most states, following the language of ABA Model Rule 7.2(b), is that "A lawyer shall not give anything of value to a person for recommending the lawyer's services. . . ." States vary significantly on their permitted exceptions to this rule. Most states allow lawyers to pay for and participate in a legal service plan or a not-for-profit lawyer referral service. Some states also allow participation in other lawyer referral services (including for-profit services) that have been approved by an appropriate regulatory authority.

Sometimes lawyers violate these prohibitions on referrals services because they are simply not aware of the boundaries of the rule. For example, would a reciprocal referral agreement with another lawyer be giving something "of value" in exchange for a referral?

Refer clients to another lawyer or a nonlawyer professional pursuant to an agreement not otherwise prohibited under these

### Referral or Marketing Arrangement?

Always carefully consider the nature of the advertising arrangements you enter rather than simply rely on labels. Advertising programs are more likely to be considered referral programs if potential clients do not have access to the entire list of participating lawyers; if potential clients contact intermediaries who direct them to a particular lawyer or actually set up appoint-ments, rather than simply providing a list of contact information; and if the "fees" for participation in the program vary according to the number of potential clients obtained from participation. If the advertisement looks like a referral service (that is, potential clients may believe they are being "matched" with an lawyer who meets their needs), but it is in fact simply a cooperative advertising program, with no effort to screen or match clients to lawyers, the advertising should be clear about that. In all instances of cooperative advertising, online directories, and referral services, you should be very clear about what you are getting into and investigate your own state's ethics rules regarding the propriety of these arrangements.

Rules that provides for the other person to refer clients or customers to the lawyer, if

1. the reciprocal referral agreement is not exclusive, and
2. the client is informed of the existence and nature of the agreement.

Sometimes the lines on referrals are less than clear. For example, states that do not permit lawyers to participate in for-profit lawyer referral services may permit lawyers to have their names listed in "directories" or participate in "cooperative advertising programs." The Internet has further blurred these lines. Where is the line between, for example, an online referral service and an online directory with search functions? Always carefully consider the nature of the advertising arrangements you enter rather than simply rely on labels. Advertising programs are more likely to be considered referral programs if potential clients do not have access to the entire list of participating lawyers; if potential clients contact intermediaries who direct them to a particular lawyer or actually set up appointments, rather than simply providing a list of contact information; and if the "fees" for participation in the program vary according to the number of potential clients obtained from participation. If the advertisement looks like a referral service (that is, potential clients may believe they are being "matched" with a lawyer who meets their needs), but it is in fact simply a cooperative advertising program, with no effort to screen or match clients to lawyers, the advertising should be clear about that. In all instances of cooperative advertising, online directories, and referral services, you should be very clear about what you are getting into and investigate your own state's ethics rules regarding the propriety of these arrangements.

Another vague line is the one separating referral fees from legitimate "fee splitting" agreements with other lawyers. Most state ethics permit lawyers who are not in the same firm to split fees only if the split is proportionate to the services performed or if each lawyer assumes joint responsibility for the representation. Some states require both that there be joint responsibility and proportionate fee splitting. States also vary on the degree to which the client must be informed of and consent to these arrangements.

Since most courts do not aggressively police amounts of proportionate-work fee splitting agreements, it is sometimes difficult to tell whether a lawyer is being paid $500 for simply referring a case to another lawyer or whether the lawyer truly has completed $500 worth of initial work on a case. Some lawyers deliberately exploit this vagueness, entering into explicit referral arrangements with other lawyers in which the receiving lawyer agrees to "split fees" with the referring lawyer at a set amount, regardless of work performed. These veiled attempts to skirt the rule prohibiting referral fees are not without significant risk. The referring lawyer has, in these circumstances, entered into a attorney-client relationship, with all the associated risks of malpractice and conflicts disqualification. The receiving lawyer runs the risk not only of violation of the rules on referral fees but also that the referring lawyer may be engaging in more than simply passive referral and may be actually soliciting clients in violation of the rules. The receiving lawyer would be equally subject to discipline for either of these violations.

Even some seemingly innocent arrangements can run afoul of the prohibition of referral fees. For example, even if a referral agreement between lawyers involves no exchange of money, but is simply a promise of reciprocal referrals, most states have opined that these arrangements

amount to "giving something of value" for a referral. So even the seemingly innocent agreement that "I'll send you my tax clients if you send me your divorce clients" can place a lawyer at risk. Likewise, courts have disapproved agreements with a current client in which the lawyer provides a discount on legal fees if the client refers additional clients. Again, you must know your own state's rules on this. The 2002 version of the ABA Model Rules 7.2(b)(4) allows reciprocal referral agreements between lawyers so long as the agreement is not exclusive and "the client is informed of the existence and nature of the agreement." This rule, however, has yet to be adopted by more than one or two states.

Bottom line on referral services and arrangements: Know the law, know the arrangement, and tread carefully (keeping a paper trail all the way).

## Mistake #5: Forsaking Professionalism for Business

Not all rules of professional conduct are antithetical to business development. Indeed, many lawyers find that plenty of business flows from attending to their professional calling "as a public citizen" to "seek improvement of the law, access to the legal system, the administration of justice and the quality of service rendered by the legal profession." Preamble, ABA Model Rules of Professional Conduct, Para. 5 (2004). For many years, solo and small-firm lawyers have provided significant pro bono legal service and civic leadership. The press of a competitive legal market may tempt you to forsake these unpaid activities in favor of more explicit "client development" activities. While forsaking the professional call to service will be unlikely to subject you to discipline, it's not especially good ethics or good business. Most lawyers still build a practice on reputation and referrals. Having your name out in the community and being known for leadership, service, and commitment are still top-notch ways to "advertise."

## Mistake #6: Not Recognizing Solicitation

Just as lawyers sometimes walk the ethical line between prohibited referral fees and acceptable fee splitting agreements, so too there are a number of lawyers who believe that in-person solicitation is acceptable if only they call it something else. Don't be misled into this viewpoint. The rules flatly prohibit in-person or live telephone or electronic communication with potential clients for the purpose of soliciting paid professional employment in all but a few limited circumstances (e.g., family members or current clients). This prohibition has survived constitutional challenge at the highest level. *Ohralik v. Ohio State Bar Association*, 436 U.S. 447 (1978).

Know what constitutes solicitation. If you ask a client to hire you, that is solicitation. Even if you are simply handing out your card at a meeting or your brochure on a street corner, you could be considered as implicitly soliciting employment. Wait to be asked! Be especially careful to avoid solicitation when providing seminars or other public information events. While the states laud the professional effort to keep the public informed about law and legal rights, when these sessions turn into "infomercials," discipline soon follows.

Solicitation is prohibited because it is private and puts a client in a position of being subject to pressure. In-person communications, telephone contact (unless a "prerecorded broadcast"), and live electronic communications (such as Internet chat room discussions) all are settings in which you may not solicit employment. By contrast, the U.S. Supreme Court has held that targeted direct mail, while solicitation in form, does not present the type of pressured environment of in-person solicitation and so cannot be subject to a flat ban.

## Where Is the Line?

**Soliciting lawyers:** You may solicit other lawyers. You can even ask them to refer business to you. In most states, however, you can't agree to pay a referral fee. Even agreeing to a quid pro quo in which they will refer cases to you if you refer cases to them violates the rule against "giving anything of value to a person for recommending the lawyer's services."

**Current clients, former clients, family, and friends:** You may solicit employment from these persons. The rules presume that there is less temptation to abuse these relationships. You may tell former client that you hope they would feel comfortable recommending you to others. You may (in most states) ask clients to provide a testimonial for your advertising. You may not ask former clients to do what you cannot yourself do: solicit employment on your behalf.

**Clients in other jurisdictions:** If you use direct mail solicitations, be careful that you know where your letters are going and that the letters comply with that jurisdiction's rules. Consider the outcome for the lawyers in *In re Coale*, 775 N.E.2d 1079 (Ind. 2002), who had violated that state's regulations regarding direct-mail solicitation. That the lawyers were not licensed in Indiana did not provide them immunity from sanction: The Indiana court barred them from practicing law within the state, including *pro hac vice* admission, until further order.

**Solicitation of potential class members:** Some of the trickiest boundaries are in class action litigation. Since many courts hold that lawyers do not represent unnamed class members until a class has been certified, in-person communications with these potential class members could be improper solicitation. Courts have broad authority to oversee communications in these cases and watch carefully for the potential abuses associated with communications to class members. For example, the court in *Waldo v. Lakeshore Estates, Inc.*, 433 F. Supp. 782 (E.D. La. 1977), commented on the "heightened susceptibilities of nonparty class members to solicitation amounting to barratry as well as the increased opportunities of the parties or counsel to 'drum up' participation in the proceeding." *Id.* at 790.

**"Public interest" solicitation:** On the same day that the U.S. Supreme Court decided *Ohralik,* authorizing flat bans on in-person solicitation by lawyers, the Court also decided *In re Primus*, 436 U.S. 412, 434 (1978). In that case the ACLU-sponsored lawyer had sent a letter to woman known to have been threatened with sterilization as condition of receiving Medicaid benefits, informing her of free legal help. The court distinguished, with respect to First Amendment protections, between solicitation of clients intended to advance political objectives and solicitation of clients for pecuniary gain.

Some states' rules prohibit solicitation only "when a significant motive for the lawyer's doing so is the lawyer's pecuniary gain" (ABA Model Rule 7.3) and interpret this provision broadly.

For example, the lawyer in *In re Teichner*, 387 N.E.2d 265 (Ill. 1979) had been asked by a pastor and community leader to come to Mississippi after a train accident and help victims understand their rights. The community leaders were concerned with the methods by which railroad representatives had been obtaining releases of liability from victims and sought representation. The lawyer, working with these community leaders, visited victims and solicited employment for pay from them. The court struggled with the First Amendment associational and speech values that were involved and refused to impose discipline for the solicitation involved in this disaster (though the lawyer was suspended for two years for solicitation of victims in other accident cases).

Lawyers should not read the "public interest" exception as a loophole through which any in-person solicitation can be justified if there are enough victims or the cause is "just." Some states take a much narrower view of the public interest exception, providing in their rules that in-person solicitation is justified only if "under the auspices of a public or charitable legal services organization; or . . . a bona fide political, social, civic, fraternal employee or trade organization whose purposes include but are not limited to providing or recommending legal services, if the legal services are related to the principal purposes of the organization." (Missouri Supreme Court Rule 4-7.2)

*Shapero v. Kentucky Bar Association*, 486 U. S. 466 (1988). Most states, however, have strict regulations regarding targeted direct mail, including disclaimers, notices, filing requirements, and waiting periods. These regulations on time, place, and manner have been upheld as constitutional. *Florida Bar v. Went For It Inc.*, 515 U.S. 618 (1995). (Florida Bar restriction that prohibited lawyers in personal injury matters from sending letters to accident victims or their families for 30 days after the accident or other triggering event held to be reasonable regulation).

## Mistake #7: Letting Others Solicit for You

If you can't do it, you can't hire someone else to do it for you. The practice of hiring "runners" whose job is to locate potential clients and solicit their representation violates the rules, even if you call the runners "investigators" and are paying them for gathering documents and evidence. The courts take these schemes very seriously. For example, lawyers who participated in "one of the largest runner-based solicitation schemes in Louisiana" recently were permanently disbarred, even though they did not originate the scheme. *In re O'Keefe*, 877 So. 2d 79 (La. 2004); *In re*

*Laudumiey*, 849 So. 2d 515 (La. 2003) (same). Even lawyers who facilitated the scheme mostly through inadvertence and inadequate supervision of staff were given significant suspensions. *In re Goff*, 837 So. 2d 1201 (La. 2002). Other lawyers have found themselves with criminal convictions for this conduct. *In the Matter of Silver*, 545 S.E.2d 886 (Ga. 2001) (lawyer disbarred after pleading nolo to a misdemeanor charge of paying runners for his firm).

Obviously, this is territory to scrupulously avoid. Train your staff carefully. Many a lawyer has been subject to disciplinary action simply because a well-meaning paralegal or secretary did not know that being "part of the team" did not mean going out into the community and "drumming up business."

## Mistake #8: Pushing the Puffing Envelope

Obviously, your advertising must be truthful. Every state prohibits advertising that is "false or misleading." However, just as the rules regulating truthfulness in negotiations recognize that "certain types of statements ordinarily are not taken as statements of material fact" (ABA Model Rule 4.1), so one might conclude that "puffing" in advertisement is permissible as well. Indeed, it can be tempting, in a world in which billions of dollars are spent competing to earn the title of "Best Super Bowl Commercial" and there is seemingly no market that cannot be created through advertising, to believe that the only effective advertisement is that which pitches "new and improved" services.

However, puffing about value in settlement negotiations and advertising the "average amount of settlements obtained" are two entirely different areas of regulation. Negotiations are ordinarily between lawyers, who have plenty of sophistication to discount your opinions and resources to check your evaluation of facts. Clients reading lawyer advertisements are on a different footing. Lawyers, by virtue of their specialized education and central role in the system of justice, can do much damage by a little puffing.

Accordingly, states tend to frown upon statements they believe to be false or misleading, or to create unrealistic expectations. When crafting your advertisements, carefully consider whether your statements can be independently verified or are likely to create unrealistic expectations. Most states consider that statements of prior case results, such as settlement figures and verdict amounts, are likely to create an unjustified expectation about results. Generally laudatory statements must be subject to independent verification, making "excellent," "outstanding," and "superior" dangerous adjectives to inject. Most states also require that comparisons to other lawyers' services be subject to independent verification.

Consider such seemingly innocent statements as "You are entitled to fair compensation" or "I will be personally responsible

## Checklist for Advertisement Content

For any advertisement you craft, ask yourself as to both the ad as a whole and as to each specific statement in the ad:

- Is the statement false?

- Is the statement misleading?

- Are any terms sufficiently abstract that different consumers could have different ideas about what that means, such that some would be misled?

- Do any statements expressly or impliedly compare the lawyer's services with other lawyers' services? If so, can that comparison be factually substantiated? Are the terms used in the comparison so subjective that they would be incapable of verification?

- Are clients likely to have expectations about results that are unrealistic? Don't presume that a "your mileage may vary" statement is sufficient to protect statements that otherwise would create unrealistic expectations.

for the performance of this legal service for you." The first statement may subject the lawyer to discipline because it does not take into account the question of liability, and therefore may be misleading and may create an unjustified expectation of results. The second statement is likewise misleading unless the lawyer will be personally handling the cases brought in from this advertisement, rather than merely supervising others. *See* Missouri Informal Ethics Opinion 950136 (1995).

Thus, for any advertisement you craft, ask yourself as to both the ad as a whole and as to each specific statement in the ad:

- Is the statement false?
- Is the statement misleading?
- Are any terms sufficiently abstract that different consumers could have different ideas about what that means, such that some would be misled?
- Do any statements expressly or impliedly compare the lawyer's services with other lawyers' services? If so, can that comparison be factually substantiated? Are the terms used in the comparison so subjective that they would be incapable of verification?
- Are clients likely to have expectations about results that are unrealistic? Don't presume

that a "your mileage may vary" statement is sufficient to protect statements that otherwise would create unrealistic expectations.

## Mistake #9: Not Saying No

So, your client development efforts have steered well clear of any regulatory minefields of advertising or solicitation restrictions. You have a strong and professional reputation and the work is pouring in. Time to congratulate yourself on an ethical and effective approach to generating business. And also time to consider turning some of that business away. Next to pure greed, some of the most serious ethical and liability risks lawyers face are created by the inability to say no.

Caseloads that are unmanageable become cases in which client communication is truncated, research and investigation corners are cut, and mistakes are easy to make and difficult to fix. Emergency hiring to cover cases solves the squeeze but creates its own risks from inadequate training and supervision.

So make sure that all you keep in mind those classic advertising positions: "quantities limited to stock on hand" and "limited time only offer." Screen your clients carefully and know when to say no.

## Mistake #10: Not Asking for Help

When you are facing issues of professional ethics in your client development, know when to ask for help and from whom. Even if you are well versed in researching issues of professional responsibility, there are times when you may want to call in an expert to assist you in assessing the current status of the law. Because lawyer advertising is subject to constitutional scrutiny, rules on the books may not represent the current state of the law. For example, are you familiar with your state's rules or statutes regulating statements of "specialization" or "certification"? Many state rules continue to have complex and idiosyncratic requirements regarding these statements, despite the U.S. Supreme Court's holdings in *Peel v. Attorney Registration and Disciplinary Comm'n*, 496 U.S. 91 (1990) (states may not categorically ban statements of specialty certification) and *Ibanez v. Florida Dep't of Bus. & Prof'l Regulation*, 512 U.S. 136 (1994) (holding unconstitutional the application of disclaimer requirement to a lawyer's advertising as "Certified Financial Planner"). If you are thinking of pushing the constitutional envelope, you'll likely want help.

Less dramatic circumstances call for an outside opinion. Since the core regulation of advertising turns on perceptions of whether a statement is "misleading," it is often useful to simply gauge the opinion of others on your advertising. After all, you know so well what you mean when you use a particular word or phrase that it may be difficult to conceive how others might interpret the same language.

Likewise, there are simply uncharted waters in the regulation of advertising and solicitation. For example, the use of computer technology and the Internet to communicate with potential clients is an area still undergoing dramatic developments. Likewise, advertising regulation has yet to respond comprehensively to the impact of transnational and international practice and the development of specialized licensing requirements (e.g., for in-house counsel).

Asking for advice on these matters is not difficult if you know where to turn. Many state disciplinary agencies provide informal ethics opinions or ethics hotlines. The ABA Center for Professional Responsibility's Ethics Search service may also be useful. See http://www.abanet.org/cpr/ethicsearch/home.html. Every law school has at least one faculty member who teaches legal ethics; many are happy to guide lawyers in researching issues of professional conduct.

Professional organizations often publish specialized guidelines for a particular area of practice (e.g., the Bounds of Advocacy by the American Academy of Matrimonial Lawyers). One need only stop and ask for directions to find one's way to ethical client development, advertising, and solicitation.

# Index

Chamber of Commerce, 13, 117, 150, 155

Civil False Claims Act, 81, 82

Clark, Alan, 238, 240, 241

client resources, 65–73

clients, 23–30
  attracting, 24–27, 116–121
    probate and estate planning clients, 112–126
  communication with, 70–72
  development, 104–109
  postcounsultation rejections, 42–43
  prospective, 69–70, 138–139
  questionnaires for, 42
  retaining, 29–30, 120–121
  screening process for, 41–42
  signing, 27–29
  turning away, 40–43

Cobbs, Nicholas H., 242

Coca-Cola, 2, 212

cold calls, 51–55
  defined, 51
  how to make, 53–55
  limitations on, 52–53

concilitator, 128

Confidential Report of Client to Attorney, 30

Connecticut, 78

consistency, 22

contact management software, 18–19

continuing legal education (CLE), 11, 90, 91, 92, 99, 132, 185, 233, 238, 239, 243

**D**

deeds, 125

DeRamus, Sterling, 240

"Documenting the Attorney-Client Relationship" (ABA 1999), 247

Dorner, Bruce, 237, 238

**E**

e-mail, 170

Elefant, Carolyn, 236

Equal Employment Opportunity Commission, 41

estate planning, 122–126

eye contact, 6

**F**

facilitator, 128

Fahle, Becki, 239, 241

Federal Bureau of Investigation (FBI), 82

Finner, Wendell, 241

*Florida Bar v. Went For It Inc.* (1995), 252

Florida Will and Trust Manual, 124

Foonberg, Jay, 236

**G**

Golden, E. Alexandra, 239

Goldenberg, Jay S., 238

Goldstein, Justin, 93

Greene and Letts, 37

Griggs, W. Garney, 234

Gulf Coast Bar Association, 15

**H**

Hawaii, 87

Hinds County Bar Golf Committee, 10

Horn, Sam, 233

*How to Meet Millionaires*, 5

Hughes, Joseph, 240

**I**

*Ibanez v. Florida Dep't of Bus. & Prof'l Regulation* (1994), 255

Initial Public Offerings (IPOs), 148

Internal Revenue Code, 84

Internal Revenue Service (IRS), 95–101

Internet law, 107

## *How to Build a Law Firm Brand*

**Corinne Cooper**

**Also available** as an e-book is the chapter *How to Build a Law Firm Brand* from this book. Not only is *How to Build a Law Firm Brand* affordable, but it is also sold as an **e-book** that you can download right now to your computer. Carry it with you to read on the road, or print out a copy for your firm resource library. **Each page includes sidebars with samples, checklists, practical tips, and real examples of branding secrets and solutions from other law firms. This e-book also has live links to valuable resources on the web.**

*For more information on this e-book, go to*

www.abanet.org/abapubs/books/5150404

*How to Build a Law Firm Brand* (2005 e-book, 22 pages) $14.99 GP Members; $19.99 Regular—product code 5150404PDF